Critical Thinking in Psychology

Biological Psychology

Minna Lyons, Neil Harrison, Gayle Brewer, Sarita Robinson and Rob Sanders

Series Editor: Dominic Upton

LearningMatters

Learning Matters
An imprint of SAGE Publications Ltd
1 Oliver's Yard
55 City Road
London EC1Y 1SP

SAGE Publications Inc.
2455 Teller Road
Thousand Oaks, California 91320

SAGE Publications India Pvt Ltd
B 1/I 1 Mohan Cooperative Industrial Area
Mathura Road
New Delhi 110 044

SAGE Publications Asia-Pacific Pte Ltd
3 Church Street
#10–04 Samsung Hub
Singapore 049483

Library of Congress Control Number: 2014930330

British Library Cataloguing in Publication data

A catalogue record for this book is available from the British Library

Editor: Miriam Davey
Production controller: Chris Marke
Project management: Diana Chambers
Marketing manager: Tamara Navaratnam
Cover design: Wendy Scott
Typeset by: Kelly Winter
Printed by: Henry Ling Limited at The Dorset Press, Dorchester, DT1 1HD

ISBN 978 0 86725 693 5 (pbk)
ISBN 978 0 86725 848 9

MIX
Paper from
responsible sources
FSC
www.fsc.org
FSC™ C013985

Contents

Series editor's introduction

Studying psychology at degree level

Being a student of psychology is an exciting experience – the study of mind and behaviour is a fascinating and sprawling journey of discovery. Yet studying psychology at degree level brings with it new experiences, skills and knowledge. This book, one in a comprehensive series, brings you this psychological knowledge, but importantly brings with it directions and guidance on the skills and experiences you should also be developing during your studies.

Psychology is a growing discipline – in scope, in breadth and in numbers. It is one of the fastest growing subjects to study at GCSE and A level, and the number of students studying the subject at university has grown considerably over the past decade. Indeed, psychology is now one of the most popular subjects in UK higher education, with the most recent data suggesting that there are some 45,000 full-time students currently enrolled on such programmes (compiled from Higher Education Statistics Agency (HESA) statistics available at www.HESA.ac.uk) and it is likely that this number has not yet peaked.

The popularity of psychology is related to a number of reasons, not the least of which is its scope and breadth – psychology is a sprawling discipline that seeks to analyse the human mind and behaviour, which is fascinating in its own right. Furthermore, psychology aims to develop other skills – numeracy, communication and critical analysis, to name but a few. For these reasons, many employers seek out psychology graduates – they bring a whole host of skills to the workplace and any activities they may be involved in. This book brings together the knowledge base associated with psychology along with these critical skills. By reading this book, and engaging with the exercises, you will develop these skills and, in this way, will do two things: excel in your studies and your assessments, and put yourself at the front of the queue of psychology graduates when it comes to demonstrating these skills to potential employers.

Developing higher-level skills

Only about 15–20 per cent of psychology graduates end up working as professional psychologists. The subject is a useful platform for many other careers because of the skills it helps you to develop. It is useful to employers because of its subject-specific skills – knowing how people act is pertinent in almost any job and is particularly relevant to those that involve working directly with people. Psychology also develops a number of generic and transferable skills that are both essential to effective undergraduate study and valuable to employers. These include higher-level intellectual skills such as critical and creative thinking, reflection, evaluation and analysis, and other skills such as communication, problem solving, understanding and using data, decision making, organisational skills, teamworking and IT skills.

The Quality Assurance Agency in Higher Education (QAA) subject benchmarks for psychology (www.qaa.ac.uk/Publications/InformationAndGuidance/Pages/Subject-benchmark-statement—-Psychology.aspx), which set out the expectations of a psychology degree programme, highlight the sorts of skills that your degree should equip you with. The British Psychological Society (BPS), which accredits your degree course, acknowledges that graduate employability is an important area of focus for universities and expects that opportunities for skills development should be well embedded within your programme of study. Indeed, this is a major focus of your study – interesting as psychology is, you will need and want employment at the end of your degree.

The activities in this book have been designed to help you build the underpinning skills that you need in order to become independent and lifelong learners, and to meet the relevant requirements of your programme of study, the QAA benchmarks and the needs of you and your potential employer.

Many students find it a challenge to develop these skills, often learning them out of context of their study of the core knowledge domains of psychology. The activities in this book aim to help you to learn these skills at the same time as developing your core psychology knowledge, giving you opportunities continuously to practise skills so that they become second nature to you. The tasks provide guidance on what the skill is, how to develop basic competence in it and how to progress to further expertise. At the same time, development of these skills will enable you to better understand and retain the core content of your course – being able to evaluate, analyse and interpret content is the key to deepening understanding.

The skills that the activities in this book will help you to develop are as presented in Table 0.1.

In addition to review and essay questions, each chapter in this book will contain novel learning activities. Your responses will be guided through these activities and you will then be able to apply these skills within the context of biological psychology.

Features in this book

At the start of each chapter there will be **learning outcomes**. These are a set of bullet points that highlight the outcomes you should achieve – both skills and knowledge – if you read and engage with

Table 0.1: Skills developed in this book

Generic skills	Transferable skills
• critical and creative thinking	• communication: oral, visual and written
• reflection	• problem solving
• analysing and evaluating	• understanding and using data
	• decision making
	• organisational skills
	• teamwork
	• information technology
	• independent learning

the chapter. This will mean at the outset of the chapter that we try to orientate you, the reader, and demonstrate the relevance of the topic.

We have also included learning features throughout the individual chapters in order to demonstrate key points and promote your learning.

- **Bulleted lists** are used within the chapter to convey key content messages.

- **Case studies** are included as part of a critical thinking activity.

- **Tasks** are a series of short review questions on the topic that will help you assess yourself and your current level of knowledge – use these to see if you can move on or whether you need to reread and review the material.

- **Critical thinking activities** allow for the review of the text by encouraging key critical and creative thinking of the psychology material presented, and provide development of the generic skills. Each of these activities is followed by a **Critical thinking review**, which unpicks the activity for you, showing how it should have been tackled, the main skill it develops and other skills you may have used in completing the activity.

- **Skill builder activities** use the psychology material presented in the text but focus on one particular transferable skill as outlined in Table 0.1. Each of these activities is followed by a **Skill builder review**, which may provide further hints and which makes explicit the skills it helps to develop and the benefits of completing the activity.

At the end of the chapter there will also be some pedagogic features that you will find useful in developing your abilities.

- **Assignments** In order to assess your awareness and understanding of the topic, we have also produced a series of questions for you to discuss and debate with your colleagues. You can also use these questions as revision materials.

- **Summary: what you have learned** At the end of each chapter we present a summary of the chapter as a series of bullet points. We hope that these will match the learning outcomes presented at the outset of the chapter.

- **Further reading** We have included items that will provide additional information – some of these are in journals and some are full texts. For each we have provided the rationale for suggesting the additional reading and we hope that these will direct you accordingly.

- **Glossary** entries are highlighted in bold in the text on their first appearance in a chapter.

- Finally, there is a full set of **references** to support all of the material presented in this text.

We hope you enjoy this text, which is part of a series of textbooks covering the complete knowledge base of psychology.

Professor Dominic Upton

March 2014

Chapter 1

Introduction to biological psychology

Learning outcomes

By the end of this chapter you should:

- *have an understanding of what is meant by the term biological psychology;*
- *have the ability to describe the diverse research methods used in biological psychology;*
- *have an understanding of the differences between proximate and ultimate levels of explanation.*

Introduction

From understanding the role of genetics in the development of anxiety in rodents to looking at brain functioning in schizophrenia, biological psychology is an extremely diverse sub-discipline of psychology, utilising many different methods in finding answers to a large number of different questions. This textbook is a collaboration of five academics who engage in both teaching and research in biological psychology. Indeed, we are hoping that our individual experiences using methods such as EEG (Meyer et al., 2013), hormonal (Robinson et al., 2008) and genetic analyses (Hamshere et al., 2011), as well as experimental methods in evolutionary psychology (Brewer and Hendrie, 2011; Lyons et al., 2013), will allow us to provide an informed, balanced account of recent research in the field. The main purpose of this book is to provide you with a critical introduction to the field of biological psychology while engaging you in an active exploration of many different topics. We hope that you enjoy completing the tasks and exercises we have included in each chapter, as this will be an excellent aid in helping you to learn about each topic.

What is biological psychology?

Biological psychology is the study of biological and evolutionary influences on behaviour. The behaviour may be that of our own species or the behaviour of a number of non-human animal species. For example, researchers investigating biological influences might be interested in the genetic make-up (and especially the interaction between **genes** and environment, or G X E) affecting individual differences in behaviour (Caspi and Moffitt, 2006). Some of this research is experimental, using **rodent models**; other research is looking at **genotypes** of humans and linking them to different environmental factors and behaviours. Biological psychology is a rapidly developing field, using innovative new methods to discover answers to important questions on varied human behaviours and traits, including mental disorders, memory, mate choice and language.

Further, the questions that we ask can be analysed at different levels. **Proximate** questions are interested in the immediate, mechanistic influences on behaviour, such as the effects of a baby's cry on the mother's behaviour. When a baby cries, the 'care' hormone **oxytocin** is released in the mother, which elicits care-giving behaviour in the mother. Thus, oxytocin can be analysed as an immediate, proximate cause for maternal care. **Ultimate questions** are interested in historical, evolutionary influences. Why has evolution produced infant vocalisations that elicit care-giving by the mother? Why do mothers look after their babies? Ultimate-level analyses are trying to find the possible evolutionary functions of behaviours. It is possible that in the ancestral babies, individuals who cried for attention received more care-giving, and had higher chances of survival. Thus, the genes of the 'cry-babies' would have been selected for by evolutionary processes.

The proximate causes often deal with biological and developmental influences on an individual. These can be things such as the neural circuitry, brain structures, hormones and neurotransmitters, learning and other social influences. These are factors that happen within the lifetime of an individual, often within the body of an individual. Ultimate causes deal with historical explanations, things that happened before the individual, in the ancestors who had genetic combinations that were selected for because they made the ancestors better adapted to their environment.

It is important to take both proximate and ultimate theories into account when trying to understand behaviour, as these interact with each other in producing behaviour that is often adapted to specific environmental circumstances. There is plenty of evidence to suggest that children may use parental care (or the lack of it) as an indicator for environmental circumstances (Del Giudice and Belsky, 2011). When care is low, children mature earlier, start reproduction earlier, and engage in more anti-social and risk-taking behaviours. Proximate explanations could look at things such as the social learning of behaviour (which would not explain the earlier maturation, though) and the role that care has on the development of biological (often neuronal and hormonal) systems that affect behavioural strategies. Ultimate explanations deal with the possible adaptiveness of different behavioural strategies. Perhaps in harsh environments it is better to start early reproduction as people die earlier, and, evolutionarily speaking, passing on your genes before you die is adaptive behaviour. Thus, although it is crucial to understand the proximate causes of behaviour, they are meaningless unless understood from the ultimate perspective too – or, as the famous evolutionary biologist Dobzhansky once wrote, 'Nothing in biology makes sense except in the light of evolution' (Dobzhansky, 1973).

Research methods in biological psychology

Biological psychologists have at their disposal a large array of techniques to measure behavioural responses and activity in the nervous system. The number of available techniques increases almost yearly due to advances in technology; often the newer techniques are able to measure more accurately, and less invasively, than the older techniques. The choice of method for a particular research study is, of course, motivated by the biological variable the researcher is interested in, but it also depends on the availability of the relevant equipment, and on ethical considerations regarding the welfare of the participants. In this section we give a brief description of the main techniques used in contemporary biological psychology. You will see that many of the experimental results you read about in later chapters have come from studies using one or more of these techniques.

When investigating the nervous system, a particular technique will generally enable researchers to examine either its structure or its function. The structure of the nervous system refers to its anatomy, and the function refers to its activity. A good way of thinking about this is to imagine that you are inspecting a car engine. Its structure would be the physical make-up of the various parts – for instance, whether they are made of metal or plastic, whether they are rusty, and so on. To get a good idea of the structure of the engine, the engine would need to be turned off. The function of the engine is how the engine actually works when it is switched on – how the various parts of the engine are coordinated to allow the car to move. To gain a full understanding of the car engine, you would need to know about both its structure and its function, and this principle is exactly the same for the nervous system.

Brain imaging techniques

You need to be aware of the main technologies that allow data about the structure and function of the nervous system to be recorded. Technologies to create structural images of the brain include **CT scans** (computerised tomography – a series of X-rays of the brain) and **MRI** (magnetic resonance imaging), which can produce very high-resolution pictures. Going beyond purely structural data, several relatively new imaging techniques can measure the function, or activity, of the brain while it is performing a task. Positron emission tomography (**PET**) measures the activity of the brain at work, but it involves the ingestion of a radioactive substance. The big breakthrough in brain imaging technology occurred in the 1990s with the discovery of functional magnetic resonance imaging (**fMRI**), which allows the activity of the brain to be precisely recorded without the need for any radioactive substance to be ingested. The ability of fMRI to record the activity of the brain relies on the fact that regions of the brain that are active use more oxygen than regions at rest. Because of brain activation, there is a change in the ratio of oxygenated to deoxygenated blood, and it is this change that the fMRI scanner is able to detect. This allows the researcher to pinpoint very precisely (in the region of several square millimetres) the regions of the brain that are working. In other words, fMRI has high **spatial resolution**. A limitation of fMRI is that it cannot provide very precise information about *when* a particular brain region becomes active, i.e. it has low **temporal resolution**. Other problems with fMRI are that it is expensive and that the environment inside the scanner is very noisy and movements are restricted, which limits the experiments that can be conducted. It is common for researchers to combine fMRI with a structural MRI scan during the same experiment, to provide both structural and functional data on the same participant.

Electrophysiological techniques

PET and fMRI are both indirect techniques for the recording of brain activity, as they *infer* neural activity from a secondary source (e.g. blood oxygen level in the case of fMRI). However, other techniques can directly record the activity of either single nerve cells or large groups of nerve cells. These techniques rely on recording the electrical activity produced by the brain cells, and thus they are called **electrophysiological** techniques. **EEG** (electroencephalography) uses electrodes placed on the scalp to record the electrical activity of large numbers of cells (hundreds of thousands of simultaneously active neurons) in the underlying brain tissue. A main advantage of EEG is the accuracy with which it can detect the time that a particular brain region becomes active. In other words, it has a very high temporal resolution, and is accurate to within a few milliseconds (thousandths of a second). Further advantages of EEG are its low cost and the fact that it is non-invasive, i.e. it causes minimal discomfort to the participant. Two main analysis techniques are applied to the EEG signals – the event-related potential (**ERP**) reflects averaged brain electrical activity in response to a particular experimental event, and event-related oscillatory analysis allows the researcher to investigate how the brain's rhythmic activity is influenced by an external event. A drawback is that EEG has rather poor spatial resolution, so it is very difficult to tell precisely which region of the brain is active at a particular time. **MEG** (magnetoencephalography) has higher spatial resolution than EEG because it measures the magnetic field changes caused by the electrical activity in the brain, and these fields are less disrupted by the layers of skull and skin through which they must pass before being recorded. However, the spatial resolution of MEG is still much lower than that of fMRI. More invasive electrophysiological techniques such as intracranial EEG (where electrodes are placed on the surface of the cortex) can increase the spatial resolution of the signals, but this is generally used only with humans who are being surgically treated for a medical disorder such as **epilepsy**. Finer spatial resolution is provided by recording electrical activity from small groups of cells (multiple-unit recording) or a single cell (**single-unit recording**), using a microelectrode. Multiple- and single-unit recordings allow a direct moment-by-moment measure of the electrical changes of single neurons or groups of neurons. They provide high spatial and temporal resolution and can be used to provide important information about the association between brain structure, brain function and behaviour. The main limitation of the multiple- and single-unit recording technique is that it is highly invasive, so it is suitable only for non-human subjects (although it is occasionally used with human patients, for example, those with Parkinson's disease.) It is also rather labour intensive to collect the data, and each study usually produces data from only one brain region.

Psychophysiological techniques

Researchers in biological psychology also need to record activity related to other processes in the body besides the central nervous system. For instance, when investigating emotions or stress, researchers want to be able to record their effects on various biological systems that are responsive to these variables. Many of the most useful measures can be recorded from the surface of the skin (these methods are known as psychophysiological measures). Among the most important psychophysiological measures are the electromyogram (**EMG**), which records muscle tension, the electrooculogram (**EOG**), which monitors eye movements, and the skin conductance response (**SCR**), which records the ability of the skin to conduct electricity, and is related to the activity of the sweat glands. Additional psychophy sociological data comes from cardiovascular activity, including heart rate (measured using an electrocardiogram (**ECG**)), blood pressure and blood volume. These non-invasive psychophysiological tools can give researchers a window into the functioning of the peripheral nervous system.

Lesions

Lesions are abnormalities in brain tissue caused by disease, trauma or surgery. Important evidence about the function of the lesioned structure can be gained by systematically testing the behaviour of a human or an animal subject with a lesion. By using laboratory animals, specific brain regions can be lesioned, allowing theories to be tested about the role of the lesioned structure. Common methods to perform lesions in animals include sectioning, where a nerve or bundle of nerves is severed, and radio-frequency lesions, where tissue is destroyed by heat using a carefully positioned electrode. Even though surgeons aim to lesion a very specific area of the brain, a major difficulty in interpreting the results of lesion studies is that nearby structures may be damaged because the structures of the brain are very small and densely packed.

Behavioural research methods

In many experiments, human or animal subjects perform some sort of behavioural task while a biological variable such as brain activity is measured. A behavioural task simply means that the subject has been given a set of instructions and is required to make a particular response in relation to what they see or hear (commonly the responses are collected via a computer keyboard). Performance on the task is a measured variable in the experiment; the most common measures are the proportion of correct responses and the speed of response (reaction time). Sometimes the paradigm for the task has been developed in a different area within psychology – for instance, in the field of cognitive psychology.

Behavioural tests are also used to assess neurological function in a patient; these are known as neuropsychological tests. These tests can identify changes in psychological functioning as a result of brain damage. A general approach to neuropsychological testing involves administering a battery of general tests followed by more specific tests to examine in more depth any deficits revealed by the general tests. The general test battery includes tests of intelligence (for example, the Wechsler Adult Intelligence Scale (WAIS)), memory and language. An example of a more specific test of neurological damage is the Wisconsin Card Sorting Test, which assesses frontal lobe function. Neuropsychological testing can be time-consuming, but the results can greatly help with the diagnosis of nervous system dysfunction, particularly in cases where a clear diagnosis cannot be made on the basis of results from brain imaging or EEG.

Biological psychologists are also interested in investigating inheritance, conducting studies trying to identify genes (or proteins) that are associated with behavioural traits. Twin studies are also a commonly used method for looking at how much inheritance plays a part in producing behaviour.

Critical thinking activity

Tools for studying the brain

Critical thinking focus: analysing and evaluating

Key question: *What are the main advantages and disadvantages of the various techniques used by biological psychologists to study the brain?*

In this activity you will practise reasoning skills and decision making to evaluate the advantages and disadvantages of some of the techniques that biological psychologists use to investigate the structure and function of the brain.

To help you do this, draw a large table with the following details. In the far left column put the heading 'technique', and underneath this include six rows labelled 'MRI', 'PET', 'fMRI', 'EEG', 'MEG', 'lesions'. Use the columns of the table to make notes about these techniques against a number of criteria. The following criteria need one column each.

Advantages. Note down the advantages and benefits of the technique. How are these advantages useful to researchers trying to understand the brain?

- Disadvantages. Record the limitations of the technique. How could the disadvantages be lessened, if at all?

- Similarities. Document any similarities between the various techniques. In what ways do they provide similar or complementary data to the other techniques?

- Differences. Note any similarities between the various techniques. In what ways do they provide different data from the other techniques?

- Overall. Provide an overall assessment of the technique based on your answers in the previous columns.

Complete the table using the information in the section on 'Research methods in biological psychology'. After completing the table, you should have an overall evaluation of each technique and also some reasons why you reached these conclusions. If you want to go even further, read other textbooks or journal articles and see if you can provide more information in each column.

Critical thinking review

This activity aids the development of analysis and evaluative skills in relation to the pros and cons of the major tools used by biological psychologists to study the brain. Being able to critically evaluate the limitations of these techniques is vital for correctly interpreting the results of experiments involving these methods. Particularly where brain imaging studies are concerned, people can be taken in by the brightly coloured brain activation maps and conclude that the results are unambiguous and important. It is therefore important to be aware of the limitations and drawbacks of these techniques.

Being able to evaluate and analyse information are important skills for being able to make your own judgements about experimental studies, and they can also be applied to ideas and theories. These skills are vital not just in academic study but also in the 'real world', where information is often biased and ambiguous.

Skill builder activity

Gene–environment interaction and epigenetics in the development of anxiety

Transferable skill focus: independent learning

Key question: *How does environment interact with genes in producing behaviour?*

Go to this learning resource maintained by the University of Utah:

> http://learn.genetics.utah.edu/content/epigenetics

Find the exercise 'Lick your rats'. In this exercise, you are pretending to be a mother rat who is giving different levels of care to her pups. The exercise shows how the GR gene, active in stress-related behaviours, can be either activated or deactivated, depending on the levels of care.

Complete the exercise twice. The first time, do not lick your pup too much. The exercise shows how the GR genes remains twisted when there are low levels of care. The second time, lick the pups more rigorously. You can see how the GR protein gets untwisted.

Read the associated information on the website and find answers to these questions.

1. What are epigenetics?

2. What is the GR gene, and how does it affect stress reactivity?

3. Can stress reactivity be adaptive?

Skill builder review

1. Epigenetics is the study of environmental influences on gene activity. Genes can be switched on or off according to life experiences, and the proteins that these genes encode for can have a major influence on behaviour. These influences can even persist across generations, and they can be evolutionarily adaptive in terms of providing organisms with means to be successful in changing environments.

2. The glucocorticoid receptor (GR) is a gene that is active in stress reactions (the fight or flight response), binding the stress hormone cortisol in the hippocampus. The more active the gene is, the quicker cortisol is bound, and the hippocampus sends a 'danger over' message to the hypothalamus. High maternal care in rats activates the GR gene, and allows the pup to cope better with stressful situations. In the pups of a low-caring mother, the gene is inactive, and the pups (even as adults) have a hard time relaxing after stress.

3. Stress reactions are not always bad. Low maternal care could be an indicator of low-resource, stressful environments where having a sensitivity to danger could be evolutionarily adaptive.

Assignments

1. Critically discuss the advantages and disadvantages of the different research methods in biological psychology.

2. Evaluate the ultimate and proximate biological causes of behaviour with reference to anti-social behaviour.

3. Discuss the ethical issues relating to the different techniques used by biological psychologists.

Summary: what you have learned

Now you have finished studying this chapter you should:

- have a basic understanding of what biological psychology is;

- understand the differences between proximate and ultimate levels of explanation;

- have an overview of different research methods in biological psychology.

Further reading

Alcock, J and Sherman, P (1994) The utility of the proximate–ultimate dichotomy in ethology. *Ethology*, 96, 58–62.

Dickins, TE and Barton, RA (2012) Reciprocal causation and the proximate–ultimate distinction. *Biology & Philosophy*, 1–10.

Two interesting articles on the proximate/ultimate distinction in biology.

Buzsaki, G (2006) *Rhythms of the brain*. New York: Oxford University Press.

A fascinating and in-depth look at what we know about how the brain functions, particularly in relation to its rhythmic activity. It includes an excellent chapter on electrophysiological techniques.

Caspi, A. and Moffitt, TE (2006) Gene–environment interactions in psychiatry: joining forces with neuroscience. *Nature Reviews Neuroscience*, 7, 583–590.

A nice paper explaining the interplay between biological systems and environment in mental disorders.

Chapter 2

The brain

Learning outcomes

By the end of this chapter you should:

- *have a good understanding of the developmental processes of the brain;*
- *have the ability to identify some of the major structures and views of the brain;*
- *understand some of the basic psychological functions in the four main lobes;*
- *have developed your organisational skills.*

Introduction

The nervous system is quite complex, with many sub-divisions within it, though the mechanisms of each of these divisions is very similar; all rely on neurons of one form or another, and the interaction between these neurons is crucial for the system to function. This similarity becomes even more obvious when nervous system development is explored – and having a good understanding of this process can help in understanding the complex interactions that are 'hard-wired' into our biological systems, so this is a helpful place to start.

The development of the central nervous system (CNS) and the brain

As any psychology student knows, humans are complex organisms, but they begin relatively simply as a single cell, the **zygote**. A zygote is the first incarnation of a new individual and is formed when fertilisation occurs (an ovum or egg joins with a sperm) through sexual reproduction. Ova and sperm are often referred to by the term **gamete**, which is simply a term for describing cells that join together during fertilisation. One of the important characteristics of gametes is that they contain only half the **DNA** of the parents – they are said to be **haploid cells**. So the sperm will contain half of your father's DNA and the ovum will contain half of your mother's DNA. On their own, then, gametes are fairly useless as they contain only half the DNA needed to make a person, but fusing them together during fertilisation results in a single cell with the full complement of DNA needed to make a person – this is referred to as a **diploid cell**. In essence, an individual begins with a single cell that is a combination of biological material from their mother and from their father. Everyone starts from this point, and a combination of the genetic material that this cell contains and the life experiences that the organism goes through over time will determine the characteristics of the organism that is produced – Hitler and Einstein both started out this way, and so did you! What is important to note here is that individuals develop according to the effects of biology and environment together – not one or the other.

One big question is how complex life forms develop from one relatively simple cell, and the answer lies in cell division. Just 12 hours after fertilisation – the creation of the zygote – the zygote divides into two cells; this cell division continues exponentially from here, so the original single-celled zygote eventually becomes a mass of many cells and is termed a **blastocyst**, which will develop into the foetus.

The nervous system contains many different types of cell, such as different types of neurons, specialised to perform certain functions. The blastocyst contains embryonic stem cells, which are a single type of cell capable of developing into any type of specialised cell that is required – from specialised neurons to specialised heart cells and so on. This aspect of embryonic stem cells makes them incredibly important as they have the potential to grow into any specialised type of cell and could therefore be used for treating almost any disorder – you would not have to transplant a specific organ into a failing body and risk organ rejection if you could use stem cells to 'grow' that particular organ.

This property of stem cells in blastocysts means that a fully functioning human with very many specialised parts can grow out of it. As the zygote develops into a blastocyst and then into a foetus, this is exactly what happens (see Figure 2.1). At around 20–21 days after fertilisation, the cell division of the zygote results in the formation of a neural tube structure. One end of this structure will develop into the brain, and the other will develop into the spinal cord. Over the next few days some distinct structures of the brain emerge, growing out of the neural tube and future spinal cord. Initially these distinct brain structures are gross differences that roughly divide the brain into three divisions (see Table 2.1). At this point it is worth bearing in mind that some sources state that there are three major divisions, while others will state that there are four, as they divide the prosencephalon into two (the telencephalon and the diencephalon).

Each major division (however many you use) contains many smaller and more specific structures that are associated with particular brain functions, and these are discussed throughout this book. For now, though, we will look at how the brain develops its more intricate structures.

Table 2.1: *Major divisions of the brain*

Also known as:	
Prosencephalon (includes telencephalon and diencephalon)	Forebrain
Mesencephalon	Midbrain
Rhombencephalon (includes cerebellum, pons and medulla)	Hindbrain

Figure 2.1: *Embryonic brain development*

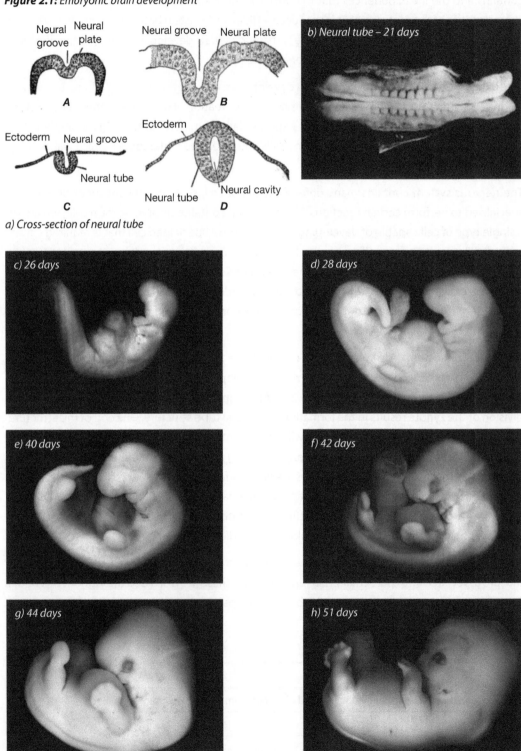

a) Cross-section of neural tube

b) Neural tube – 21 days

c) 26 days

d) 28 days

e) 40 days

f) 42 days

g) 44 days

h) 51 days

Developmental stages

The gross morphology of the developing brain needs to be populated by neurons of different types and functions, and this population of the gross morphology takes place in several stages.

1. Neural proliferation.

2. Neural migration.

3. Neural differentiation.

4. Synaptogenesis.

5. Neuronal survival.

6. Synaptic survival.

It is important to note that these stages are not performed serially. Each stage does not need to be complete before the next one begins; all of these stages may be in process at any one time. Understanding the processes involved at each of these stages can give us a good insight into some of the power and flexibility of the brain, and it is worth spending some time understanding these.

Neural proliferation

Through cell division, the foetus develops and grows by increasing the number of cells that it has. For the brain and nervous system, the cells of the neural tube divide and proliferate, giving rise to a large number of stem cells that will become different types of neuron or **glial cells** (see Chapter 3 for a more detailed description of glial cells). Once these cells have developed into neurons or glia, they no longer divide – only the neural tube stem cells can divide and proliferate. This fact led to an early idea that humans were born with a fixed number of neurons that could not be replaced or added to through cell division (Whatson and Sterling, 1998) – essentially, you got what you were born with and no more. This is no longer considered to be accurate, as Shankle et al. (1998) demonstrated significant post-natal neuronal cell growth between the ages of 15 months and 6 years. So the neuronal proliferation stage, once thought to end around the time of birth, has been noted to continue up until the age of at least 6 years. In fact, a longer period of neuronal generation throughout brain development may have significant evolutionary advantages by encouraging diversity of functioning (Hoffman, 2010). That is to say, the longer that the individual can generate new neurons during their development the more likely they are to develop more specialised and more diverse neuronal systems, which can help the individual survive or adapt to their environment.

At this point you should also be able to appreciate some of the potential of harvesting or using embryonic stem cells for treatment purposes, particularly for diseases that involve neuronal degeneration, such as Parkinson's disease. If the disease process results in the 'death' of neurons, and neuronal generation ends relatively early in the developmental process – perhaps around the age of 6 – then it would be advantageous to be able to transplant stem cells into a diseased brain in the hope of these generating new, healthy neurons. The therapeutic effects of such therapy have, however, proved less than convincing after two decades of experimental treatments (Vidaltamavo et al., 2010).

Neural migration

Once cells have been generated at the neural tube they have to move into place throughout the developing nervous system or brain. This is accomplished using a 'scaffolding' system of glial cells known as radial glial cells (Rakic, 2003). These glial cells radiate out from the centre of the neural tube (the ventricle) to the surface of the neural tube in a structured way and provide a 'scaffold' along which cells can migrate throughout the nervous system, 'crawling' along the scaffold toward the surface. As more cells migrate along the scaffold and arrive at the surface, the surface becomes crowded with more and more cells eventually resembling a complex mass of interconnected cells, which can be seen in a more mature brain. At this point the cells that have migrated along the radial glia remain undifferentiated – that is to say, they do not yet possess any of the specialised qualities of neurons found in certain regions of the brain or nervous system. These relatively basic cells that have completed migration need to undergo the next stage of development, which is differentiation.

Neural differentiation

Neural differentiation is the process by which basic neuronal-type cells develop into the specialised types of neuron required by the area of the nervous system they have migrated to. So cells that have migrated to an area of sensory input into the nervous system (e.g. touch) may develop into unipolar (sensory) neurons; cells that have migrated to an area interacting with muscles may develop into motor neurons; and so on.

The interesting question is how such basic non-specialised cells develop into the 'right' kind of specialised neuron for the area of the nervous system they have migrated to. The answer lies in the genetic material in each cell. Gene expression moderates the development of the neuron, controlling the growth of axons (nerve fibres that project from neurons) and dendrites (nerve fibres that axons of adjacent neurons send signals to) from the initial cell. Gene expression is the term given to whether a particular gene has been activated or not.

Each cell at this stage is diploid, that is, it has a full set of DNA containing many thousands of genes, each of which has a specific function. If one of these genes is activated, it will set in motion a range of chemical processes that produce a protein, and this protein is used to create cell structures such as axons and dendrites. So if a gene is expressed, or switched on, a protein will be created and perhaps a dendrite formed; if the gene is not expressed, no dendrite will be formed. In this way the complex morphology of a neuron is controlled.

So what determines if a gene is expressed or not? A complex number of factors are involved, and they occur both within and without the cell – the intrinsic and extrinsic cellular environments that play a role in gene expression.

- Intrinsic cellular environments are specific to each cell and usually relate to the levels of chemicals within that cell, the presence of glucose or oxygen, which may trigger gene expression.

- Extrinsic cellular environments refers to the environments outside the cell, which may be the presence of particular chemicals in connecting cells or, more broadly, the nutrient status of the mother, which can provide rich material for development or toxic materials such as alcohol, which may impede development.

In essence, then, for neuronal differentiation there is an interplay between intrinsic and extrinsic cellular environments. The correct chemicals need to be present in order to 'switch' the gene on, and, following this, the correct chemicals need to be present in order for the gene to be able to build a protein from these building blocks.

Synaptogenesis

At this stage in the developmental process, cells have been created, they have migrated into position, and they have become differentiated in their morphology by growing axons and dendrites. The next stage is for these neurons to connect up to each other, and to other structures, and form synapses. In order to do that, the axons and dendrites of various neurons need to grow towards each other.

The tip of the developing axon or dendrite is referred to as the growth cone (Gordon-Weeks, 2000), and this tip has fine outgrowths on it. Some of these are hair-like structures known as filopodia, and some are sheet-like structures known as lamellipodia. Both filopodia and lamellipodia react to the extrinsic cellular environments around them, moving towards certain chemicals and 'dragging' the growing axon or dendrite behind it.

The source of attraction for the filopodia and lamellipodia are chemicals released from target nerve cells or structures (such as muscles) that may attract or repel the growth cones. As the growth cones detect the presence of a chemical attractant in the extrinsic cell environment, the growth cone will orient towards it and 'follow' the signal. The signal becomes more concentrated nearer to its source, so by following the concentration of the chemical attractant the growth cone will drag the axon or dendrite to its source, and once there a synapse will be formed. This is termed chemotropic guidance and it is in this way that many synapses may be formed.

Neuronal survival

During the development of the nervous system, large numbers of neurons are created, though not all of them survive. In fact, it has been estimated that between 20 per cent and 80 per cent of neurons may die in various locations in the nervous system (Toates, 2006).

In order to survive, a neuron must make a connection, or synapse, with another cell or structure. Once this connection is made, the target cell releases a neurotrophic factor that is taken into the neuron; neurons that receive such neurotrophic factors survive while neurons that do not receive the neurotrophic factor die.

The term neurotrophic factor is a term that refers generally to the life-giving chemical that is given to the neuron by the target cell, though this can take several specific forms. Perhaps the most common form of neurotrophic factor is nerve growth factor, also known as NGF (Levi-Montalcini, 1982). NGF is produced by the target cells but is taken up along the axon of the neuron into its cell body where it prevents the neuron from dying.

Cells which do not receive such neurotrophic factors die through a process of programmed cell death (Burek and Oppenheim, 1996), which is a genetically driven process of cell 'suicide', determined, in part, by the failure to make any synaptic connections or receive any neurotrophic factor.

At this point you should be able to see that the developmental process of the nervous system and the brain is a competitive one – many neurons are created, but not all survive. Competition is rife between the neurons to make synapses with other cells, so that they may receive a neurotrophic factor such as NGF and therefore survive in the first instance. Of course, neurons need to survive over a longer term too, which is where the next stage of development comes in.

Synaptic survival

Making a synaptic connection with another cell and receiving an initial boost of a neurotrophic factor in order to avoid programmed cell death is fine in the short term, but the synapse needs to be maintained over the longer term if it is to be effective; it is no use having a synaptic connection that lasts for only a matter of days. So while the synapse needs to be made in order for the neuron to survive, the synapse must be an effective working connection if the synapse is to survive. An active working synapse will maintain a flow of the neurotrophic factor, stabilising the survival of the neuron and its connection, while an inactive non-working synapse will not allow enough of the neurotrophic factor into the neuron for it to survive.

In order for the synapse to survive it must be used by the organism on a fairly regular basis. Regular use reinforces the synaptic connection and ensures the survival of that connection and of the neuron itself.

While this is relatively simple to understand, it does have some important consequences. Imagine that the synapse in question is between the brain and a leg muscle, so it involves a motor neuron. If the organism can walk around activating the leg muscle repeatedly, the synapse will survive. However, if the individual is in an environment where walking is impossible (confined in a small cage, say), then any synapse between the brain and leg that occurs will not be reinforced through use and will eventually die. In this sense the environment can have a significant impact upon neuronal survival. The futility of arguing whether nature or nurture is responsible for any behaviour becomes obvious – nature and nurture work together in developing the nervous system and neuronal synapses.

The survival of synapses, and neurons, can be seen in terms of evolutionary natural selection – the survival of the fittest (Edelman, 1987). Only strong and useful synapses continue to exist, while the rest are 'pruned' as neurons succumb to programmed cell death and inactive synapses wither. In fact, the number of neurons in the brain doubles between the ages of 15 months and 6 years (Shankle et al., 1998) while the number of synapses increases from birth to a peak at the age of 3 years before being pruned again by the time of puberty (Bruer, 1998). In this way our development begins with an 'over-production' of neurons seeking to make synapses; however, many of these synapses will not be reinforced through interactions with the environment so they will 'die'. This ability to over-produce what is needed and then 'weed out' neurons or synapses that are not needed reflects just such an evolutionary process of development.

Task — Take some time now to go over the stages of development outlined above and review your understanding of them. Once you have an understanding of the mechanisms, consider what consequences this has for understanding how psychological functions develop.

Up to this point the chapter has focused quite intensely on the *mechanics* of the nervous system and brain, and it is helpful to pause here and reflect on the impact they may have on the *functions* of the nervous system or brain. You should be able to see that complex functions are not fully developed from the moment of conception or birth but rather develop over time from much simpler functions; for example, you cannot produce spoken language without first having motor-neuronal control of your lips, tongue, breathing and so on.

Genetics plays a role in providing the raw instructions for the development of the neurons involved, but the environment can help to generate, maintain or kill off the neurons and synapses that are produced. So two people may have motor neurone disease but for very different reasons; one individual may have an abnormality in a particular gene (SOD1, superoxide dismutase 1) that has produced an enzyme that is toxic to motor neurons; or the disease may be due to some environmental factor. Only around 10 per cent of cases of motor neurone disease are thought to have an inherited genetic cause (Siddique and Deng, 1996), and it may be that the toxic factor has been ingested via diet for some cases.

The adult brain

Having discussed how the brain starts out, let us turn to the brain that you may be more familiar with from its wrinkled image. It was tempting to call this section 'the fully formed brain', but that is very misleading as the brain is, in many ways, in continuous development, developing new synapses in response to the environment, repairing damaged tissue, and even possibly growing new neurons over time. This makes the study of the brain incredibly complex, as individuals' different life environments result in individual reinforcement of synapses and neurons, giving each brain an individualised content.

In many ways brains are like faces: most faces are the same in that they have two eyes, a nose, a mouth, ears, and so on, but each face is also unique. Just as most faces have commonalities in their structure so too do brains and we will discuss them here. It is worth noting at this point that in order to discuss the various aspects of the brain you will need to become familiar with some quite odd terminology that has come from a variety of sources (Greek, Latin, medicine, biology, to name a few). This also means that some parts of the brain have more than one name – one that was the 'original' and one that may be a more modern term – so when you go away to read around the subject be ready for the terminology to change from one book to the next, even though they are talking about the same thing.

Views of the brain

One of the other things you will need to do is to learn to visualise the brain, so that you can interpret diagrams and photos that you will see. As the brain is a three-dimensional object you can look at it from different angles and directions, and these have been named to make interpretation of diagrams and photos a little easier. Table 2.2 lists some of these.

Not only do these terms refer to viewing angles of the whole brain, they are often used to refer to specific parts of larger brain structures. So the dorsal aspect of some structure will be 'the bit towards the top', while the posterior aspect of some structure will be referring to 'the bit towards

Table 2.2: Viewpoints of the brain

Viewpoint	Terminology	Alternative terminology
Looking down on to the brain	Dorsal view	Superior view
Looking from the front (face on)	Rostral view	Anterior view
Looking from underneath	Ventral view	Inferior view
Looking from the back	Caudal view	Posterior view

the back'. In addition, there are a couple of other terms that are often used: 'lateral', which means 'towards the sides', and 'medial', which means 'towards the middle'.

There are different ways of slicing brains open to look inside, and these have specific names too. Brain 'slices' sounds a little too gruesome, so they are properly referred to as brain sections. A **sagittal section** is sliced vertically between the eyes; an **axial section** is sliced horizontally (as if taking the tops of both ears and the top of the head off); and the third and final section is the **coronal section**, which is a vertical slice through both shoulders (as if taking the face off). The resulting images of the brain are much less gruesome than all this sounds, and some examples are given in Figure 2.2.

Main structures of the brain

There is no doubt that the brain is an extremely complex structure, so to get a handle on how it works we need to divide it into a number of different parts. There are a number of different systems of classification of the various regions of the brain, but one of the best ways of simplifying the parts of the brain is to divide it into four parts: the brainstem, the limbic system, the cerebellum and the cerebral cortex. We will briefly look at the functions of these parts next, concentrating mainly on the cerebral cortex where many of the so-called 'higher' functions – such as perception and planning – reside.

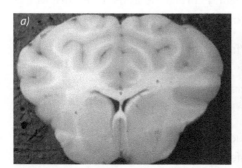

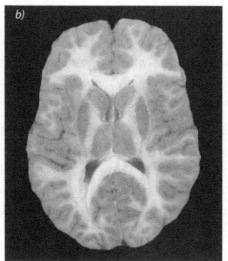

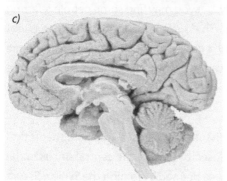

Figure 2.2: Brain sections
a) a coronal section
b) a sagittal section
c) an axial section

The brainstem, limbic system and cerebellum

These three parts of the brain are known as 'sub-cortical' regions, both because they are located under the cerebral cortex and because they are older in an evolutionary sense. The brainstem, which sits at the top of the spinal cord, controls many of the most basic functions that are necessary for the survival of the organism, including heartbeat, breathing and blood pressure. The limbic system contains regions that are responsible for our emotional reactions to events, and it can initiate hormonal responses. Regions in the limbic system include the amygdala, the hippocampus, the hypothalamus and the thalamus. The **amygdala** is crucial for emotional processing, particularly for negative emotions such as fear and threat, while the **hypothalamus** controls thirst, mood, hunger and temperature. Activity in the hippocampus is related to memory and learning, among other functions, while parts of the thalamus receive incoming signals from the various senses such as vision and hearing. The cerebellum (often known as 'the little brain') is located at the back of the brain, and plays an important role in motor movements and balance.

The cerebral cortex

One of the things you should notice from the coronal and axial sections of Figure 2.2 is that the brain seems to appear darker around the edges. The dark edges you see in these sections are the outer layer of the brain known as the cerebral **cortex**, which is a six-layered sheet of tissue densely packed with neurons; because of its dark colour it is known as **grey matter**. Inside this outer layer is the white matter – mainly myelinated axons connecting cortical neurons to the rest of the nervous system or to cortical neurons in other regions of the cortex.

As the cortex is one large sheet of tissue, it needs to be 'folded up' to fit into your head. These folds are what give the brain its wrinkled appearance. Happily for us, almost all cortices are folded up in the same way, giving rise to very specific patterns of folds that, like eyes and ears, we all have but in a unique configuration.

It has been at least a couple of paragraphs since introducing some terminology so it is about time for some more. The folds or creases in the cortex are referred to as sulci (the singular is **sulcus**) or fissures; sometimes these terms are used interchangeably, but you may find some people referring to shallow folds as sulci and deeper folds as fissures. The surface of the cortex that is not disappearing into a crease is known as a **gyrus** (the plural is gyri). Almost all brains have the same sulci and gyri in roughly the same places, and these can act as the landmarks by which we can navigate around the cortex. Some important landmarks that use sulci and gyri are shown in Figure 2.3.

The central sulcus, Sylvian fissure and parietal-occipital fissure can be used to create theoretical divisions of the brain. The anterior area of the cortex enclosed by joining the central sulcus to the Sylvian fissure is known as the frontal cortex; the inferior area defined by joining the Sylvian fissure

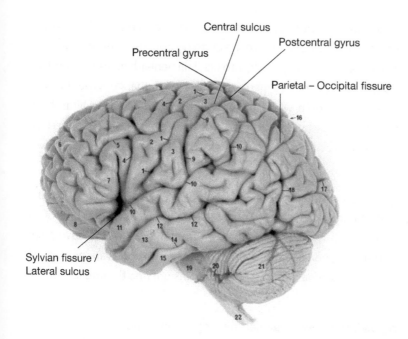

Central sulcus

Postcentral gyrus

Precentral gyrus

Parietal – Occipital fissure

Figure 2.3: Landmarks of the cortex

Sylvian fissure /
Lateral sulcus

to the parietal-occipital fissure is known as the temporal cortex; the superior area defined by the Sylvian fissure, the central sulcus and the parietal-occipital fissure is known as the parietal cortex; and the remaining posterior area is known as the occipital cortex. You will see articles referring to frontal, temporal, parietal and occipital lobes – this refers to the whole section of brain covered by these areas of the cortex, as the cortex is just the outer layer. Essentially, then, the frontal cortex is the outer layer of the brain towards the front of the brain, while the frontal lobe is all of the brain in that area – the outer layer *and* the inner layers.

These four areas of the cortex are associated with specific behaviours and psychological processes that we will discuss in more detail.

The frontal lobes

Perhaps the most famous case used to illustrate the characteristics of frontal lobe functioning is that of Phineas Gage in 1848 (Macmillan, 2008). Phineas Gage was a foreman working for the Rutland and Burlington Railroad company laying tracks across Vermont in the USA. In order to lay railway tracks the ground has to be reasonably level, so any large rocky obstacles either have to be avoided or blown up to make a level route. Part of Phineas's job was overseeing the demolition of such obstacles – drilling holes in the rock, filling them with gunpowder and setting a charge to create an explosion and so on. In particular, Phineas used to 'tamp-down' the explosive in the hole by hitting the loose powder with an iron bar known as a tamping iron. By hitting the powder with the bar, the powder becomes more tightly packed giving more energy and destructive force to the subsequent explosion.

However, one Wednesday afternoon in September 1848, an accident occurred as Phineas was tamping down the explosives. As he hit the powder with the tamping iron, the explosive went off, sending the tamping iron flying back through his hands, into his skull beneath his left eye and out of the top of his skull, eventually landing about 20 metres behind him. Remarkably, he survived. He was carried to a cart, which took him home, where he climbed down from the cart himself, sat on his veranda and told the story to passers-by until a doctor arrived. The medical care he received was probably a key factor in Phineas's continued survival until his death in 1860, some 12 years after the accident.

What makes this case so interesting for students of bio-psychology is Phineas's behaviour in the 12 years following the accident. Though there is some debate as to the actual areas of his brain that were damaged by this accident, it is clear to see that the frontal lobes would have been affected to some degree by the tamping iron passing through his head. The observations made at that time about the changes in Phineas's behaviour can provide an insight into the implications of frontal lobe damage.

Phineas recovered reasonably well but never regained his original job, and his post-accident behaviour was described by his doctor as irreverent, grossly profane, impatient and capricious about his plans for his future, with the balance between his intellect and 'animal propensities' destroyed. This was clearly at odds with his behaviour prior to the accident, which was said to be efficient, shrewd and capable. Clearly, then, the frontal lobes may be seen either to mediate 'animalistic urges' or to control 'civilised, intellectual behaviour'. Phineas's case has often been retrospectively, perhaps even incorrectly, reported as an example of what can happen when the civilising effects of the frontal lobes are removed, resulting in an animal-like 'frontal lobe syndrome'.

One of the difficulties of Phineas's case is the lack of solid evidence about his behaviour in the historical record. However, evidence is available from more contemporary sources to suggest such a complex, 'executive' role for frontal lobe functions. Luria et al. (1964) noted a patient, 'Zav', who had frontal lobe damage and was unable to copy sequences of movement or reproduce a series of rhythmical taps even though she could understand the instructions to do so. From observations of Zav, Luria and colleagues concluded that frontal lobe damage resulted in being unable to inhibit impulsive reactions, seemingly responding instead to the demands of the environment, which may account for Phineas's capricious and profane manner.

This pattern of behaviour has been found in a number of patients with frontal lobe damage (Konow and Pribram, 1970; Wallis, 2007) and led to the idea of a frontal lobe 'syndrome' consisting of disinhibited and impulsive behaviour. This 'syndrome', though, is by no means found in all patients with frontal lobe damage; the pattern of impairment observed in such patients is often varied and can include emotional blunting, poor memory performance or an inability to shift between tasks.

One attempt to explain this variety of deficits over and above the use of a purely descriptive phrase such as 'frontal lobe syndrome' refers to executive functions or goal-directed behaviour. Aspects of the (intact) frontal lobes are thought to play a role in complex behaviours required to complete certain goals, and goal completion is thought to require some organisational function that controls and manages simpler psychological functions that need to be strung together to complete more complex goals. For example, going out to eat may be a relatively straightforward goal, but in order to complete this task, you need to manage and combine several simpler behaviours (using a telephone, driving a car, reading a menu, communicating with your guests and the waiter). Executive functions take on the task of ordering these simpler tasks and initiating them as and when appropriate; it is this executive functioning that is thought to be affected by frontal lobe damage.

If these executive functions are damaged in some way, then individuals may not be able to self-initiate sequences of actions, and consequently they either perform the same action repeatedly (known as perseveration) or they act only in response to the environment rather than under their own initiative. An individual with such deficits could be said to be capricious or animalistic, just as Phineas Gage was described.

The parietal lobes

The range of psychological functioning mainly associated with the parietal lobes is visuo-motor guidance – tasks that involve making use of visual information or coordinating motor movements of the body to visual information from the environment. In its simplest form this may be a simple 'find the letter' task; for example, when you are looking through a word search puzzle to find specific letters or words, it is your parietal lobe that is active. This activation of the parietal lobe can be shown by examining fMRI or PET activity when participants are asked to visually search for, and locate, specific targets (see Corbetta, 1998, for a review). What such studies show is that there is a network of activity that becomes active when individuals are asked to perform such visual searches – a network that spans both the frontal and the parietal lobes.

Not only does activity in the parietal lobe increase in response to visual searches, the area is also active when individuals are asked to visually imagine objects and then manipulate (usually rotate) them (Kosslyn et al., 1998). In order to activate your parietal lobe right now, imagine the letter 'A', and then rotate it in your mind – it is this kind of mental rotation that requires parietal lobe functioning. Kosslyn and colleagues discovered that there seemed to be two distinct 'circuits' of activity activated by different stimuli; if the imagery was a geometric shape, then the parietal and occipital lobes were activated; however, when the imagery was a human hand, then parietal, occipital and frontal lobes were activated. This suggests there are different systems at work – one for mental rotation and one for preparatory motor movements (as participants were imagining rotating their own hands when using the hand stimuli).

The parietal lobe has also been implicated in the function of corollary discharge, which is essentially a signal from the brain to itself about what it is doing. That sounds complicated, so an example may help at this point. Put the book down for a second and jump up and down. As you move, you will perceive yourself moving through the environment, moving up and down or side to side. What you do not perceive is that the environment is suddenly moving, as it might in an earthquake. The reason for this is that in order to jump, your brain is sending lots of signals to your muscles, but at the same time it is sending messages back to itself to let you know that it is not an earthquake – it is actually you causing the disturbance. This feedback signal is known as corollary discharge and it lets us know what we are doing and what we are not doing so that we can accurately perceive the world around us – it is also why we cannot tickle ourselves. Corollary discharge originates in the frontal lobes but terminates in the parietal lobes in an area known as the somatosensory cortex, a strip of cortex that represents sensation throughout our bodies – we will discuss this in more detail in Chapter 4.

Up to this point the evidence for parietal lobe function (visuo-motor guidance) is based on observing activation levels in the brain during certain tasks, but what happens if the parietal lobe is damaged in some way? As you may imagine, damage in this area results in a visuo-motor disturbance and this is known as visual neglect (McFie and Zangwill, 1960). Visual neglect is a rather rare and strange condition where individuals are unable to 'see' parts of the world around them, often behaving as if they do not exist. Typically, neglect stems from stroke damage to the right parietal lobe and shows contra-lateral effects; that is, if the damage is in the right hemisphere, the neglected area of the world is on the patient's left side. In some cases, the damage is so great that an entire side of space is neglected by the individual and such encompassing one-sided neglect is referred to as hemi-neglect.

If asked to copy a drawing, individuals with neglect will often do so but miss out aspects of the original drawing that fall in the neglected area; they may not attempt to dress the left side of their bodies; or they may misread hyphenated words such as 'visuo-motor' simply as 'motor'. Clearly such a deficit would be frustrating and at times dangerous to live with. It is thought that such damage to the right parietal lobe results in a deficit in visual attention rather than in the visual system itself, so those with neglect are able to see a whole scene but are unable to attend to all of it.

The occipital lobes

The function most associated with the occipital lobes is the sensory processes of vision, and while the majority of the occipital lobes are devoted to vision, visual processing is not confined to the occipital lobes alone. The occipital lobes are home to the primary visual cortex, which processes the visual information it receives via a certain route from the eyes. If damage occurs to cells at any point in the visual pathway from the eye to the visual cortex in the occipital lobe, then the result can be blindness or impaired vision, depending on the extent of the damage. Blindness or, more commonly, impaired vision from occipital lobe damage is referred to as cortical blindness, as the eyes still retain their full functioning but the signals they send are not processed.

The 'map' of visual information in the primary visual cortex is said to be topographic. This means that the relationship between specific points of the visual field are retained by the cortex – if you damage one area of the cortex, then the corresponding area of the visual field will be impaired. Although this cortical representation is topographic, it is inverted, with the top of the visual field being represented by the bottom of the visual cortex and the left side of the visual field being represented by the right side of the visual cortex. So damage to the left ventral visual cortex results in an area of impaired vision for the upper right of the visual field. Such an area of impaired vision is known as a scotoma. Scotomas are not areas of blindness or blackness in your vision but rather areas that are just not perceived, rather like the blind spot we all have in each eye but do not notice.

Other visual problems can be related to damage of the occipital lobe, and because of the complex organisation and pathways of the visual system, such damage can result in some quite different experiences. One such experience is **visual agnosia** (a deficit in object recognition).

Perhaps the most widely reported instance of this is the man who mistook his wife for a hat (Sacks, 1985) – Dr P, to give him his proper pseudonym. Dr P was a music teacher who developed a large growing tumour in his occipital lobe, resulting in his rather odd visually related behaviour that is indicative of visual agnosia. Although Dr P's sight was fine, his processing of visual information was disrupted in that he was unable to recognise objects or faces from vision alone; thus he attempted to grasp his wife's head, lift it off and place it on his own, believing her to be a hat. More poignantly, he was unable to recognise his family, friends, colleagues or students from their photographs alone; instead, he had developed a method of recognising distinctive features and using these to trigger his memory for the person. He was therefore able to recognise his brother from a photograph because of his brother's big teeth and square jaw, and he was able to recognise a student from the way they moved, but without these cues Dr P was at a loss to recognise them.

The temporal lobes

In order to illustrate some of the functions attributed to the temporal lobe we will return to case studies again, but this time to one that is a little more modern. In 1957 Scoville and Milner reported the case of HM, who from an early age had experienced epileptic seizures. They were increasing in severity – so much so that at the age of 27 it was decided to treat his condition through neurosurgery, bilaterally removing his medial temporal lobes as this was where the epileptic foci were. Now you know your terminology, you should be able to work out that bilateral medial temporal lobe removal involves removing the middle (medial) parts of the temporal lobe from both (bilateral) sides of the brain.

This surgery led to a successful cessation of seizures, but it had a noticeable impact on HM's psychological functioning – it impacted quite drastically on his memory. Following the operation HM would quite happily sit and read the same magazine over and over, would complete the same jigsaw puzzle repeatedly without any recognition or familiarity. He would even be unable to remember what he had had for lunch or even that he had had lunch as little as half an hour after eating it.

HM eventually worked in protected employment in a state rehabilitation centre in the USA, performing quite repetitive work (for example, putting cigarette lighters into cardboard display cases), and he successfully lived alone in his own bungalow. However, six months after starting this work he was unable to recall his place of work, his job, or the route to and from his workplace. Since his surgery HM clearly had difficulties in forming new memories (known as **anterograde amnesia**), and his case, along with many others, has led to the idea that the temporal lobes are important in memory functioning.

Mr B developed a tumour in his left temporal lobe at around the age of 38 when he had become a successful and well-respected oil company executive. Following the tumour his memory performance markedly decreased and he had difficulty maintaining performance in his job. In fact, his memory was particularly poor for verbal narratives but seemed unimpaired for recalling digits or shapes. This curious pattern of memory deficit may be due to the tumour affecting only his left temporal lobe, leaving the right temporal lobe functioning quite typically, which suggests that the right and left temporal lobes may play different roles in memory functioning.

The memory deficits of Ms C further this argument as she developed a tumour in her right temporal lobe at around the age of 22. Ms C was a promising student prior to the tumour, but afterwards she developed specific memory deficits, in that she had problems with recalling shapes but had no difficulties with her memory for verbal narratives. It is possible, then, that the left temporal lobe is required for verbally based memories while the right temporal lobe is required for visually based memories.

You might at this point start to question whether we therefore have different kinds of memories, performed by different regions of the temporal lobe or brain, and you would be right to do so. Memory is not one psychological function but a whole array of different and interacting processes, and we will explore this in more detail in Chapter 6. As well as not underestimating the complexity of the psychological processes discussed here, it is also important not to underestimate the complexity of the brain. The temporal lobes are a great example of this, for not only are they implicated in memory functioning, they are implicated in other processes too. For example, the temporal lobes are the end-point for all incoming information from our auditory (hearing) system, sometimes referred to as the auditory cortex, and damage to this area can result in impairments in understanding language. So while reviewing the functions of the lobes it is worth remembering that the lobes which we have been discussing are large brain areas that include many structures carrying out different functions, so any attempt to define just one function that a lobe carries out is inherently over-generalised. So you need to be aware that the functions of the lobes we have discussed really are just the tip of the iceberg – we will explore some of these issues further in later chapters.

Critical thinking activity

The role of the cerebral cortex in controlling sexual impulses – a case study

Critical thinking focus: analysing and evaluating

Key question: *What can case studies tell us about the importance of the brain in controlling impulses?*

For this activity, you should locate and read the following paper:

> Burns, JM and Swerdlow, RH (2003) Right orbitofrontal tumor with pedophilia symptom and constructional apraxia sign. *Archives of Neurology*, 60, 437.

If there are any words or ideas that you do not understand, please use an online dictionary to check what they mean.

The paper reviews a case study of a 40-year-old male who suddenly develops an interest in child pornography, and has no control over his sexual urges. Read the paper, and think about the following questions.

1. What does the section on personal history tell us about this man? Does his paedophilia and lack of sexual impulse control seem out of character?

2. The man was diagnosed with a tumour in the orbito frontal cortex (OFC). What does his behaviour tell about the function of the OFC? What does the report name as the functions of the OFC?

3. How can the researchers justify their idea that the tumour is linked to inappropriate sexual behaviour?

4. Are case studies useful in understanding how the brain works? What criticism can you think for case studies?

Critical thinking review

1. The fairly detailed personal history that is reported in the paper is interesting, and reveals a fair amount of information about the previous behaviour of the patient. It seems that paedophilia and lack of control for sexual impulses are out of character. The report reveals that he started developing an interest in child pornography in a very short space of time, and started molesting his step-daughter after living with her for some years without having sexual interest in her. Thus it seems that something 'triggered' the sudden paedophilia and inappropriate sexual behaviour, and that the behaviour escalated and spiralled out of control very rapidly.

2. OFC is important in the development of social and moral behaviour. Especially in adults, damage in the OFC can result in the inability to control impulses that are not socially acceptable. Patients with OFC lesions have their moral judgements intact (i.e. they know what is right and what is wrong), but they are not able to control their behaviour, even though they would like to be able to control it. Thus, OFC has a crucial role in keeping our behaviour in check, and controlling socially unacceptable behaviours.

3. The case study report reveals close links between the OFC tumour and sexually inappropriate behaviour. The paedophilic tendencies coincided with the migraines and the growth of the tumour. When the tumour was removed, the patient reported that the sexual urges were also gone. Further, the year following the operation, the patient started developing migraines and inappropriate sexual interests again. An MRI scan revealed that the tumour had reappeared. It is clear that the repeated appearance of the tumour, coupled with the migraines and the poor sexual impulse control, are closely linked to each other. It is safe to say that the OFC tumour made a major contribution to the paedophilic interests of the patient.

4. Case studies can be useful because they reveal richer information about the patient that can be used in understanding how brain tumours are related to behaviour. Case studies should always be discussed in relation to existing research, as the authors of the article being studied here have done successfully. Case studies can be used only to support existing quantitative research, as we cannot generalise from a single person to the whole population. So, for example, if we find that in one person OFC damage is linked to paedophilia, we cannot conclude that this is the case for all OFC patients unless other research has found a statistically significant relationship in studies with multiple patients.

Skill builder activity

Mapping the main structures of the brain

Transferable skill focus: communication

Key question: *What are the main structures of the brain?*

The communication of concepts, theories and facts is an important task of a scientific researcher. While the primary form of communication is generally the written or spoken word, a valuable and often efficient way of communication is by visual image. Pictures and diagrams can often convey large amounts of information in an economical way, proving true the old saying that 'a picture is worth a thousand words'. This task is an opportunity for you to develop your skills of communication by visual image. At the same time, the process of creating images or pictures of the structures of the brain should help you to remember the different areas of the brain.

The activity should be completed with pens and a large piece of paper. The aim is to draw three pictures of the human brain – your pictures can be as creative and colourful as you like. The first picture should be a diagram of the different views of the brain (see Table 2.2). The second picture should be of the lateral surface of the left hemisphere, and should include the four major cortical lobes and some details about the major functional roles of each lobe. The third picture should be a medial view of the brain, showing the cortex, the parts of the limbic system, the cerebellum and the brainstem. Again, you should include some details of the important functions of these brain regions. For the last two pictures, it may help to do an internet search of images of the brain.

Skill builder review

This activity helps you to develop your visual communication skills, which can be a very effective way to communicate complex information. Sometimes people can grasp ideas or facts more easily when they see a diagram or an image. Also, by making a drawing of the various regions of the brain, you may improve your chances of remembering these details in the future. Lastly, you spent some time drawing, which is always a fun skill to practise.

Assignments

1. Can the brain change in adults as a result of learning? Review this with regard to spatial knowledge and grey matter volume in the hippocampus.

2. How does the brain grow? Discuss the different processes of neural growth during brain development in infancy.

3. Are females and males different? Find out evidence for sex differences in the neuronal wiring and structure of the brain.

Summary: what you have learned

- You should have a good understanding of the six main developmental stages during the maturation of the brain.

- You should have a solid understanding of how the brain is structured.

- You should be able to locate the different lobes in the cerebral cortex, and understand what their basic functions are.

- You should be able to discuss normal brain functioning, and what happens when there are tumours or lesions.

Further reading

http://thebrain.mcgill.ca/

A good educational website for exploring the brain:

www.sciencemuseum.org.uk/WhoAmI/FindOutMore.aspx

Another good website, maintained by the Science Museum in London.

Blakemore, SJ (2012) Development of the social brain in adolescence. *JRSM*, 105, 111–116. (You can download a copy on academic search engines.)

Interesting article on adolescence brain development.

Huttenlocher, PR (2009) Neural plasticity: the effects of environment on the development of the cerebral cortex. Cambridge, MA: Harvard University Press.

A good book on neural plasticity of the human brain.

Chapter 3

The nervous system

Learning outcomes

By the end of this chapter you should:

- *have a good understanding of the divisions of the nervous system;*
- *have developed your critical thinking skills in reflection;*
- *have developed your independent learning skills;*
- *have a good understanding of the 'mechanics' of the nervous system, that is, the structure and function of the individual cells in the nervous system.*

The organisation of the nervous system

The nervous system is a large and complex interconnecting network of cells and nerves that weaves its way throughout most of the body, carrying out some very important functions. Although it is all interconnected, some parts of the system carry out very different functions to others, and it is useful to be able to differentiate between these different parts. To this end the nervous system is conceptually divided into several distinct networks (the major sub-divisions), each offering something unique to the way we function as humans (see Figure 3.1).

The first major sub-division to note is the distinction between the **central nervous system** (CNS) and the **peripheral nervous system** (PNS). The CNS consists of the brain and the spinal cord, while the PNS refers to the rest of the nervous system in our bodies.

The central nervous system (CNS)

The brain is undoubtedly the centre of the CNS, carrying out numerous functions that we often take for granted but that make us innately human. Our brains give us the ability to think and perceive and experience the world around us by receiving sensation from our environments and initiating our own behaviours in order to explore and interact with those environments. The brain is often the end point for all incoming stimuli and the beginning of our wilful actions, and is so complex that the whole of the previous chapter was devoted to it.

Figure 3.1: *Flow chart of nervous system components*

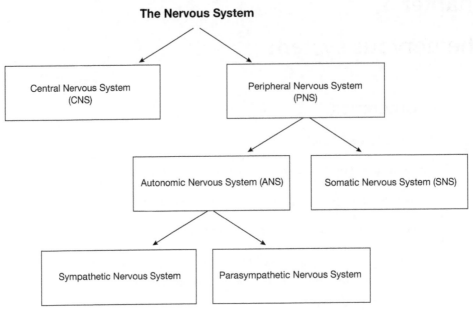

The spinal cord is the second component of the CNS and is just as important, if not as complex, as the brain. Like the brain, the spinal cord is conceptually divided into specific areas. These are (from the skull downwards):

- the cranial section;
- the cervical section;
- the thoracic section;
- the lumbar section;
- the sacral section;
- the coccygeal section.

The spinal cord acts as a pathway to and from the brain, allowing information to travel from the brain to various parts of your body to effect action (e.g. activating muscles to walk, talk or breathe) and allowing information to travel from various parts of your body into your brain to enable perceptions (e.g. sending pain information from your big toe to your brain if someone stands on your foot, or from your heart to your brain if you have a heart attack).

The brain and the spinal cord are so important to our biological functioning that evolution has provided the CNS with its own unique form of protection by evolving a bony shield to help protect it from damage. The bony skull and the spine surround the soft nerve tissues of the brain and spinal cord in order to protect these most valuable components of our biology; without this protection it would be like wearing your heart on your sleeve, revealing a vulnerable and vital part of yourself to the world around you.

The peripheral nervous system (PNS)

The PNS is made up of the nerves that radiate out from your spinal cord to many locations and organs within your body. Some of these are afferent nerves (they direct information towards the brain and spinal cord), and some of them are efferent nerves (directing information away from your brain and spinal cord). Afferent nerves typically carry sensory information from the outside world and from your internal organs into your CNS. These are the nerves that convey tactile information about the texture of the book you are holding or let you know that you have indigestion in your stomach, for example. They provide useful information about your environment and about your internal bodily state. By contrast, efferent nerves convey information from your CNS to your body, activating muscles so that you can walk or talk or take deep breaths.

Nerves that innervate lower areas of your body (providing sensation in your feet or controlling your bowels) will connect to a lower point of the spinal cord (e.g. lumbar, sacral or coccygeal sections); similarly, nerves that innervate higher areas of your body (providing sensation in your shoulders or controlling your heart rate) will connect to a higher point of the spinal cord (e.g. cervical or thoracic sections). This is why the location of spinal injuries is so important; a higher site of injury will result in more areas of your body being disconnected from your CNS. The PNS may be unimpaired, but its communication with the brain will be disconnected, affecting all afferent nerve pathways (resulting in a loss of sensation) and all efferent pathways (resulting in a loss of willed muscle control).

Sub-divisions of the peripheral nervous system

Different components of the PNS serve different functions and are distinguished accordingly:

- the **autonomic nervous system** (ANS);
- the **somatic nervous system** (SNS), which includes the cranial nerves.

These sub-types contain both afferent and efferent nerves.

The autonomic and enteric nervous systems

The ANS is essentially the collection of nerves that act as the manager of your internal organs. They control your heart rate, your blood pressure, your perspiration and so on. Some texts also refer to a sub-set of the ANS known as the **enteric nervous system**, which refers to a fine network of nerves that are found only in the walls of the digestive tract and control the digestive process.

You may have noticed that you cannot deliberately increase or decrease your heart rate (or other internal processes) by will alone. This is because your autonomic nervous system is under 'automatic' control and not subject to conscious influence. The ANS can function independently (autonomically) of the CNS and the SNS, which is why individuals with spinal cord injury are still able to regulate their heart rates and control other internal, visceral systems.

The sympathetic and parasympathetic autonomic nervous systems

There is also a further division of the ANS into the **sympathetic autonomic nervous system** (sANS) and the **parasympathetic autonomic nervous system** (pANS), which serve distinct functions within the ANS (see Figure 3.2). Essentially, the sANS refers to the autonomic nerves that prepare your internal systems for emergency action (the fight or flight response), while the pANS refers to the autonomic nerves that prepare your internal systems for calm. The sANS and the pANS are not different messages going through the same nervous system; they are different networks of nerves that innervate your internal systems, so any internal organ will be connected to one set of nerves that can prepare that organ for fight or flight, and will also be connected to another set of nerves that can prepare that organ for calm. To reinforce the idea of these being two entirely

Figure 3.2: *Sympathetic and parasympathetic divisions of the autonomic nervous system*

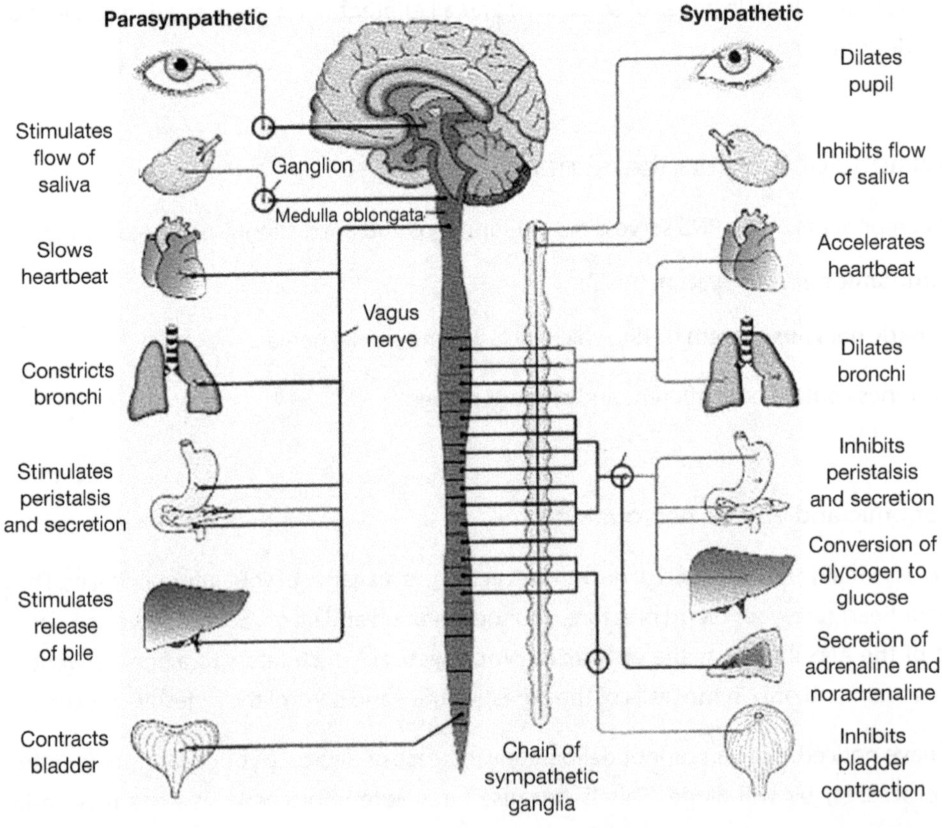

separate systems you should note that the sANS connects to the thoracic and lumbar regions of the spinal cord, while the pANS is connected to the cranial and sacral regions of the spinal cord.

Actions related to the sANS include: dilating the bronchia (a passage conducting air towards the lungs); accelerating the heart rate; increasing secretion by the sweat glands in your skin; inhibiting digestion; increasing secretion of adrenaline and noradrenaline; and inhibiting muscular contractions of the bladder. All of these actions ready the body for fight or flight by increasing the intake of oxygen, increasing the amount of oxygen directed to the muscles via increased blood flow, and directing resources away from less important tasks in emergency situations (water retention, 'secondary' muscular contractions). Taken together, the functioning of the sANS can explain many of the physiological reactions noticeable during an emergency situation (reddened face from increased blood flow, a sense of a pounding heart from increased heart rate, emptying of the bowels and/or bladder).

The actions performed by the pANS are opposite to the sANS, in order to promote relaxation and calm, and they include: constricting the bronchia; decreasing the heart rate; decreasing sweating; stimulating digestion; decreasing the secretion of adrenaline and noradrenaline; and contracting the bladder.

The somatic nervous system

The SNS, like the ANS, is comprised of afferent and efferent nerves; however, unlike the ANS, the SNS allows us to interact with our external environments through sensation (through afferent nerves taking information towards the brain) and movement (through efferent nerves carrying information away from the brain).

The somatic nervous system nerves join the spinal cord at all levels: cranial, cervical, thoracic, lumbar, sacral and coccygeal.

The somatic nerves connect to the spinal column through spaces in the bony vertebrae that occur at regular intervals, allowing access to the spinal cord. As you can see from the cross-sectional diagram of the spinal column (Figure 3.3), the nerves connect to the spinal cord on the left and the right side of the vertebra and do so in two places on each side – towards the front (known as ventral) and towards the back (known as dorsal). The ventral connections, or roots, convey sensory information while the dorsal roots convey motor information. This means that the two aspects of the somatic nervous system are functionally distinct and physically separate – one deals with the senses and one deals with movement (motor control). This separation remains within the spinal cord, with sensory information being transmitted vertically upwards (to the brain) within the spinal cord via a distinct ventral pathway, and motor information being transmitted vertically (from the brain) within the dorsal pathway of the spinal cord.

Figure 3.3: *Cross-section of spinal cord*

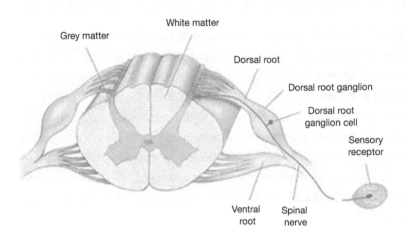

There are occasions when information within the somatic nervous system is not transmitted to or from the brain but is instead dealt with wholly within the spinal cord. These occasions are reflex actions where sensory information (being hit on the knee with a rubber hammer) enters the spinal cord through the ventral root and almost immediately causes motor information (a knee jerk) to be transmitted out of the dorsal root. In this way we can sense and act without the brain's direct involvement at all. You may have seen such tests of reflex being carried out by neurologists to assess where there may be any damage to the nervous system that is independent of brain functioning.

Task — Take some time out now and map out on a blank piece of paper the divisions of the nervous system encountered so far. Write a brief description of the functions that each division of the peripheral nervous system serves and include the two distinct pathways within the spinal cord. This activity checks your understanding of the gross organisation of the nervous system. As you progress through the book and learn more about the biology involved, you may find it helpful to pause and create such notes for yourself so that the overall organisation of the biological system is firmly embedded in your mind; understanding the biological aspects well will make it easier to comprehend the many functions associated with each biological aspect.

The cranial nerves

The cranial nerves are part of the somatic nervous system and, like the rest of the somatic nervous system, convey both sensory and motor information to and from the brain. As the cranial nerves connect either directly into the brain or into the very beginnings of the spinal cord at the base of the brain (the brainstem), bypassing the spinal column, they are typically identified as being separate to the rest of the SNS, which utilises the ventral and dorsal pathways of the spinal cord.

There are 12 cranial nerves in total, each referred to by one of the Roman numerals I–XII and each carrying out specific functions. Some cranial nerves are solely sensory, some are solely motor, and some are both. However, cranial nerves that serve both sensory and motor functions have separate pathways for each, rather than one nerve that is both motor and sensory.

- Cranial nerves I, II and VII serve olfactory (smell), optical (vision), and vestibulocochlear (inner ear) senses respectively, and are solely sensory afferent nerves.

- Cranial nerves III, IV, VI, XI and XII serve motor functions of the eye (oculomotor, trochlear and abducens), the neck (spinal accessory), and the tongue muscles (hyperglossal) respectively, and are solely efferent motor nerves.

- The remaining cranial nerves – V, VII, IX and X – serve both motor and sensory functions through different pathways; these are the trigeminal nerve (face, teeth, sinus, jaw muscles), facial nerve (tongue, facial muscles, salivary and tear glands), glossopharyngeal nerve (taste), and the vagus nerve (internal organs) respectively.

So far we have seen that the nervous system can be divided into distinct sub-divisions that serve specific functions within our bodies; now would be good time to review your understanding of them and to consider some of the consequences of this structure.

Critical thinking activity

Nervous system sub-divisions

Critical thinking focus: analysing and evaluating

Key question: *How useful is nervous system measurement as an indicator of lying in a forensic context?*

Go to the British Psychological Society's journals website (www.bps.org.uk/publications), and access Ben-Shakhar's (2008) paper, The case against the use of polygraph examinations to monitor post-conviction sex offenders. *Legal and Criminological Psychology*, 13, 191–207.

As you read through the paper it may be helpful to have some of the following questions in your mind.

- What components of the nervous system are measured by polygraph examinations?

- Why are these components chosen?

- Is there a certain response that indicates lying?

- How is lying indicated by the polygraph?

Critical thinking review

One of the things you may notice from your understanding of the nervous system is that some divisions of the nervous system are under conscious control (e.g. the central nervous system) and some are not (e.g. the autonomic nervous system). As the central nervous system is under conscious control, we can make it do what we choose. It can initiate speech and determine what we say to others, for example; this can be truthful or deceitful – whichever we have consciously chosen. In contrast, we cannot consciously control our autonomic nervous system – it will react to our environments. If you are sitting in a warm room reading this, you may be sweating; if it is a cold room, you may have 'goose bumps'. This is due to your autonomic nervous system and you cannot consciously do anything to stop your body shivering or sweating. Your autonomic nervous system, then, is 'honest', reacting in appropriate ways to your environment with no possible way of 'faking' the response. This simple aspect of the divisions of the nervous system is the principle behind lie detector tests or polygraphs – you cannot consciously 'fake' an ANS response.

However, as Ben-Shakhar points out, there is a great deal of individual difference in ANS response, so there is no objective score on a polygraph that indicates lying; polygraphs must make within-subject comparisons of ANS responses from one individual to a number of questions. Polygraphs measure many aspects of an individual's autonomic nervous system during questioning to determine how they are autonomically reacting to what they are consciously saying. As Ben-Shakhar notes, at least three measures of ANS arousal are used, which usually include respiration rate, electrodermal activity and blood pressure – all aspects that are under ANS control.

In particular, the polygrapher will look for differential responses to control and critical questions, the assumption being that the stress or guilt of lying will result in measurable and uncontrollable ANS activity across some or all of the domains being measured. While the notion of a measurable response that cannot be consciously controlled is clearly an attractive one for lie detection, there is no identifiable pattern of ANS activity that denotes lying; it is the relative differences in ANS activity between the control and critical questions that is thought to be suggestive of deceit.

Take a moment to consider if there are other aspects of ANS measurement that may be problematic for a lie detection test.

Issues that have been raised as criticisms of this approach are that the ANS activity is reacting to the environment, and the environment can be thought of as containing many variables, including the physical environment (e.g. the temperature of the room, or a drawing pin in sticking into you) as well as the psychological environment (e.g. an emotional reaction to the question or answer or the stressful nature of the procedure). As such, it is difficult to claim that a person's ANS response is solely in response to the answer they give; in other words, their ANS could be reacting to any number of things in the immediate environment.

Further to this, the entire paradigm rests on a comparison of activity between control and critical questions. If this is to be scientifically accurate, then the control and critical questions should be identical, apart from the one critically manipulated aspect. In this way the polygrapher can be sure that any differences in response are due to the single manipulated aspect rather than other differences between control and critical questions. Frequently this tight control on question wording is not done, rendering the 'scientific' approach flawed.

One further criticism of the polygraph approach is the way in which the ANS measures are quantified and the different responses to control and critical questions compared. It is not difficult to accurately measure the size of responses in each physiological domain (respiration, blood pressure, etc.) and then analyse these using appropriate statistical tests of difference. However, this is rarely the case in polygraphy, with comparisons often being made on subjective grounds, as Ben-Shakhar outlines.

Many biological psychologists (e.g. Kozel et al., 2009; Monteleone et al., 2009) acknowledge these criticisms and are now investigating whether changes can be detected in the consciously controlled divisions of the nervous system (for example, using functional imaging of brain activity) as this is where the conscious decision to lie actually takes place.

The cells of the nervous system

Now that we have discussed the gross organisation of the nervous system and thought about some of its implications, it is important to focus on the detail – that is, the cells that allow it to communicate and perform the wide range of functions that make us human. The cells that make up the nervous system can be divided into two main categories: glial cells and neurons.

Glial cells

Glial cells are found throughout the nervous system and are often referred to as supporting cells as their role is not to transfer information from one part of the nervous system to another but rather to provide an optimal environment for the neurons, whose role is to transfer information around the nervous system. These 'housekeeping' activities of the glial cells range from attacking invading organisms to promoting neuron repair and maintenance to providing insulation for the electrochemical communications that the neurons send and receive to modulating neuro-transmission (the communication between neurons). So although the glial cells themselves do not participate directly in our psychological and behavioural functioning, they do make such functioning possible and are an essential part of the nervous system.

There are several different types of glial cell, which can be roughly categorised as microglia or macroglia. **Microglia** are, as the name suggests, relatively small and can be considered to be the immune system of the CNS, attacking invading organisms or promoting tissue repair. **Macroglia**, in contrast, are larger cells that perform a range of activities throughout the entire nervous system. These activities may be aiding the insulation of the electrochemical messaging of the neurons (e.g. Schwann cells) or providing a 'scaffold' along which developing neurons may grow (radial glial cells).

Neurons: structure

Neurons are at the very centre of the functioning of the nervous system and are the means by which communication occurs within the nervous system. As such, it is incredibly important to understand their mechanisms of action in order to be able to understand the biological actions underlying any behaviour. It is estimated that there are approximately 150 billion neurons in the brain alone, and it is these that give us our 'processing power', allowing us to interact with the world around us, to create inner worlds we escape to, and to actively take part in our lives.

Like glial cells, neurons are found throughout the nervous system and also come in various types, which are distinguished by their shape or morphology and are therefore adapted to certain functions.

Task — As you can see from Figure 3.4, there are a variety of shapes and sizes of neurons, and these can be found throughout the nervous system, though some are so specialised they are found only in certain locations. One example is the motor neuron, which connects the nervous system to the muscles of the body. Reflect for a moment on these highly specialised cells and consider the following questions.

– What kinds of muscles will require nervous system control?

– What do those muscles do?

– What would be the consequences of a disease process affecting motor neurons only?

Figure 3.4: *A typical neuron and other neuronal morphologies*

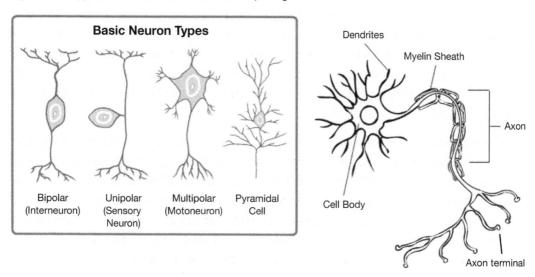

You may immediately think of muscles that control skeletal movement and enable us to walk or move; if you think a little more, you will realise that muscles also control non-skeletal movement (you need muscles to move your eyes over the words on this page). You may also have realised that many of the visceral functions of your body require some degree of muscular control, and these can be vital for our existence (moving our diaphragm so that we may breathe, making our heart beat, for example). Now that you have given some thought to the range of functions that require muscular involvement, consider what would happen if a disease process affected just one type of neuron – the motor neuron. In fact, that is what motor-neurone disease is – a disease that attacks motor neurons, causing the degeneration of the motor neurons, which causes interruption to the flow of information from the nervous system. Given what you now know about the role of muscles, what do you think would be the symptoms and outcome of motor neurone disease?

The typical signs and symptoms of motor neurone disease can be very wide ranging and may include impaired reflex actions and muscle weakness, resulting in a lack of motor control and eventually muscle wastage as the muscle is not being used; this can result in symptoms such as a dragging foot, slurred speech and even paralysis.

The muscles of the visceral system are affected too, which means that vital life systems can be impaired. Indeed, motor neurone disease is fatal, with death typically resulting from a loss of diaphragm function, which results in an inability to breathe. So you can see that the impact and function of just one neuronal type can be incredibly important to the whole biological system.

Despite the different varieties of neuronal shape, all neurons have some features and mechanisms in common in terms of their basic structure. Each neuron possesses certain common elements that are required for the general functioning of the neuron as an 'information processor', and these are the dendrite, the cell body (or soma), the nucleus, the axon, the axon terminal and the myelin sheath (see Figure 3.4). You will also notice that the neuron is defined by its membrane or cell wall, which holds everything in place. Inside the cell membrane is intracellular fluid, while outside the membrane the fluid in between the neurons is known as interstitial fluid. The neuronal membrane is semi-permeable, which means that it can change its configuration to let some, but not all, chemicals through (letting chemicals in the intracellular fluid out and letting chemicals from the interstitial fluid in).

The flow of information – or, more accurately, electrochemical transmissions – from many neurons enters the neuron through its dendrites. The input from many sources is then 'summed' in the cell body. Depending on whether this summed input reaches a certain level or not, the neuron will initiate its own electrochemical signal to pass on and continue the message along its axon (or not as the case may be). The axon carries the message right to its end at numerous axon terminals in order to pass the message on to numerous other neurons. The message is passed on because the axon terminals form connections (or synapses) with the dendrites of other neurons. Therefore each neuron receives inputs from many neurons and passes its own message on to many other neurons. In this way, great networks of activity (neural networks) are created throughout the nervous system and brain.

While each neuron alone cannot make complex decisions about data, the immense processing power of the brain comes from the whole network of neurons that function in parallel rather than serially. It is the sheer number of connections that provides this processing power rather than any single neuron being responsible on its own. There have been many attempts to replicate this processing power through artificial neural-like networks, and these have formed the basis of many artificial intelligence programmes. In order to better understand the role of biology in psychological processing and functioning, it is therefore important to understand these neuronal communications and connections in more detail.

Neurons: action

The basis of neuronal action is electro-chemistry, the electrical properties of various chemical particles found in the nervous system. You may recall from school chemistry lessons that atoms contain charged particles: electrons, which carry a negative charge, and protons, which carry a positive charge. Atoms can be combined together in different ways to form different chemical molecules; these chemical molecules may have an imbalance of protons or electrons, resulting in a slight electric charge. When molecules have a slight electric charge, they are known as ions. Ions have either an excess of protons, thereby being slightly positively charged (cations), or an excess of electrons, thereby being slightly negatively charged (anions). When two negatively charged ions (anions) or two positively charged ions (cations) are brought together, they repel each other; however, when two oppositely charged ions are brought together (an anion and a cation), they attract each other. Just like magnets, like charges repel each other and opposite charges attract each other. This is important, as ions are found both within the neuron, in intracellular fluid, and outside the neuron in interstitial fluid.

Inside the neuronal membrane in the intracellular fluid are large protein molecules that have a slight negative charge and that are too large to pass outside through the neuron's semi-permeable membrane; this gives the resting or inactive neuron a slightly negative charge overall of around –70mV (millivolts), known as the resting potential. So what happens when a neuron is activated?

A neuron may be activated by receiving input through its dendrites that originated from other neurons' outputs (i.e. they are part of a chain of neurons activating each other); neurons that are sensory receptors are activated directly from the environment (e.g. light hitting the neurons in the retina of the eye). However activation occurs, a neuron usually responds by changing the permeability of its membrane. This change in permeability does not let the large negative protein molecules out, but it does allow smaller ions (usually sodium ions) to get inside the neuron's membrane. The smaller ions that can now move through the membrane will be positively charged ions (cations) as these will be attracted to the negatively charged protein molecules (remember, opposite charges attract).

Once the neuron is active, then, the permeability of the membrane changes and allows an influx of positive ions inside the neuron. The effect of this is to gradually change the overall charge on the resting neuron, making it gradually more positive – this is known as depolarisation. As a consequence, the overall charge on the neuron gradually moves from its resting charge of approximately –70mV to –69mV, then –68mV and so on. As well as each neuron having a resting potential, each neuron also possesses a threshold potential, typically around –55mV. Once the overall charge of the neuron reaches this threshold level, the floodgates open and the neuron's membrane 'opens up' to allow even more positive ions to flood in, resulting in a brief positive spike where the overall charge on the neuron becomes positive for a brief moment. This spike in positive charge is known as the action potential and is how a neuron 'fires'. The size of the spike is always the same at approximately +40mV, regardless of the amount or size of the input to the neuron.

Once an action potential has fired, the neuron must return to its previous resting state, or resting potential, so that it can be ready to fire again if needed. It does this by closing the gaps in its membrane that have allowed positive sodium ions through, and by beginning to open potassium channels in its membrane, which allow the positive potassium ions to leave the neuron, return to the interstitial fluid and so make the overall charge on the neuron more negative. This process of the neuron becoming more negatively charged is termed hyperpolarisation. Hyperpolarisation often overshoots the resting potential, making the overall charge on the neuron even more negative than its resting potential of –70mV; this overshoot is often termed an afterpotential and it may take some time for the neuron to regain its resting potential balance via the movement of ions across the membrane.

All of this takes time, of course, typically in the order of milliseconds, which is remarkably fast. However, the short time between the cell reaching its threshold potential and the time when the cell re-establishes its resting potential is a refractory period when no matter what input the cell receives, it cannot fire an action potential, thus limiting the firing rate of the neuron.

Where does the action potential go?

The mechanism by which an action potential is created, described above, occurs in the cell body of the neuron, the point at which the neuron's dendrites converge. In order for the neuron to communicate with other neurons, the action potential needs to get down the axon, through the axon terminals and on to the next neuron(s).

In order to understand the journey of the action potential it helps to look at the cross-section of an axon (as shown in Figure 3.5). As you can see, the axon is surrounded by a myelin sheath, which is an electrically insulating material generated by glial cells. This insulation gives the nerve impulse direction by helping the action potential travel down the length of the axon rather than radiating

Figure 3.5: *Cross-section of an axon*

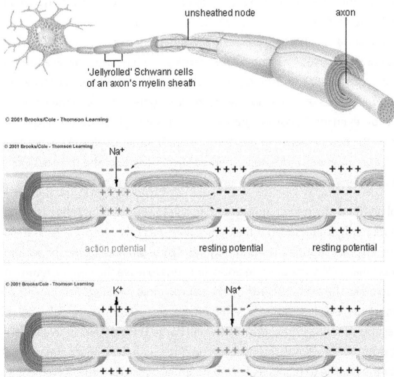

Myelin Sheath

A series of Schwann cells

Sheath blocks ion movements

Action potential must 'jump' from node to node

out from the axon. As you can see, the myelin sheath does not completely cover the length of the axon and there are 'gaps' where the axon can access the interstitial fluid – these 'gaps' are the nodes of Ranvier and are essential for the action potential's journey from the cell body to the tip of the axon.

Action potentials occur at the nodes of Ranvier but not in between; this is because for an action potential to fire, the cell's membrane needs to allow positive ions into the cell – this can only happen where the membrane is exposed to the interstitial fluid and not covered by myelin (i.e. at the nodes of Ranvier). In essence, then, the action potential does not 'flow' smoothly along an axon, but rather 'jumps' from one node of Ranvier to the next in a sequence of action potentials.

Each action potential at a node can travel a short distance beneath a myelinated section of an axon and begin to change the permeability of the membrane of the axon at the next node of Ranvier – this change in permeability lets positive ions flow into the axon, allowing the new action potential to be initiated. In this way the action potential is constantly regenerated along the length of the axon. This is a very useful means of transmission, as the signal (action potential) initiated at the cell body does not diminish or fade by the time it reaches the end of the axon. In fact, this continually self-regenerating 'jumping' transmission not only occurs within the axon of one neuron, but also occurs when neurons communicate with each other; each neuron will generate a new action potential as it passes the 'signal' on from one neuron to another.

Neuronal interaction

Gap junctions

There are two basic types of connections that neurons make with each other where axon terminals from one neuron connect with the dendrites of another neuron. The first of these connection types are known as gap junctions. Paradoxically, gap junctions have virtually no gap, they are junctions where the axon terminal is structurally continuous with a dendrite, that is, they are physically connected together, and the action potential can jump from one neuron to the next much like it can jump from one node of Ranvier to the next within an axon.

This type of connection has some distinct advantages in that it maximises the speed of transmission from one neuron to another and also allows for easier synchronisation of neurons, factors that can be important when the neurons are involved in processes that require the fast accurate transmission of signals. This type of neuronal interaction is relatively rare in the brain but is fairly widespread in retinal neurons, which provide us with visual information about the environment around us. From an evolutionary perspective, this information needs to provide precise details about the visual world that can be quickly updated so that we may respond to threats or opportunities.

The disadvantages of the gap junction are that there is little or no diversity available when passing signals from one neuron to the next. Adding diversity to a signal is vitally important in our psychological processing, allowing other thoughts or stimuli to influence our processing, allowing us to be creative, or simply allowing us to change our minds – to take an input from one source and alter it or process it so that it becomes changed in some way. This is where the second type of neuronal connections, synapses, are advantageous.

Synapses and the role of neurotransmitters

Confusingly, synaptic connections actually have a larger gap between axon terminals and dendrites than gap junctions do. This physical space between the axon terminal of one neuron and the dendrite of another is known as the synaptic cleft; the term pre-synaptic is used to refer to elements of the neuron that are sending the signal, and the term post-synaptic refers to elements of the neuron that are receiving the signal.

Inside the pre-synaptic neuron are packages of neurotransmitters – neurochemicals – that are used to communicate between neurons. The packages themselves are referred to as vesicles and are self-contained in that they have their own membranes (if it helps, think of them as balloons filled with neurotransmitters). As an action potential reaches the synapse the vesicles fuse with the neuron's membrane and release the neurotransmitter into the synaptic cleft. Here, the neurotransmitter can either inactively 'float around' in the interstitial fluid in the synaptic cleft or it can bind to a receptor site on the membrane of the post-synaptic neuron.

Neurotransmitters can only bind to certain types of receptor sites because of their respective chemical properties, so if a post-synaptic neuron only has receptors for the neurotransmitter **serotonin** and the pre-synaptic neuron has released the neurotransmitter **dopamine**, no binding will occur. However, if the pre-synaptic neuron releases dopamine and the post-synaptic neuron has dopamine receptors, then binding will occur. The effect of binding is to alter the permeability of the post-synaptic neuron's membrane, making the charge on the post-synaptic neuron either more positive, and therefore more likely to fire an action potential (excitatory), or more negative, and therefore less likely to fire an action potential (inhibitory).

Once the moment of neurotransmitter release and possible binding to receptors has occurred, the synapse needs to be returned to its former state so that further communication may take place. To do this any 'excess' neurotransmitters need to be 'deactivated' through a process of re-absorption by the pre-synaptic neuron, known as re-uptake, or broken down into its constituent parts (metabolites), known as degradation; additionally, the pre-synaptic neuron needs to create more of the neurotransmitter through synthesis, to replace what it lost from its synaptic vesicles.

This process of neurotransmission at a synapse can be disrupted in various artificial ways through the administration of drugs in order to alter neuronal functioning. Neuronal functioning can be altered in two essential ways: by increasing the excitatory effects of the neurotransmitters or by increasing the inhibitory effects of the neurotransmitters.

Medications may be agonists, that is, they increase the effectiveness of a neurotransmitter, or they may be antagonists, that is, they decrease the effectiveness of a neurotransmitter. These two basic effects can be created in a number of ways. **Agonists** may stimulate the release of a neuro-transmitter from the pre-synaptic neuron; they may block the re-uptake of the neurotransmitter by the pre-synaptic neuron; or they may block the degradation of the neurotransmitter. In all of these cases the net effect is that there is an increase in the action of the neurotransmitter at the synapse. By contrast, **antagonists** may block pre-synaptic neurotransmitter release; they may block post-synaptic receptor binding sites, preventing the neurotransmitter from binding; they may increase degradation of the neurotransmitter; or they may block the pre-synaptic neuron from synthesising the neurotransmitter. In all of these cases there is a net decrease in the action of the neurotransmitter at the synapse.

We hope you have been able to see the importance of synapses for transmitting information and the usefulness of understanding the neurotransmitter systems in order to be able to manipulate them for pharmacological treatments. It is also worth taking some time to consider the mechanics of pharmacological treatment and the effects such treatment may have, particularly as you know that one neurotransmitter may be implicated in many illnesses or functions of the nervous system.

One of the earliest ideas about the cause of schizophrenia was the dopamine hypothesis. This hypothesis (since found to be vastly over-simplified) noted that drugs such as cocaine, which act as dopamine agonists (increasing the amount of dopamine available at the synapse), can result in behaviour and experiences that are similar to those found in schizophrenia. Additionally, it was noted that dopamine antagonistic drugs such as chlorpromazine (which decreases the amount of dopamine available at the synapse) could alleviate some of the signs and symptoms of schizophrenia. However, if the dosage of chlorpromazine was too high, then side effects such as the Parkinson's disease-like movement disorder, tardive dyskinesia, could occur.

Conversely, the movement disorder Parkinson's disease has been linked with a dearth of dopamine in the brain and can be treated with dopamine agonist drugs such as levodopa. Considering what you now know about the dopamine hypothesis in schizophrenia, what do you expect the side-effects of a dopamine agonist to be? They can in some circumstances include perceptual disturbances, or hallucinations, which are common symptoms of schizophrenia. This over-simplified example illustrates the possibilities, and problems, of disrupting neurotransmitter functioning.

Task — Try doing an internet search for 'dopamine-related disorders' or 'serotonin-related disorders' to see how many different disorders are affected by these neurotransmitter systems.

Your internet search should demonstrate that it is, in fact, quite common for one neurotransmitter to be implicated in many disorders. In reality, it is highly unlikely that any naturally occurring disease process that affects neurotransmitters would affect one type alone; in fact, there are not enough neurotransmitters in existence for there to be a one-to-one relationship with a disorder. It is likely that there will be a number of neurotransmitters involved in any such disorder and any one neurotransmitter will feature in numerous disorders.

Skill builder activity

Using neurotransmitters as treatment: psychopharmacology

Transferable skill focus: independent learning

Key question: *What is the continuing role of psychopharmacology as a treatment paradigm?*

Read the recent editorial paper by Cowen (2011), Has psychopharmacology got a future? *The British Journal of Psychiatry*, 198, 333–335, which is available free online via the archives at http://bjp.rcpsych.org) and write a short synopsis of the paper (maximum of 500 words). In formulating your synopsis consider the following.

- What are the main points of Cowen's argument?

- What evidence or arguments does he put forward for each of these points?

Now look at the references for Cowen's paper and do some follow-up reading of Moncrieff and Cohen (2009), How do psychiatric drugs work? *British Medical Journal*, 338, 1535–1537, available free online via the archives at www.bmj.com. As you read through, bear in mind the following questions.

- What are the main points of Moncrieff and Cohen's paper?

- Does Cowen (2011) summarise their paper accurately?

Skill builder review

Independent learning is a key skill for any student or any professional wanting to keep up to date, and vital to increasing your understanding of a topic (it also helps immensely in gaining better grades). There are a number of skills involved in independent learning, from being able to understand the content of various papers to being able to organise your own further reading, and the tasks above should help you achieve this. Writing a synopsis can help clarify the main points of any paper and give you easy bullet points to remember. Using one paper's references to create your own follow-up reading list helps broaden your knowledge and develop a wider perspective on a given topic. Use these techniques to broaden your reading and understanding on future topics that we will come across.

You should have been able to see that Cowen's paper is an editorial rather than a fully fledged research paper. This is an important difference to recognise in your reading, as editorials typically present an opinion on a topic rather than an informed argument supported by research findings. As such, it is useful to be more sceptical of papers presented without empirical (evidenced) support, though they can be very useful in summarising some of the opinions on a topic and generating your own ideas. Some of the points Cowen raises in his editorial paper are these.

Questioning the objective nature of developing psychopharmacological treatments. Cowen voices concern that a withdrawal of drug company activity in developing new psychopharmacological treatments may lead to a cessation of new treatments being discovered. Reliance on drug companies for conducting expensive drug development and clinical trials can often result in accusations of drug companies marketing their products with dubious evidence of their effectiveness. Cowen adds that involving clinicians and researchers in this process to counter such accusations only results in further accusations that the individual clinicians and researchers have lost their objectivity.

Questioning whether there is a demand for developing psychopharmacological treatments. Drug treatments for psychiatric/psychological disorders are often perceived in a negative light as they may be deemed to ignore the personal or social context of patients, particularly if given against the patient's will; they require little understanding or psychotherapeutic skill to administer; and can cause unpleasant side-effects, so there may be little desire from clinicians and patients to develop these kinds of treatments.

Questioning the usefulness of psychopharmacological treatments. In the final few paragraphs of the paper, Cowen argues that drug treatments are often generalised, as the goal of evidence-based personalised treatment has not been reached. Indeed, Cowen stresses that there is a lack of understanding of the biological bases of psychiatric disorders generally. Psychopharmacological treatments, then, may be improved through a better understanding of the neurobiology underlying mental disorders combined with a more collaborative therapeutic relationship with the patient.

You should be able to see that Cowen's argument about the lack of specificity of psychopharmacological treatments fits neatly with the idea that there are a limited number of neurotransmitters and that one neurotransmitter can be implicated in many different disorders. Thus dopamine may be out of balance in a number of disorders and administering dopamine-based treatments may be indicated for a variety of disorders. Moncrieff and Cohen (2009), however, suggest that the idea of neurotransmitters being out of balance for certain disorders and that medications realign this balance may be a mistaken belief. They suggest that medications create a different, altered mental state that may be beneficial to the individual – a drug-centred rather than a disease-centred model. They argue that recognising this effect of drug treatments and discouraging the view that pharmacological drugs are disease-specific treatments would encourage more careful consideration in treatment selection, more collaboration between patients and clinicians, and periodic rather than continuous drug treatment. Cowen (2011) accurately summarises this view as 'highly critical' of psychopharmacology but accepting of its potential benefits as a treatment approach – suggesting Cowen's opinion of the literature is, in this case at least, an accurate one.

So, while you may begin to understand the role that neurotransmitters play in the signalling processes of neurons and how these may be manipulated for treatment purposes, the independent learning exercise should demonstrate that there are many other issues to consider in this process.

The role of hormones

Another important chemical signalling system within our bodies that can affect our behaviour is that based on hormones and is known as the **endocrine system**. Just as neurotransmitters are chemicals that can aid the communication between neurons within the nervous system, hormones are chemicals that can aid communication between the hormone-producing parts of our bodies (endocrine glands) and cells distributed more distantly throughout our bodies.

Hormones are produced at various locations in our bodies, including areas of the brain (hypothalamus, pineal gland, pituitary gland), thyroid, pancreas, gut, testes and ovaries, to name a few. At each location endocrine glands synthesise and store hormones, much as the pre-synaptic neuron may synthesise and store neurotransmitters within vesicles. When released, the hormone enters the bloodstream for transportation throughout the body. Hormones will bind with target cells throughout the body if the target cell possesses an appropriate receptor site, and this in turn triggers a particular response by the cell, that can trigger certain effects. Typical effects associated with the action of hormones are on functions of the autonomic nervous system that affect the fight or flight response, and on sexual responses; other effects include the control of metabolism, hunger, menstrual cycles, puberty, growth and the immune system. As you may expect, these effects do not occur milliseconds after hormone secretion but rather take much longer than the extremely short timescales evidenced in neurotransmission – typically seconds or even minutes.

As with neurotransmitters, the endocrine system can be artificially manipulated through the administration of medications to produce specific results. For example, increasing the amount of oestrogen by taking oestrogen-containing contraceptive medications can be used to prevent fertilisation for women; similarly, oestrogen-containing medications may be used as a treatment for the alleviation of menopausal symptoms as the naturally occurring hormone can influence a range of things – from stimulating endometrial growth to reducing muscle mass, increasing fat stores and increasing bone formation.

Of course, the endocrine system, like the neurotransmitter system, cannot continuously produce and release hormones (or neurotransmitters) indefinitely. As with the neurotransmitter system, which can 'clear' the synaptic cleft of excess neurotransmitter through reabsorption or degradation, there has to be a mechanism to return the endocrine system to homeostasis; this system is a variety of negative feedback loops that signal to the endocrine glands to stop producing and releasing their hormone. There are several ways this is accomplished, but all share the same basic negative feedback properties. For example, the endocrine gland may produce a hormone that acts on target cells but also acts on itself to prevent any more hormone release. There may also be another mechanism whereby the endocrine gland releases a hormone that acts on a target cell, and one of the actions of the target cell is then to feedback to the endocrine gland to reduce hormone release. Through these methods the body can control its hormone levels so that the endocrine glands are not constantly releasing hormones.

Assignments

1. Describe the major conceptual divisions of the nervous system and their functions.

2. Explain in detail the signalling systems used within the cells of the nervous system. How are these signals propagated from one cell to the next?

3. Explain the mechanism of action of psychopharmacological treatments.

Summary: what you have learned

Throughout this chapter we have focused on the major conceptual divisions of the human nervous system in order to better understand the biological systems that help us control our bodies and help us interact with the world around us using afferent and efferent nerves. The chapter introduced the notion of a central nervous system (brain and spine) and discussed the sub-divisions and functions of the peripheral nervous system. The major sections of the spinal cord were outlined, and its function as a conduit for nerve signals to and from the brain were described – you should also recall that the spinal cord can effect action independently of the brain through reflexes.

We have also looked at the nervous system at a much more detailed level, discussing the structure and function of nerve cells found throughout the nervous system. We have seen the way in which they utilise electro-chemistry to initiate signals (action potentials) in response to stimuli and how these signals may be passed on to other nerve cells throughout the nervous system. The mechanisms of passing signals from one nerve cell to another have also been discussed, and you should understand the mechanisms of action of the two basic types of 'junction' between nerve cells – gap junctions and synapses. By understanding how the nervous system is structured, the mechanisms by which it transmits signals, and the way these signals may be affected by neurotransmitters or hormones, we can better understand how humans work.

In addition to this content, you should have learned, and practised, some valuable study skills, particularly skills of reflection and independent learning through the critical thinking and skills activities. Remember that you can apply these skills to any topic in order to increase your under-standing – remember to think past the content presented and consider the wider implications of the work, and remember to read around the topic areas using reference sections to create your own reading lists.

Further reading

Becker, JB, Breedlove, SM, Crews, D and McCarthy, MM (eds) (2002) *Behavioural endocrinology*, 2nd edn. Cambridge, MA: MIT Press.

This is a good overview of the role of hormones and how they affect a range of behaviours, both in humans and in animals.

Crossman, AR and Neary, D (2010) *Neuroanatomy: an illustrated colour text*, 4th edn. London: Churchill Livingstone Elsevier.

This text contains good colour illustrations and photographs to illustrate relevant aspects of the nervous system alongside an informative text – it also has a nice glossary.

Stahl, SM (2001) *Essential psychopharmacology: neuroscientific basis and practical applications*, 2nd edn. Cambridge: Cambridge University Press.

This describes the neurochemistry underlying psychopharmacology, giving a good account of the basic principles underlying chemical neurotransmission and how it can be manipulated in order to treat mental disorders.

Chapter 4

Sensation and perception

Learning outcomes

By the end of this chapter you should:

- understand the fundamental organisation and evolutionary significance of sensory systems;

- appreciate the similarities, as well as the differences, between the sensory systems;

- understand how receptor organs convert energy into neural signals;

- be able to identify specific sensory pathways;

- understand how the cortex represents and processes sensory information;

- be able to use reflection to consider a topic in depth;

- have developed your organisational and literature searching skills.

Introduction

Our biological systems play a key role in all aspects of our functioning, from obtaining information about the world around us to using that information, or processing it, in many different ways. Before we move on to discuss how we process information, we need to understand how we get that information in the first place. All the information we have about the world around us comes through our sensory systems. There are a number of sensory systems in our bodies allowing us to gain a rich experience and a variety of information from our environments – more than the standard five senses (sight, sound, taste, smell and touch). While each of these sensory systems (or, to use a different term, sensory **modalities**) are specialised for receiving and processing their own particular form of information, they all share some common elements too.

In this chapter the main focus will be on vision and somatosensation (somatosensation refers to the sensory systems that are involved in sensing stimuli from our bodies – from the Greek word 'soma' for body), and we also look at hearing. Vision, somatosensation and hearing are the dominant senses for most humans, and scientific studies of sensory systems have tended to concentrate on these. However, it is crucial to realise that for many species, other senses – for instance, smell and taste – are the most important senses for providing information about the external world. Indeed, many species have evolved highly specialised sensory systems that detect very different types of energies, for instance, the echolocation system in bats. Many of the same basic principles of sensory processing that you will learn about in this chapter can also be applied to these other more exotic senses.

Before we go further, it is worth considering the fact that the external world is not perceived as being fragmented into separate experiences based on the different senses. For example, when you are talking to someone, you do not hear the other person's words as separate from the sight of their mouth moving. Instead, you perceive a single, unified impression of someone speaking. The combination of information from each of the senses is known as **multisensory integration**, and this is an important, but sometimes overlooked, feature of sensory processing that we will look at towards the end of this chapter.

From sensation to perception

All sensory systems require, at some point, neurons that can react or change in relation to different stimuli in the internal or external environment. As these 'sensory neurons' react to environmental stimuli they fire action potentials that are sent through their axons, typically ending at some location in our brain. This basic idea of sensory neurons reacting to the environment and 'sending' that information to the brain is a good starting point for understanding the many sensory systems we possess. These systems may be described as either **exteroceptive** (reacting to stimuli from environments external to our bodies) or **interoceptive** (reacting to stimuli from our internal environments).

Sensory systems are often described as involving the *detection* of stimuli, whereas perceptual systems are seen as being involved in the *interpretation* of the detected stimuli. To some extent the division between these two systems is rather artificial, as we will see later in this chapter. For instance, the retina of the eye, which is responsible for the detection of light, also carries out basic processing on the detected information. Thus, in many ways it makes more sense to think of the process of acquiring and interpreting information from the internal or external environment as being parts of one integrated system.

There are two key theories that are often used to explain how perceptual systems make sense of the incoming stimuli. One theory is the **bottom-up** approach to perception, which is also known as a 'data-driven' approach. In this theory, perception depends only on the information available to the sensory neurons. An influential bottom-up theory of perception was Gibson's direct perception model (Gibson, 1966), in which perception is not influenced by higher cognitive processes. By contrast, **top-down** approaches to perception emphasise the interpretive nature of perception, and highlight how higher-level contextual information such as expectations, knowledge and goals influences what we perceive. An influential top-down theory was Gregory's indirect perception model (Gregory, 1974); strong support for Gregory's theory came from experiments using illusions and ambiguous stimuli, where the perceptual system must use prior knowledge and other contextual information to make sense of the stimulus. In many instances, the same physical stimulus can be perceived as several different objects, depending on the top-down internal 'set' of the viewer. More recent approaches tend to view a combination of bottom-up and top-down processing as vital for perception. For example, in the theory of predictive coding, the brain is viewed as constantly making predictions about upcoming sensory stimuli (for a review (see Clark, 2013). The (top-down) predictions are compared with the incoming (bottom-up) signals, and discrepancies between the expected and the actual signals are used to modify future predictions.

Critical thinking activity

Fundamental issues in perception

Critical thinking focus: reflection

Key question: *How do we perceive the world?*

In this activity you will practise a skill called reflection. In general terms, reflection is thinking about a particular subject in great depth by considering it from several different perspectives. The subject of a reflection is often your own experiences, feelings and actions, but the subject can equally be someone else's experience.

In this activity reflect on the process of perceiving the external world, and how what we perceive is as much the result of the design of our own sensory apparatus as it is the external world that triggers the senses. This is an interesting topic that may help to shed light on some of the fascinating issues raised by the study of perception. While reflecting on this topic, try to consider some or all of the following issues.

- As you look around, to what extent is the external world that you perceive a result of your own previous behaviour?

- Imagine that a tree falls down in a forest, but no one is there to hear it. Does the falling tree make a sound?

- Try to think of some concrete examples of when your expectations have influenced your perception.

- Try to imagine the kind of world that is perceived by a bat using echolocation, and then the kind of world that is experienced by certain species of snake that can 'see' heat.

Critical thinking review

This task helps you to reflect on some of the more philosophical aspects of the study of perception that our scientific knowledge may be starting to be able to answer. There are many possible answers to these questions, and the more closely you reflect on the topic, the more you may become aware of the numerous different aspects raised by each question. Reflection often goes hand in hand with creative thinking, as some of the insights you gain through the act of reflection may be used to inform future problem-solving tasks or creative endeavours.

Vision

The scientific study of sensory systems has tended to be heavily weighted towards the visual modality. One of the main reasons is that, for humans at least, vision is the dominant modality. When asked which sense they would least like to lose, most people would probably answer 'vision'. This is because vision provides such a wealth of information about crucial features of the world – such as colour, space and motion – that it is hard to imagine what life would be like without it. In this section you will learn how light energy is transformed by the eye into neural signals, and how these signals are processed by the parts of the brain that are specialised to process visual information.

Task

In an online scientific database (such as ScienceDirect), pick a time period (say, from 2010 to the present) and find the total number of studies that contain the word 'visual', then search for 'auditory', then search for 'tactile'. What do you notice about the number of results you get for these three searches?

Light and the eye

Light is the physical stimulus that is detected by the visual system. Visible light is the part of the spectrum of electromagnetic radiation that can be detected by the human perceptual system. Visible light has a wavelength between around 400 to 700 nanometres (billionths of a metre); electromagnetic radiation that is not detectable by the human eye includes such things as X-rays and gamma rays. Determining the wavelength of light detected by the eye is a crucial part of the visual system involved in the perception of *colour*.

The eye is the **receptor organ** for vision – that is, the eye is the organ that is specialised to detect the physical energy associated with vision, i.e. light. Light passes through the transparent outer layer of the eye (the cornea), then passes through the pupil (the hole in the middle of the iris), and the lens brings the light to a focus on the retina at the back of the eye. The retina is the part of the eye where the physical energy of light is converted into neural signals that the brain can process. This process of converting a physical stimulus into neural impulses is known as **transduction**. The specific cells in the retina sensitive to light are the rods and cones; these are known as the sensory receptor cells. In humans there are approximately 130 million receptor cells in each eye. In the presence of light, the receptors change their electrical state, which conveys a message that light has been detected to other cells in the retina called bipolar cells. According to the **duplexity theory of vision**, cones and rods mediate different kinds of vision. Rods are sensitive to low levels of light, while cones are concerned with the perception of detail and colour at greater intensities of light. Rods and cones are not distributed evenly across the retina; the greatest density of cones is found in the central region of the retina (the **fovea**), which allows the sharpest vision (i.e. greatest **acuity**) of images at the centre of the visual field. The number of cones falls off sharply further away from the fovea, and at the portion of the retina corresponding to the edge of the visual field there are rods but no cones. This is why the perception of colour is greatly diminished at the boundaries of the visual field, but why dim objects can still be perceived out of the corner of your eye.

It is important to reiterate that the visual system does not simply create a direct copy of the external world. Instead, visual information is already being transformed and interpreted in the five layers of cells that make up the retina. One of the ways that the visual information is transformed in the retina is via a process called **convergence**. Although there are around 130 million photo-receptors per eye, there are only around 2 million ganglion cells carrying the signals from the retina to the brain. Many photoreceptor cells may therefore converge onto (i.e. connect with) one ganglion cell, especially in the periphery of the visual field. This convergence increases the sensitivity of cells in the periphery to detect light, at the cost of precision (i.e. acuity). In contrast, at the fovea there is a one-to-one convergence between the cone photoreceptors and the ganglion cells, which increases acuity but at the cost of sensitivity to light.

Another way that visual information is transformed by the arrangement of neurons in the visual system, starting in the retina, is via a particular property that sensory neurons possess called a **receptive field**. This is an important concept to understand as it applies not only to visual processing but also to the auditory system and the somatosensory systems. In all three systems, sensory neurons have receptive fields that limit the detection of stimulus – if a stimulus acts outside the receptive field of a sensory neuron, then it will not be 'detected' by that sensory neuron (but may be detected by others). Sensory neurons with large receptive fields can react to stimuli acting anywhere in that large area, but what they gain in overall area, they lack in detail.

Visual pathways

You have just seen how photoreceptors in the retina send a signal to bipolar cells; they then relay the signal to retinal ganglion cells, whose axons make up the optic nerve. Next we will look at the possible routes that the visual signals can take from the retina into the brain. Nerves that carry information inwards from the receptor organ to a cortical region specialised for processing that **sensory modality** are known as **afferent** nerves (nerves that carry signals in the opposite direction i.e., away from the central nervous system, are known as **efferent** nerves). The main visual pathway is called the retina-geniculate-striate pathway, and this pathway carries signals from the retina to the visual cortex (via the thalamus) for extensive processing. However, there are also several subcortical visual pathways that are specialised for certain types of more basic, but nevertheless highly important, processing. An important feature of the visual system (and of some other sensory systems) is that signals from the left side of space are transmitted to the right side of the brain, and signals from the right visual field are processed by the left side of the brain. It is not really clear, though, why the brain has evolved to processes information from the **contra-lateral** (i.e. the opposite) visual field.

Subcortical visual pathways

The majority of axons of the retinal ganglion cells terminate in the lateral geniculate nucleus of the thalamus, a subcortical region where further basic processing of the visual signals is carried out. The thalamus plays an important role in all sensory processing as we will see; in fact, you can think of the thalamus as a sort of 'gateway to the senses'. Signals are sent from the thalamus to the cortical region specialised for visual processing (the primary visual cortex in the occipital lobe in the case of vision). The retina-geniculate-striate pathway is referred to as the cortical visual pathway.

Some axons of the optic nerve, however, do not connect to the thalamus at all; instead they form so-called subcortical circuits. One such circuit involves a structure called the suprachiasmatic nucleus. Neurons in this structure regulate daily biological rhythms such as the sleep–wake cycle, by signalling to the brain the presence or absence of light. Other fibres from the optic nerve connect to a structure called the superior colliculus, which controls reflexes for quickly orientating the eyes and head to important external events. As we will see at the end of the chapter, some neurons in the superior colliculus are multisensory cells, so they respond to visual and sound information; for instance, they would respond if you saw a flash of light and heard a loud bang at the same time. The superior colliculus also sends signals to the amygdala via the pulvinar nucleus of the thalamus. The amygdala is specialised for emotional processing, and in particular for the detection and identification of threatening or fearful stimuli. Therefore, this subcortical pathway is concerned with the rapid processing of potentially dangerous events or objects that may require a swift 'fight or flight' response.

Cortical visual pathways

The place where the most extensive visual processing takes place is in the visual cortex. Most axons from the lateral geniculate nucleus of the thalamus terminate in the primary visual cortex (also known as the striate cortex because it has a striped appearance under a microscope). The primary visual cortex consists of six layers of cells; neurons in layer 4 receive projections from the lateral geniculate nucleus, and cells in layers 1 and 5 project to further regions of the visual cortex. These further regions are known as extrastriate visual cortex, and here the neurons are specialised for the processing of more complex features of visual information, such as colour and motion.

An important organisational principle of the visual system (and of other sensory systems) is **topographic mapping**, which is the ordered projection of cells from the receptor organ to the brain, and this serves to organise sensory information. A primary example of this in the visual system involves retinotopic maps. Here, adjacent regions of the retina are represented by adjacent neurons in the visual cortex, thus preserving in the brain the spatial features of the visual input. Another noteworthy feature of the organisation of the primary visual cortex is cortical magnification – much more of the primary visual cortex is devoted to the processing of signals from the fovea, compared to the visual periphery. This allows the brain to process much more extensively the high acuity visual images from the central region of the retina.

The cells in the primary visual cortex respond to basic visual properties such as orientation and motion. The particular response properties of neurons in the primary visual cortex have been discovered by experiments using single-cell recordings. The first researchers to characterise the receptive field properties of cells in the primary visual cortex research were Hubel and Wiesel (1962), who won the Nobel Prize in 1981 for their pioneering research.

After basic processing in the primary visual cortex, what then happens to the visual signals? Further processing is required to extract higher-level visual information such as identifying an object, or detecting the direction that an object is travelling. This occurs in the extrastriate visual areas that are dedicated to extract specific features from the visual information. In an influential theory of visual processing proposed by Ungerleider and Mishkin (1982), there are two main pathways or 'streams' that the visual signals can follow through the cortex – the 'what' pathway and the 'where' pathway. These two pathways are also known as the ventral pathway and the dorsal pathway, respectively, because the 'what' pathway extends ventrally from the primary visual cortex to the inferior temporal lobe, and the 'where' pathway extends upwards to the parietal cortex. The 'where' pathway is specialised for spatial processing, and processes features such as location, movement, spatial relations and spatial transformations. The 'what' pathway is dedicated to object processing, and processes colour, texture, pictorial detail, shape and size. The evidence for the existence of separate ventral and dorsal pathways came primarily from lesion studies in monkeys, where deficits related to lesions within either the dorsal or ventral pathways provided support for the pathway's involvement in either spatial processing or object identity. The 'what' and the 'where' pathway model was updated in Milner and Goodale's action-perception model (Milner and Goodale, 1995). This model suggests that the dorsal pathway should more accurately be called the 'how' pathway because this system is involved with the visual control of motor behaviour – for example, reaching or grasping for an object (see Table 4.1). Processing in the 'how'

Table 4.1: Main characteristics of Milner and Goodale's 'what' and 'how' pathways

	'What' pathway	'How' pathway
Cortical route	Ventral	Dorsal
Function	Object identification and recognition	Visual control of motor behaviour
Speed	Slow	Fast
Sensitive to	Details	Motion

pathway is carried out faster compared to the ventral stream, as swift responses are necessary for the moment-by-moment control of action. The 'how' pathway is specialised for processing motion, whereas the ventral pathway is specialised for processing visual pictorial details. While the ventral and dorsal visual pathways have often been viewed as completely separate, it is important to realise that there are dense interconnections between the neurons in the different regions of the visual system and that results from several lines of research challenge the view that the two pathways are absolutely independent (see Schenk and McIntosh, 2010). At this stage of our knowledge of the visual system, it is probably best to think of the two streams as being a useful way of thinking about the organisation of visual processing in the brain, but to be aware that the dorsal and ventral pathways are relatively but not absolutely independent.

The extent to which particular regions of the visual cortex are specialised for processing specific visual features (i.e. the domain specificity of a region) is a topic of great current interest and debate. For example, the so-called fusiform face area (FFA), a region within the right fusiform cortex along the ventral 'what' pathway, is often described as being specialised for the processing of faces (Kanwisher et al., 1997). Much of the evidence for the face-specificity of the FFA has come from fMRI experiments where brain activation when viewing faces and viewing non-face objects (such as houses) is compared. A large number of studies using this type of paradigm have found that the FFA responds preferentially to faces compared to non-face objects, and shows more activation to normal faces compared to scrambled faces (for a review, see Kanwisher and Yovel, 2006). However, the face-specificity of the FFA has been challenged by evidence showing that the FFA may not be responding to faces per se, but rather to the fact that faces are well-known objects that we are all expert at viewing, in the sense that we are all 'face experts'. Evidence for this so-called expertise effect in FFA comes from fMRI studies showing that experts in a particular domain (for example, bird watchers) show activation in the FFA when viewing objects they are expert at (in this case, birds) compared to viewing objects that they are not expert at (for example, cars) (Gauthier et al., 2000). This debate about the domain specificity of the fusiform face area is still ongoing and highlights some of the difficulties that researchers face in trying to decide whether a particular region of the visual cortex responds only to a certain defined class of stimuli.

Skill builder activity

Face perception

Transferable skill focus: IT and organisational skills

Key question: *Is the fusiform face area (FFA) face-specific?*

In an online database such as ScienceDirect or PsycArticles, use the 'Advanced search option' to perform a search for the terms 'FFA' and 'face-specific'. Combine the two search terms together using the 'AND' symbol. You should see a large number of results. Randomly select around six results, and read the abstracts of these articles. Next, create a table with four columns. In the first column, enter the surnames of the authors, followed by the year of publication. Call the second column 'Supports', the third column 'Contradicts' and the fourth column 'Neither'. Place a tick in the second column if the results of the article support the conclusion that the FFA is face-specific, or place a tick in the third column if the authors report that activation in the FFA was not specific to faces. If it is not clear from the results whether the face-specificity of the FFA is supported or contradicted, place a tick in the fourth column.

Have a look at your completed table. Think about what the table is telling you about the controversy over the face-specificity of the FFA. Does it look like the evidence is in favour of the FFA being face-specific? Look at the dates of publication of the articles you selected – do you think the controversy is still continuing? If you have some more time available, you could select more than six articles. Do you think that you could improve your ability to do this task by changing the search terms, or by altering any other feature of the literature search?

Skill builder review

This activity helps develop your database searching skills using information technology, by performing an online literature search. This is a vital skill, as researchers must be able to make efficient use of technology to access previous published studies. Additionally, the task demands an evaluation of the results of the studies that you found, and requires a decision on how to classify the findings with respect to a theory. Together, these skills will be necessary whenever you write a research report, as you will have to cite papers that support a particular theory, and cite other papers reporting evidence against the theory.

Somatosensation

Somatosensation includes sensations of touch, as you may expect, but also sensations of temperature and pain, as well as something called proprioception, which we will come on to later. As you are learning, all sensory systems possess sensory receptor neurons that can react to specific stimuli from the environment, and the somatosensory systems are no different in this respect. There are over 20 different types of somatosensory neurons that enable us to react to our environment by detecting different types of stimuli. While each 'class' of somatosensory neurons is specialised to detect specific kinds of stimuli, the general principle remains true across a whole range of different stimuli; somatosensory neurons react to environmental stimuli and are afferent nerves, firing action potentials along our nervous system to allow us to be aware of that stimulus.

Touch

Let us begin by looking at some of the somatosensory neurons in our layers of skin that provide the input for our perception of touch (see Table 4.2 and Figure 4.1). These types of neuron may be referred to as **mechanoreceptors** as, in order to initiate an action potential, they must be stimulated mechanically, that is, physically moved in some way.

For example, in order to sense vibration or pressure through your skin, the Pacinian corpuscle must be mechanically 'deformed' by a stimulus. The corpuscle is made up of several layers of tissue surrounding an axon, and to activate the so-called generator potentials the layers of tissue need to be squashed against each other. This deformation results in small generator potentials occurring within the corpuscle; the more intense the physical stimulus (or deformation) the greater the generator potential, and this relationship between deformation and potential is a directly proportional relationship. If the generator potential reaches the threshold potential of the neuron, the neuron will fire an action potential along its axon and along the nervous system; in fact, the neuron will fire the same action potential whether the generator potential just reaches the threshold or is well over the threshold.

Table 4.2: Somatosensory neurons in skin associated with touch

Somatosensory neuron	Associated perception
Pacinian corpuscle	Vibration/pressure
Meissner's corpuscle	Fast reaction to skin touch
Merkel's disc	Slow reaction to skin touch
Ruffini ending	Stretching of the skin
Free nerve ending	Skin touch
Free nerve ending associated with hair follicle	Hair movement

Figure 4.1: *Sensory neurons in skin*

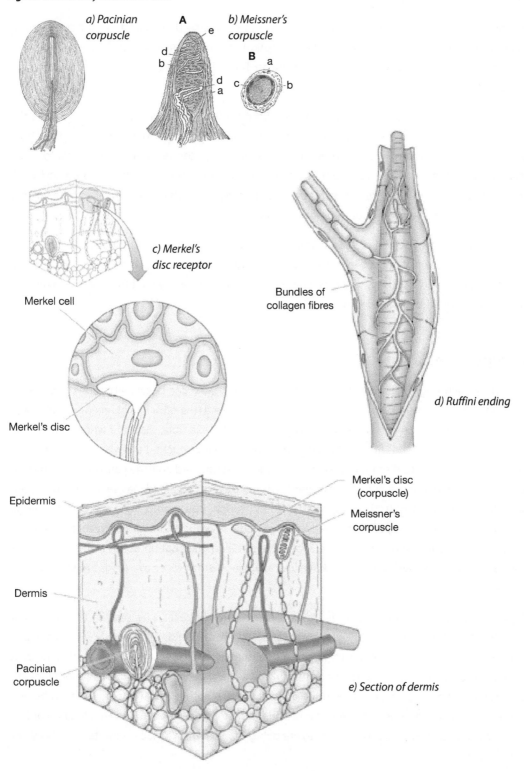

a) Pacinian corpuscle

b) Meissner's corpuscle

c) Merkel's disc receptor

Merkel cell

Merkel's disc

Bundles of collagen fibres

d) Ruffini ending

Epidermis

Dermis

Pacinian corpuscle

Merkel's disc (corpuscle)

Meissner's corpuscle

e) Section of dermis

Magnitude of touch

Action potentials can therefore be thought of as binary signals – they indicate whether a stimulus is present or absent – so how do we get a perception of stimulus magnitude if anything equal to or above the threshold will fire an action potential? There are two ways that sensory neurons can indicate this.

One answer lies in the fact that while the amplitude of the corpuscle's response indicates the presence or absence of a stimulus (i.e. whether the generator potential reaches the threshold potential of the neuron), it is the frequency of the action potentials that informs us about the magnitude of the stimulus – for example, to enable us to discriminate between large and small vibrations of our skin). The higher the frequency of action potentials generated by a single sensory neuron, the more intense the stimulus is perceived to be.

A second method by which we can perceive stimulus magnitude lies in the fact that multiple sensory neurons can be utilised to represent touch, with each neuron having a different threshold of activation. So some sensory neurons may respond to light touch while others require a heavier touch, indicating the magnitude of the stimulus.

Receptive fields of touch

Of course, each single Pacinian corpuscle is a specific size, so it can detect vibrations or pressure only in the area it covers, which is known as its receptive field (the principle of receptive fields was introduced in the section on visual processing.) Imagine, for example, that your whole hand is one large sensory neuron that fires one action potential if you are touched anywhere on your hand; you would be unable to discriminate between stimuli that touched only the palm from stimuli that touched only your fingers, or just one finger. Such a large receptive field may serve a purpose, but in order to be able to discriminate more detailed touch, you would need to replace a large receptive field with a cluster of smaller receptive fields. As you can imagine, clusters of neurons with small receptive fields can provide a lot more detailed information about a stimulus. In this way large receptive fields are said to have low acuity and small receptive fields are said to have high acuity.

A great example of differences in acuity across receptive fields can be seen in the two-point threshold task. This is a simple task where you touch a person's skin simultaneously with two points that can be varying distances apart (imagine a geometric compass you may have used in the past to help you draw circles, with a point on one arm and a sharp pencil on the other). Without looking at the stimulus poking you, it can be quite difficult to tell whether you are being touched by one point or by two; the two-point threshold is the minimum distance needed between the two points for the person to be able to sense that they are being touched in two places simultaneously rather than just one.

The ability to detect two points requires that each point 'hits' a different receptive field triggering action potentials in two sensory neurons; if the two points both 'hit' the same receptive field, then they will trigger just one action potential in the sensory neuron attached to that receptive field. So, if a circular receptive field is 2mm and the points are 5mm apart, then two points would be detected (because if one point is in one receptive field the other point must be in another receptive field if it is 5mm away). Similarly, points that are 5mm apart would find it difficult to 'hit' two receptive fields if the receptive fields were 100mm in diameter. Figure 4.2 shows average two-point thresholds for tactile stimuli on skin at various locations on the body. This clearly shows that the area with the smallest two-point thresholds (that is, with the smallest receptive fields) is, unsurprisingly, on the hands, as these are most often used to explore detailed tactile stimuli.

Somatosensory pathways

Hopefully, you now have some idea of how somatosensory neurons can be activated by environmental stimuli and consequently fire action potentials, but where do these action potentials go?

Figure 4.2: *Two-point thresholds*

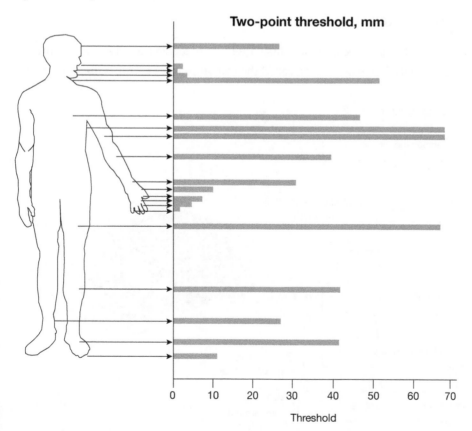

Each sensory modality can initiate action potentials along its own afferent sensory pathways. For sensations of touch using somatosensory neurons, these sensory pathways extend from where the initial stimulus was received on the body, into the spinal cord and up into the brain. Stimuli received lower down the body – for example, on the big toe – would join the spinal cord at the lower, sacral section while stimuli from higher locations on the body (e.g. the shoulder) would join the spinal cord at a higher section such as the cervical section.

Action potentials from somatosensory neurons travel along the axon and enter the spinal cord through the dorsal root ganglion and ascend to the medulla of the brainstem along a dorsal spinothalamic tract, and from there into a specific part of the thalamus known as the ventral posterolateral nucleus (see Figure 4.3). Importantly, as the axons travel from the spinal column to the brainstem they cross over so that the axons from the left side of your body enter the right brainstem, and vice versa. This 'switch over' remains after this point so that once past the brainstem all somatosensory axons remain contralateral; so, for example, damage to the thalamus in the right hemisphere would result in impairment in sensation on the left side of the body. From the thalamus the somatosensory pathway projects on to a specific area of cortex known as the primary somatosensory cortex.

Somatosensory cortex

The somatosensory cortex is a specific area of the cortex where tactile stimuli are represented in terms of neuronal activity. The specific area called the somatosensory cortex is the post-central

Figure 4.3: *Somatosensory pathway*

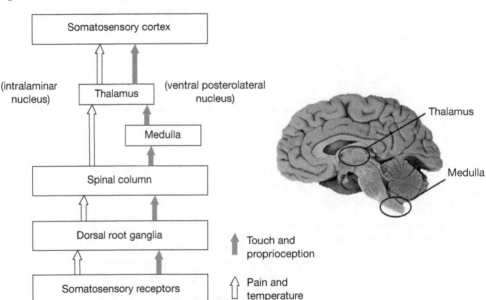

gyrus and each area of the gyrus corresponds to sensation at particular contralateral points of our bodies (see Figure 4.4).

You will notice that the somatosensory cortex is organised in a manner that is akin to our physical bodies, but you can also see that not all of our body is represented by the same amount of cortex – the arm takes up less cortex than the face, for example. The amount of cortex devoted to a body part indicates the density of somatosensory neurons in that body part – so the face and hands are densely packed with such sensory receptors, allowing for finer discrimination in touch sense, while the arm and trunk are less densely packed. You could think of this as illustrating how important touch sensation is to each of our body parts – the greater the area of cortex devoted to it, the more important it is to us; if you compare this with Figure 4.2, you will notice how the areas with larger cortical representation have smaller two-point detection thresholds.

The sensory homunculus was identified originally by Penfield (Penfield and Boldrey, 1937) during neurosurgery as he probed the post-central gyrus with electrodes and asked the patients what effects the electrode stimulation had on them. As there are no somatosensory neurons in the brain itself to indicate sensations of touch or pain, brain surgery can be, and often is, conducted using just local anaesthetic to 'numb' the skin on the scalp, leaving the patient conscious, aware and able to respond to questions. Using this technique Penfield would electrically stimulate points of the exposed brain and converse with the patients about the subjective effects of such stimulation – in this case patients reporting a feeling of being touched in specific locations on their body.

Figure 4.4: *Representation of tactile stimuli in the somatosensory cortex of the left hemisphere*

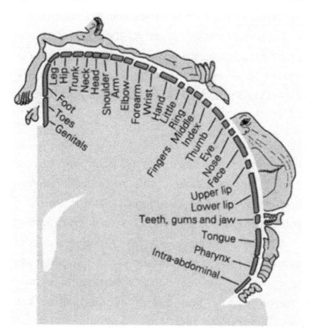

Proprioception

The eagle eyed among you will have noticed from Figure 4.3 that there is more than one somatosensory pathway. So far we have discussed just one aspect of one pathway – the one related to touch and the mechanoreceptors listed in Table 4.1. The other 'body sense' that shares the pathway with touch is proprioception.

Proprioception is our sense of where our limbs and body are currently positioned in space, and this sense is gained from monitoring our muscles and joints. This is actually a lot more important than it sounds, as we need to know how our body is positioned (upright, sitting down, standing on one leg, etc.) in order to plan our actions. If I wish to walk across the room I need to know what position I am starting from, as the sequence of movements I need to initiate will be different depending on my starting position. Proprioception is also an important sense cultivated by many athletes where very specific physical movements are required to carry out particular tasks – for example, in gymnastics or golf.

The sense of proprioception relies on two main types of sensory neurons: muscle spindles and Golgi tendon organs. From their names you will have guessed that muscle spindles are located in our muscles and help monitor the action and position of those; while Golgi tendon organs are located at our joints and provide information about joint position.

Muscle spindles

A muscle spindle is the term used to describe the situation where the free nerve ending of a somatosensory neuron wraps around muscle fibres within the muscle itself, akin to the free nerve endings associated with hair follicles in the skin that detect movement of the hair. For muscle spindles, though, the nerve endings are wrapped directly around muscle fibres within the muscle, so that as a particular muscle fibre stretches, the nerve endings will stretch and fire an action potential. In this way, a cluster of muscle spindles can indicate the stretch of the muscle in some detail.

The degree to which our muscles stretch depends upon the position of our limbs – if your arm is straight, the bicep muscle is flattened but it squashes up when you bring your hand to your shoulder, so the muscle stretch relates to the position of your arm. Muscle spindles therefore provide an effective feedback system to help notify us of the position of our body without requiring any visual input. You can test out your own sensation from muscle spindles by standing up and letting your arms hang straight down with the palms facing forward, closing your eyes to avoid any visual feedback. Now raise your forearms up (bending at the elbow) and stop when you think your forearms are at 90 degrees to your upper arm. The information you are using to make the judgement about the position of your forearms comes from the action potentials of your muscle spindles (and most people are fairly accurate at doing this).

Golgi tendon organs

Another way to receive proprioceptive feedback relies on somatosensory neurons known as Golgi tendon organs located in tendons, which attach muscle to bone. These neurons, like muscle spindles, work on the principle of stretch in that they will fire action potentials when the tendon, and consequently the Golgi tendon organ, stretches. What stretches the tendon is not the position of the limb but rather the load placed on the muscle itself, so the Golgi tendon organs detect when load is placed on a muscle.

Let us return to our biceps to illustrate this point. The bicep muscle is connected to the bone in your arm by tendons at the elbow and at the shoulder. At your elbow, your bicep is actually attached to one of your forearm bones (the radius). As your bicep contracts it 'pulls' on the radius and moves your forearm, which does not put too much strain on the tendon connecting the bicep to the radius. Now imagine you are in a gym going through the same movement but with a heavy weight in your hand. You can imagine this puts a lot more strain on the tendon holding your bicep to your radius – in fact, your tendon will stretch a little in response to this extra strain and it is this stretch that the Golgi tendon organs detect.

Somatosensory adaptation

So far we have discussed somatosensations of touch and proprioception that have some basic properties in common – they both rely on mechanoreceptors and both follow the same afferent pathway back to the brain, which is the dorsal column pathway indicated in Figure 4.3 (sometimes also referred to as the dorsal spinothalamic tract).

One other property that touch and proprioception share is that they both relay action potentials through the use of relatively large, myelinated axons, allowing the action potentials they transmit to travel relatively quickly. This speed in relaying action potentials from somatosensory neurons makes good sense, as we need to be able to detect such stimuli as quickly as possible in our everyday lives; it would not be helpful to know that your limbs were in a certain position several seconds ago.

While all mechanoreceptors have myelinated axons, insulating and improving the transmission of the electrical potential, not all mechanoreceptors react to stimuli in the same way. Some mechanoreceptors fire action potentials when stimuli are present and continue to fire action potentials for as long as the stimuli are present, letting you know it is still there; the only limiting factor in the number of action potentials fired is the amount of time it takes a neuron to hyperpolarise and return to its resting potential ready to fire again. These neurons are said to show no adaptation and are referred to as **slow adaptors**. Merkel's discs do not show adaptation, so they will fire if a stimulus is present and continue to fire as long as the stimulus remains present.

By contrast, some mechanoreceptors may fire action potentials when a stimulus first triggers the mechanoreceptors but will cease to fire if the stimulus persists. These neurons are said to show adaptation and are referred to as **fast adaptors**. Meissner's corpuscles are fast adapting mechanoreceptors, which means that they will eventually stop firing if a stimulus remains present – which is why you may not be aware of some constantly present tactile stimuli on your skin, such as your hair.

These two types of mechanoreceptors, the fast and the slow adaptors, are useful in signalling two important aspects of tactile somatosensation: *when* a stimulus occurs and *whether* it is still occurring. These aspects can both serve important functions, allowing us to respond as soon as we encounter stimuli (for example, by letting us know when we touch something we have reached for) and also letting us know that we are still in contact with tactile stimuli (for example, when we are carrying something). We can also think of these functions as being useful in evolutionary terms, in that we can reach out and explore our environments, making use of slow adaptors, and we can use our fast adapting mechanoreceptors to enable us to grip or carry objects by being aware of the constant pressure against our skin.

Pain

Another aspect of somatosensation that has an important evolutionary role is the detection of pain. It is tempting to think of pain as merely very intense sensation from our touch receptors; however, this is not the case. After all, the action potential of a sensory neuron is the same magnitude whether the activating stimuli just passes the threshold potential of the sensory neuron or whether the activating stimuli go way over that threshold potential. So how do we detect pain? In order to answer that, we need to realise that pain is not just ordinary tactile stimuli at a really intense level; rather, pain is a noxious (harmful) stimulus that can damage our tissue. Sensory neurons for pain therefore need to detect tissue damage rather than tactile stimuli, and the neurons that do this are termed **nociceptors**. Nociceptors are free nerve endings that initiate action potentials when they are irritated or damaged by mechanical or thermal noxious stimuli that can cause tissue damage.

Nociceptors

The receptive field of nociceptive neurons is dependent upon the distribution of the free nerve endings, with a wide distribution relating to a large receptive field and vice versa for small receptive fields. One exception to this is that if neighbouring cells are damaged, they will release various chemicals that can increase the chances of the nociceptor firing, so the receptive field can be 'extended' in this sense. If the nociceptor is activated, either by noxious stimuli on the free nerve endings or by neighbouring cell damage, then it will send an action potential along its axon.

The pathway of nociceptor axons enters the spinal cord through the dorsal root ganglia (just like those of the mechanoreceptors), but instead of forming the dorsal spinothalamic tract to the brain, nociceptor axons 'switch over' to the opposite side of the spinal column and form the ventral spinothalamic tract. While the mechanoreceptors for touch remain on the same side of the body until they reach the brainstem where they become contralateral, the nociceptor pathway becomes contralateral much earlier in its journey to the brain. Therefore, a unilateral (single-sided) injury to the left side of the spinal column would result in difficulties in sensing touch on the same side of the body (ipsilateral), but would result in difficulties in sensing pain on the opposite side of the body (contralateral).

Moving on from the ventral spinothalamic tract, the nociceptor axons terminate in the thalamus before ascending to other cortical areas such as the somatosensory cortex and the anterior cingulate cortex. Action potentials from nociceptors also reach the reticular activating system (RAS) in the brainstem; the RAS, in turn, sends signals to many cortical areas. Interestingly, the functional role of the RAS is in modulating sleeping and waking behaviour, so one can see how pain may interrupt sleep functions or aid in general levels of arousal (wakefulness).

For people in chronic pain, pain-relieving medication is often unable to relieve the experience of pain, and more dramatic solutions can be sought. One such approach is to lesion (selectively destroy) the nociceptor pathway involved in the pain, the rationale being that if there is no nociceptor pathway activity, then there can be no experience of pain. Unfortunately, while this drastic approach may result in some temporary relief, it is very common for the experience of pain to return even when the nociceptor pathway is destroyed (Melzack, 1993). This then poses some very serious questions over the role of the nociceptor pathway in the perception of pain if you can still perceive it in the absence of any functioning nociceptor pathway.

Other experiences of pain similarly cast doubt over the sole role of the nociceptor pathway. In addition to situations where the nociceptor pathway is lesioned and pain is still experienced, there are amputees who have had whole limbs (including their nociceptor pathways) removed yet continue to experience pain in their missing limbs. This phenomenon, known as phantom limb pain, affects up to 80 per cent of amputees (Ephraim et al., 2005) so it is by no means a rare occurrence.

In order to attempt to explain these phenomena, Melzack (1993) points out that in cases such as these – where nociceptor pathways are lesioned or removed – it is only the initiating or afferent components of the system that are affected. The remaining nociceptor pathway in the spinal column or brain, above the point of removal or lesion, remains intact. Melzack postulates that activity in the remaining nociceptor pathway results in experiences of pain identical to pain experienced before any lesion or amputation; the final cortical activation is identical but has just been initiated by other means than free nerve endings in a limb – rather like Penfield electrically stimulating brain areas directly rather than through mechanoreceptors (Penfield and Boldrey, 1937).

The question of how and why the cortical representation of nociception is activated is a question that is yet to be solved, though clearly cognition and emotion have roles to play, as our thoughts and emotions can quite clearly affect our experiences of pain, through placebo effects, for example.

Temperature

The ability to be able to sense temperature and temperature change within one's own body is, like the ability to detect pain, an important evolutionary function, as survival is only possible within a finite temperature range. While the average temperature of the human body (37°C) may vary by 0.5–1°C each day with little or no adverse effects, a change in body temperature of plus or minus 10°C would prove fatal. It is therefore important for our survival that we can sense temperature change and respond to it to ensure we do not place our lives at risk.

External temperatures can affect your internal and external body, so you need to be aware of both. Take an increase in external temperature as an example. If it is a warm day, your (internal) body temperature will begin to increase and you would need to take action to keep your body temperature around 37°C. If you have a different external temperature rise – say, a candle flame in contact with your external body – then this may cause tissue damage (pain) and you would need to withdraw your hand from the flame. You can therefore see that it is important for you to be able to detect both external and internal temperature changes, and, as you can see from Figure 4.3, pain and temperature share the same afferent pathway – the ventral spinothalamic tract.

Temperature change that can cause tissue damage will be sensed through nociceptor neurons and pathways responsive to thermal tissue damage – causing a perception of pain and the reaction of withdrawing your body part from the extreme temperature. Any change in the external temperature causing a similar change in internal body temperature, moving it away from the average 37°C, will be detected by thermal neurons in the central nervous system, most typically in the hypothalamus or the pre-optic area. Thermal neurons in the hypothalamus can act to regulate your body temperature through initiating conscious behaviours (such as putting on a coat or opening a window) or through initiating autonomic nervous system responses (such as shivering or sweating).

So-called 'warm neurons' in the hypothalamus or pre-optic area fire action potentials in response to raised temperatures, while 'cold neurons' fire in response to lowered temperatures. Interestingly, lesion studies carried out in animals demonstrate that lesions of thermal neurons in the pre-optic area result in impaired physiological autonomic responses to temperature change but leave behavioural responses intact. Conversely, lesions of thermal neurons in the hypothalamus result in the impairment of behaviour responses yet leave autonomic responses intact (Van Zoeren and Stricker, 1977).

Evidence from these lesion studies therefore suggests that there are two quite distinct systems for regulating temperature: one behavioural, cortical system, of which we are consciously aware and one physiological, or autonomic, of which we are not consciously aware.

Hearing

Hearing is a vitally important sense, and is particularly crucial for species such as humans that communicate using spoken language. Hearing can provide crucial information about the identity and position of objects or events in low-light conditions, and it can enable us to perceive events that occur behind our head. Hearing is often referred to as 'audition', hence the system for hearing is often called the auditory system. In this section you will learn the basics of auditory processing and how, in many ways, similar principles of sensory processing that you have learned about in the previous sections on vision and somatosensation can be applied to the processing of sound.

Sound and the ear

The auditory system senses pressure waves travelling through the air or through water. The pressure waves that can be detected by humans (i.e. sound waves) have a frequency of between around 20 and 20,000 cycles per second. Sound waves have three important dimensions that relate to three perceptual characteristics of hearing: the size of the wave is related to its loudness; the frequency (i.e. the number of cycles per second) relates to its pitch; and the complexity of the wave relates to its tonal quality (the distinctiveness of the sound).

You will remember that in the visual system transduction referred to the process whereby light waves are converted into neural signals by retinal cells in the eye. For auditory processing, the process of transduction refers to the conversion of mechanical sound waves by the ear into neural impulses that are processed by the brain. The inner ear contains the specialised structures for transduction, but the outer ear (the auditory canal and the external fleshy part of the ear) is also important as it transforms the sound slightly differently, depending on whether the sound is coming from behind or in front of the head. This allows the auditory system to decide if a sound is located in front of or behind the listener. The middle ear comprises the tympanic membrane (the eardrum) and three tiny bones (the smallest bones in the human body) called the ossicles, which transmit the vibrations of the tympanic membrane across to the inner ear. Here, the sound vibrations are converted into neural impulses by the auditory receptor organ – the organ of Corti – which is housed in the snail-shaped, fluid-filled structure called the cochlea. The organ of Corti contains the hair cells, which are the auditory receptor cells, and these cells convert the vibration of the fluid in the cochlea into neural impulses that travel down the spiral ganglion cells of the auditory nerve into the brain. An important feature of the organ of Corti is that different frequencies produce maximal stimulation of hair cells at different points along the cochlea. Low-frequency sounds produce maximal stimulation towards the tip of the cochlea and high-frequency sounds produce maximal stimulation towards the base; this arrangement is called **cochlear coding**, and it means that the auditory system represents important information about the frequency of a sound.

Auditory pathways

The structure of the auditory pathway is more complex than that of the visual system in that there are several subcortical structures on the route that goes from the ear to the auditory cortex, multiple crossovers of signals from one ear to structures on the opposite side of the brain, and several different routes that the signals can take. The cochlear nucleus in the brainstem is the first structure that receives input from the auditory nerve. From here, a large number of auditory nerve axons cross the brain and have synaptic connections with neurons coming from the opposite ear, in the superior olivary complex. This arrangement allows the auditory system to compute the location of a sound source by comparing the time of arrival of the sound at one ear with the time of arrival at the opposite ear. The spatial localisation of a sound can also be inferred from the relative loudness of the sound at one ear compared to the other, and specialised auditory neurons are sensitive to differences in intensity between the left and right ears. Signals from the superior olive are then sent to the inferior colliculus in the midbrain, and then on to the thalamus. Remember that the thalamus also receives visual and somatosensory signals, but the auditory signals are received by a part of the thalamus called the medial geniculate nucleus.

The primary auditory cortex receives the majority of the auditory output from the thalamus. The primary auditory cortex is situated in the temporal lobe, and consists of a core region and a number of surrounding regions called 'belt' and 'parabelt' regions. Less is known about the functionality of the auditory cortex compared to our knowledge of the visual cortex, but the core region is thought to be involved in pitch processing and spatial location, while the belt and parabelt regions process more complex sound signals. A fundamental feature of all of the structures in the auditory pathway is their tonotopic organisation, whereby adjacent frequencies are represented by adjacent neurons. This is the auditory equivalent of the retinotopic organisation of the visual system, and it serves to preserve the frequency information of the sound across different brain structures. As with the visual system, signals are sent down a descending pathway so that the results of processing from higher-level areas can influence neural activity at lower levels. This feedback mechanism allows top-down control at all levels of the auditory system so that higher-level processes such as expectations and attention can modulate the incoming auditory signals.

Multisensory processing

Traditionally, the different sensory systems have tended to be studied in isolation from one another. In many ways, this approach has proven very useful and given us an incredible amount of knowledge about how the brain processes information from the external world. However, this approach fails to understand the crucial ways in which information from the different senses is combined together so that we perceive a coherent, unified picture of the world. In the real world, our brains are receiving information simultaneously from many different sensory modalities, not just from one sense on its own. A major contemporary area of research in perception is the study of multisensory processing, where researchers investigate how the brain is able to integrate information from several different senses.

Since the 1970s it has been known that certain regions of the brain, such as the superior colliculus, contain neurons that are responsive to stimulation in more than one sense (Stein and Arigbede, 1972). Since then, researchers have made great advances in our understanding of how perception in one sense affects processing in a different sense (for a review, see Driver and Noesselt, 2008). It is now known that many areas of the cortex are multisensory, i.e. they are involved in the processing of more than one type of sensory information. The ability of the brain to combine information from more than one sense has several important consequences. For instance, when we combine information about the same event in more than one modality (for example, we see a flash and hear a bang), we are able to act and identify the event faster than if we had only visual or only auditory information (e.g. Harrison et al., 2010). Sometimes, the information in one sense can influence or distort our perception of the signals in a second modality. For example, it has been shown that if you are presented with a brief flash of light and at the same time you hear two beeps in quick succession, most of the time you will perceive seeing two flashes of light (Shams et al., 2000). This has been called the double-flash illusion, and is a nice experimental example of how information in one modality can affect perception in a different sense.

Finally, recent investigations into multisensory processing in the brain have challenged the view of totally separate sensory-specific areas for the processing of visual, auditory and somatosensory signals. Instead, research has begun to reveal how areas that were once thought of as purely 'sensory-specific' (i.e. designed to process signals from just one sensory modality) may in fact also respond to signals in a separate modality (Ghazanfar and Schroeder, 2006). Research into multisensory processing has revealed the large amount of collaboration between the various sensory systems, but in a way this should come as no great surprise, as the brain has evolved in a multisensory environment and must constantly process and interpret signals from multiple senses simultaneously.

Assignments

1. Critically evaluate the claim that the fusiform face area (FFA) is dedicated to the processing of faces.

2. To what extent does the evidence support the theory of separate 'what' and 'how' visual pathways?

3. Critically discuss the 'top-down' theory of perception.

Summary: what you have learned

Now that you have finished studying this chapter, you should:

- understand the fundamental organisation and evolutionary significance of sensory systems;

- appreciate the similarities, as well as the differences, between the sensory systems;

- understand how receptor organs convert energy into neural signals;

- be able to identify specific sensory pathways;

- understand how the cortex represents and processes sensory information;

- be able to use reflection to consider a topic in depth;

- have developed your organisational and literature-searching skills.

Further reading

Clark, A (2013) Whatever next? Predictive brains, situated agents, and the future of cognitive science. *Behavioural and Brain Sciences*, 36, 181–204.

An excellent in-depth critical review of combined top-down and bottom-up processing approaches, focusing on the strengths, limitations and potential applicability of predictive coding theories.

Driver, J and Noesselt, T (2008) Multisensory interplay reveals crossmodal influences on 'sensory-specific' brain regions, neural responses, and judgments. *Neuron*, 10, 11–23.

An accessible review of many important brain and behavioural features of multisensory processing

Melzack, R (2011) The story of pain. *The Psychologist*, 24, 470–471.

A clearly written introductory look at the perception of pain.

Schenk, T and McIntosh, RD (2010) Do we have independent visual streams for perception and action? *Cognitive Neuroscience*, 1, 52–62.

An important critical evaluation of the theory of independent visual streams for 'what' and 'how' processing.

Chapter 5

Emotions

Learning outcomes

By the end of this chapter you should:

- *understand two theories of emotion;*
- *be able to discuss the adaptive benefits of key emotions;*
- *recognise sex differences and individual variation in emotional responses;*
- *be able to identify the brain regions and hormones associated with specific emotions;*
- *understand the biological mechanisms associated with the recognition and processing of emotional expressions;*
- *have developed the ability to process and evaluate written information.*

Introduction

In our own species we often refer to emotions when discussing subjective feelings. It is the physiological and behavioural responses to these subjective feelings, however, that are most important. Emotions can be conceptualised as adaptive response patterns shaped by natural selection. These responses increase the likelihood of survival by facilitating adaptation to new situations and enhance reproductive success through the effective formation and maintenance of social relationships. Emotions therefore impact on our decision making (Oatley and Johnson-Laird, 1987) and prepare us for appropriate action (Frijda, 1986). While the current chapter focuses on human emotion, in *The expression of the emotions in man and animals* (1872) Darwin discusses a number of similarities between species for primary emotions such as fear and anger. These similarities highlight an important continuity of species that extends beyond mere physical characteristics, and you should consider both human and non-human emotions when reading this chapter.

Specific emotions are evoked by distinct threats. This chapter discusses a number of important emotions, establishing their evolutionary function and the physiological mechanisms responsible for these emotional responses. Though these emotions will be discussed separately, it is important to note that emotions often interact to increase the appropriateness of the response (Panksepp and Biven, 2012). For example, it is possible to feel both jealous and angry at the same time.

The chapter also outlines the adaptive benefit of expressing emotions and recognising the emotions of other individuals. Displaying emotions provides important opportunities to influence social relationships and manipulate others – for example, communicating disappointment can encourage others to cooperate (Wubben et al., 2009). Emotions should therefore be considered in this social and interpersonal context.

Theories of emotion

The James-Lange theory

When thinking about or discussing emotions we often focus on the way in which feelings encourage us to behave or respond in a particular way. For example, if I am walking alone at night and I hear footsteps behind me, the fear I feel may prompt me to become more vigilant, looking for potential sources of help or starting to run from danger. However, James (1884, 1890) and Lange (1885/1912) suggested that emotions are the *consequence* not the *cause* of physiological changes. While these researchers developed their theories separately, we typically refer to the 'James-Lange' theory because of the similarity of their explanations. James and Lange propose that the brain processes stimuli (e.g. the sound of the footsteps), and if they are emotionally relevant, the autonomic nervous system reacts. The brain receives feedback about this physiological arousal, which is then consciously interpreted in terms of emotional states.

Though research investigating the order of physiological responses and subjective feelings is inconsistent, physiological reactions can precede subjective experiences (Damasio et al., 2000), providing some support for the James-Lange theory. In addition, Hohmann (1966) found that emotions are less intense among those with higher spinal cord injury, which makes the brain insensitive to a greater proportion of the body. However, other studies involving spinal cord patients – such as that of Cobos et al. (2002) – have not found impaired subjective experiences or physiological responses (e.g. heart rate). According to the James-Lange theory, different emotions have distinct physiological patterns. The feelings of anger and love therefore differ because they are associated with different biological responses. There is some support for this argument, with research finding specific autonomic responses relating to emotions and facial expressions (Ekman et al., 1983; Rainville et al., 2006; Stemmler, 2004), though overlap between physiological response is expected (Cacioppo et al., 2000).

The Cannon-Bard theory

Cannon (1927) and Bard (1934) criticised the James-Lange approach, arguing that the emotion is not dependent on an initial physical response. Using injections of adrenalin, Cannon (1927) demonstrated that people are able to experience a physiological response without interpreting these reactions as an emotion. In other species, Cannon (1915) found that it is possible to display emotional behaviours such as hissing when autonomic feedback is not available (i.e. following lesions). It was further argued that the physiological responses associated with emotions such as fear and anger are rather similar (e.g. the increased heart rate that prepares the body for action) and therefore not varied enough to account for the wide range of emotions experienced. Cannon instead proposed that the brain stimulated the autonomic nervous system to produce a physiological response at the same time as producing the conscious interpretation.

Anger and aggression

Aggression is a basic human emotion, and it is displayed in all cultures (McCall and Shields, 2008). It represents an adaptive response to potentially threatening stimuli (Daly and Wilson, 1994). Anger is associated with a range of physiological responses such as increased heart rate, muscle tension and body temperature that prepare the body for action (Panksepp, 1998). Anger and aggression can increase access to a range of valued resources including social status and mates (Daly and Wilson, 1994), and this emotion typically increases if few resources are available (Harding, 1983). The extent to which a person behaves aggressively is important because while moderate levels of aggression may be adaptive (Ferguson, 2008; Smith, 2007), extreme aggression may threaten survival and become maladaptive. Extreme levels of aggression may result from an increased aggressive drive or impaired inhibition of the aggressive drive.

Testosterone and serotonin

Testosterone is the hormone most commonly associated with aggression (Giammanco et al., 2005). In non-human animals there is a clear relationship between aggression and testosterone, though animals with complex social systems may require relevant stimuli such as the presence of a rival to become aggressive. In humans, there is a weak positive relationship between testosterone and aggression (Book et al., 2001), and testosterone may be more closely related to dominance than to aggression (Archer, 2006). Research in this area is hindered by the fact that testosterone levels display daily and seasonal fluctuation (Bernstein et al., 1983) and further vary across the lifespan (Mazur and Booth, 1998). In addition, changes to social status or dominance may influence testosterone levels (Mazur and Booth, 1998). This process may also be adaptive as reduced testosterone levels in response to defeat encourage submission and withdrawal from potentially harmful competitions.

Serotonin is the **monoamine** most closely associated with aggression (Miczek and Fish, 2006). It appears to inhibit aggression in a range of species (Summers and Winberg, 2006), and aggressive animals demonstrate lower levels of serotonin (de Boer et al., 2003). Furthermore, manipulating the serotonin precursor tryptophan also impacts on aggressive behaviour (Manuck et al., 2006).

Specifically, serotonin influences activity in the prefrontal cortical regions (e.g. the anterior cingulate cortex and orbital frontal cortex), which inhibits instinctive and impulsive behaviours and is negatively related to violence (Moore et al., 2002). In addition, a range of studies indicate a genetic influence on aggression (Guo et al., 2007; Morley and Hall, 2003) and related variables such as antisocial behaviour (Volavka et al., 2004). It has also been argued that impairments to the frontal lobe (Mercer et al., 2005) – which contributes to impulse control and brain asymmetry (Rohlfs and Ramirez, 2006) – are associated with aggressive and violent behaviour.

Male and female aggression

In most mammals, males are more aggressive than females (Gottschalk and Ellis, 2009; Wrangham et al., 2006), and in humans, women are consistently less aggressive than men (see Cross and Campbell, 2011, for a review of female aggression). These sex differences are most apparent for extreme violence. There is no difference in male and female levels of anger or indirect (i.e. non-physical) aggression (Archer, 2004), suggesting that it is the expression of aggression rather than the feeling of anger that differs between men and women. These sex differences reflect the fact that men and women are faced with different evolutionary challenges. In particular, the consequences of conception are much greater for women than for men, and so women are typically more sexually cautious. In this context, male competition for the female attention creates a specific selection pressure for male–male aggression (Wang, 2002).

Women typically spend greater time and energy than men caring for children, and women's survival has a greater impact than men's survival on the survival of their child (Sear and Mace, 2008). As a consequence, women are more reluctant to engage in potentially fatal or damaging aggression. Consistent with this suggestion, women experience greater fear than men (Else-Quest et al., 2009) and greater physiological responses to fear-relevant stimuli (Bradley et al., 2001). Rather than physical violence, women may be more likely to compete intra-sexually through ostracism and exclusion than through physical aggression, though female–female competition does increase if few suitable mates are available. Female aggression may be influenced by oxytocin, which inhibits aggression towards offspring and facilitates aggression towards others (Debiec, 2005; Pedersen, 2004). In fact, it is argued that similar levels of physical intimate partner violence displayed by men and women reflect the lower fear that women experience when faced with a partner, which may be mediated by oxytocin (Cross and Campbell, 2011).

Disgust

Disgust research typically focuses on the disgust evoked by the origin of food and its ability to contaminate, often referred to as 'core disgust' (Rozin et al., 2000). It is argued that this form of disgust is an adaptation that motivates avoidance behaviour, reducing the likelihood of contamination and subsequent bacterial, parasitic or viral infection (Curtis et al., 2004; Oaten et al., 2009). Disgust can therefore be conceptualised as part of the behavioural immune system that motivates our avoidance of potentially harmful objects and reduces the threat of disease.

In particular, disgust reduces appetite (Rozin et al., 2000), is associated with nausea and vomiting (Rozin et al., 2000) and promotes behaviours such as washing (Ritter and Preston, 2011). These behaviours may prevent ingestion of pathogens and toxins, encourage learned aversions to particular foods, and therefore reduce the likelihood of disease (Aiello et al., 2008; Bernstein, 1999). Behaviours that reduce the threat of disease are apparent in a range of species. For example, sheep avoid eating grass in areas contaminated with faeces (Cooper et al., 2000). The avoidance behaviours motivated by disgust are further supported by a range of biological defences (e.g. stomach acid) that reduce the threat of infection.

Variation in disgust sensitivity

Individuals vary in their disgust sensitivity (de Jong and Merckelbach, 1998). For example, disgust sensitivity decreases with age (Fessler and Navarrete, 2003) and is associated with a range of personality traits (Olatunji et al., 2008). Importantly, disgust and contamination sensitivity are related to the frequency and timing of infection (Stevenson et al., 2009). More frequent infection is associated with heightened contamination sensitivity (Stevenson et al., 2009), highlighting the flexibility of the disgust response and the importance of the disgust response when the person is most vulnerable to infection. Similarly, stress (which increases vulnerability to disease) is also associated with increased disgust sensitivity (Al-Shawaf and Lewis, 2013).

Research consistently demonstrates that women are more sensitive to disgust than men (Al-Shawaf and Lewis, 2013; Curtis, et al., 2004), reflecting the increased likelihood of disease transmission to children. Women are particularly sensitive to disgusting stimuli during the luteal phase of the ovulatory cycle when the immune system is compromised (Fleischman and Fessler, 2011). Women's immune systems are also compromised during the first trimester of pregnancy, increasing the vulnerability of both the woman and the foetus (Fessler, 2002). Consequently, women demonstrate heightened disgust sensitivity (particularly for foods) in the first trimester of pregnancy (Fessler et al., 2005). Increased nausea and vomiting during the first trimester (Lacroix et al., 2000) further reduces the likelihood that contaminants will be ingested during this vulnerable period (Flaxman and Sherman, 2000) and demonstrates the importance of both behavioural and biological responses to threats.

While avoiding potential sources of infection is adaptive, in some situations (e.g. caring for others) it may be necessary to come into contact with sources of disgust (e.g. faeces). If a woman experiences a strong disgust reaction each time she is exposed to her child's faeces or vomit she may find it difficult to care for the child or to develop an attachment bond (see the section on love).

Consequently, women perceive the smell of their own baby's faeces as less disgusting than the faeces from other babies (Case et al., 2006), demonstrating the adaptive nature of the disgust response. Disgust responses may be costly in other respects; for example, greater time and energy may be expended sourcing suitable food. Consequently, disgust sensitivity may vary according to the relevant benefits and costs of contamination and selectivity. For example, hunger also impacts on women's sensitivity to disgust (Al-Shawaf and Lewis, 2013).

Other forms of disgust

The majority of disgust research focuses on the manner in which disgust may prevent the ingestion of pathogens and toxins. Though disgust may have evolved to reduce the threat of pathogens or disease, it also extends to social contexts, and a number of disgust types exist. These include interpersonal and socio-moral disgust (Rozin et al., 2000). People experience disgust when sexual taboos such as incest are violated (Gutierrez and Giner-Sorolla, 2007), and this disgust sensitivity is related to willingness to engage in sexual behaviour (Rempel and Baumgartner, 2003). The disgusted reaction encourages men and women to avoid sexual behaviours that inhibit reproductive success and offspring fitness (Cosmides and Tooby, 2000). Furthermore, contact with out-groups (Cottrell and Neuberg, 2005) and rejected religions evoke disgust (Ritter and Preston, 2011). In this context, disgust may function to protect moral beliefs (Ritter and Preston, 2011) and promote cohesion within the in-group.

Biological responses

Important interactions occur between the behavioural and biological immune system. In particular, there is evidence of a preparatory immune response, i.e. increased levels of TNF-A (and albumin) in response to disgusting images (Stevenson et al., 2011). Disgust responses also raise body temperature (Stevenson et al., 2012), which facilitates a physical response to potential infection. Viewing stimuli that are associated with disgust, such as the symptoms of disease, leads to a more aggressive immune response to infection (Schaller et al., 2010), further indicating that important interactions occur between the behavioural and physical immune responses.

With regard to brain regions, the insular cortex is particularly important for the processing of disgust-relevant stimuli. The insula is activated both when experiencing disgust and when viewing disgusted facial expressions (Wicker et al., 2003), suggesting that the neural representation of disgust in response to the disgust response displayed by another person is automatic. Additional findings indicate that damage to the insula can impact on the perception (Phillips et al., 1997) and experience (Hayes et al., 2007) of disgust. The insula may be important for the avoidance of core disgust, with the area involved in the processing of immune relevant signals (Pacheco-Lopez and Bermudez-Rattoni, 2011) and conditioning the immune response to pathogens (Oaten et al.,

2009). Activation of the insula is not restricted to core disgust, however; it also occurs in response to social or moral violations (Borg et al., 2008).

Fear

Fear is a powerful emotion occurring in response to threatening stimuli. Fear confers important evolutionary advantages and promotes fast effective responses to potential threats. The ability to experience fear is therefore essential for survival. Specific fears may develop when most beneficial; for example, fear of heights develops before infants start to crawl (Scarr and Salapatek, 1970). A fearful response to the threat, such as freezing, may reduce the likelihood of accidents and injury, further highlighting the adaptive benefit of this emotion.

According to Seligman's (1970, 1971) preparedness model, four features distinguish specific phobias from conditioned fears. These are: irrationality; ease of acquisition; high resistance to extinction; and greater prevalence for specific stimuli. Some stimuli may be particularly salient for a species, reflecting a recurrent threat experienced during evolutionary history. Seligman argued that phobias were a consequence of biologically 'prepared' learning, and that individuals may display fear to biologically relevant stimuli without prior experience of the object or learning (Menzies and Clarke, 1995). Developing this concept, Ohman and Mineka (2001) argue that there is an evolved module for fear elicitation and learning, which demonstrates selectivity with regard to stimuli that elicit a fear response (Mineka and Ohman, 2002). More recently, it has been suggested that the perceived dangerousness, disgustingness, predictability and uncontrollability of an object contribute to a 'vulnerability schema' that is automatically activated on presentation of a fear-relevant stimulus (Armfield, 2006). Once the vulnerability schema is activated, there is an automatic affective reaction and a controlled cognitive appraisal of the stimulus. Individual traits and experience may, however, influence perceived vulnerability.

The detection of fear has an important survival value, allowing individuals to learn from the experience of others (Williams et al., 2007). The reactions of other people therefore influence whether a stimulus is interpreted as threatening. For example, children observe the reaction of a caregiver when faced with a potentially threatening stranger or visual cliff (Marks, 1987). A similar process occurs in other species. For example, rhesus monkeys reared in a laboratory environment do not display fear of snakes until they observe the fearful reactions of others. The fear of snakes is then developed quickly compared to other stimuli (Mineka et al., 1984). Fear has an important influence on cognition and behaviour (Stefanucci and Proffitt, 2009). For example, when fearful, auditory stimuli are perceived as physically closer (Gagnon et al., 2013) and louder (Siegel and Stefanucci, 2011), allowing individuals to avoid potential threats.

The amygdala

The amygdala is important for the processing of threat-related information (Adolphs, 2002a) and is active following presentation of fearful stimuli (Zald, 2003). The amygdala is actively involved in the regulation of arousal and vigilance for potential threat (Davies and Whalen, 2001). It is suggested that the ventral amygdala may be particularly active in the processing of threat-related stimuli. The right amygdala is involved in the detection of salient emotional signals, and the left amygdala is involved in continued stimulus evaluation (Wager et al., 2003; Whalen et al., 2001). Important sex differences occur in response to fear: males show attenuation of the right amygdala while females show greater right-sided amygdala activity. In addition, amygdala activation persists for longer in females following presentation of fear-relevant stimuli (Williams et al., 2005). This continued amygdala arousal may promote vigilance for further threat-related information (Williams et al., 2001).

Love and attachment

Romantic love is near universal and though difficult to define, it involves **attachment** (a selective emotional or social bond), care-giving and sexual attraction (Mikulincer and Goodman, 2006). The actual experience of love is associated with a range of intense feelings and behaviours. These include intrusive thoughts, emotional dependency, increased energy and behaviours intended to produce a response (Leckman and Mayes, 1999), though this altered mental state is temporary and limited to the early stages of romantic relationships (Marazziti et al., 1999). Romantic love provides a number of adaptive benefits (Hatfield and Rapson, 2002). In particular, it promotes courtship behaviour, resulting in enhanced fitness and reproduction (Buss, 1988b; Fisher, 2004). Romantic relationships may also enhance positive emotions and reduce stress and anxiety, contributing to greater overall health and well-being (Esch and Stefano, 2005). There are therefore clear evolutionary advantages for those falling in love. These benefits are, of course, influenced by the type of person that we fall in love with.

Though the process of falling in love described above is observed in the majority of societies, the experience of love differs (Landis and O'Shea, 2000). Social rules that vary cross-culturally may influence the selection of a partner, the timing of a relationship or the expression of love (Doherty et al, 1994; Hatfield and Rapson, 1996). The extent to which love is an integral part of long-term sexual relationships also varies cross-culturally. Less than 5 per cent of Americans would marry without love compared to 50 per cent of participants in Pakistan (Levine et al., 1995). In part, these cultural differences may reflect the level of ecological stress experienced (Rohner and Britner, 2002). In stable environments with adequate resources, long-term planning, high investment and committed relationships are most adaptive. In contrast, distant emotional attachments, short-term relationships and lower levels of love may be adaptive in high-stress, unpredictable environments (Schmitt et al., 2004).

Brain activation

A range of brain areas, particularly those forming part of the reward system, are activated by romantic love (de Boer et al., 2012). These include the anterior cingulate cortex, hippocampus, hypothalamus, medial insula, nucleus accumbens and stratum (Zeki, 2007). In addition, a number of areas such as the amygdala and frontal cortex are deactivated (Zeki, 2007), which may reduce the likelihood of negative emotions, judgement of the romantic partner and calculated assessment of their intentions. This is described as a push–pull mechanism that rewards social interaction and suppresses negative emotions and critical judgement (Bartels and Zeki, 2004). A number of studies suggest that brain activity (or deactivation) during the early stages of a romantic relationship may predict a range of relationship outcomes such as satisfaction, commitment and happiness (Acevedo et al., 2012; Xu et al., 2011). In addition, Xu et al. (2012) demonstrate that long-term relationship outcomes are associated with brain areas involved in emotion regulation, social evaluation and inhibitory cognitive control and extend beyond the reward and motivation centres.

Hormonal influence

Oxytocin and **vasopressin** are produced by the hypothalamus and released by the pituitary gland (Debiec, 2007). Oxytocin is associated with the parasympathetic aspect of the autonomic nervous system, reduction of stress and regulation of the **hypothalamic–pituitary–adrenal (HPA) axis** (Engelmann, et al., 2004). Physiological systems involving oxytocin may inhibit the defensive behaviours associated with anxiety and encourage trust (Keri and Kiss, 2011). Oxytocin is associated with social interaction and bonding in a number of species (Olazabal and Young, 2006) and stimulates a range of social behaviours (Bartz et al., 2011). However, both individual and environmental differences influence the impact of oxytocin on social behaviour, affect and cognition (Bartz et al., 2011).

Vasopressin regulates the parasympathetic nervous system (Dreifuss et al., 1992). Oxytocin and vasopressin act on various pathways within the brain (Lim and Young, 2006) and receptors are present in a number of brain areas associated with romantic love. Oxytocin and vasopressin may allow sexual behaviour to be adapted to the social and physical environment, and concentrations of both oxytocin and vasopressin increase during the intense stages of romantic love (Carter, 1992). Research indicates that while males may be more sensitive to vasopressin (Winslow et al., 1993), females may be more sensitive to oxytocin (Insel and Hulihan, 1995).

Oxytocin and vasopressin interact with the **dopaminergic system** and can stimulate dopamine release by the hypothalamus (Young and Wang, 2004). The dopaminergic pathways activated through romantic love produce a pleasurable, rewarding feeling. These pathways are also associated with addictive behaviour, reflecting the dependency that characterises romantic love

(Edwards and Self, 2006). Increased levels of dopamine are associated with depleted serotonin levels. Low levels of serotonin during the early stages of romantic love characterised by obsessive intrusive thoughts (Zeki, 2007) are consistent with the low serotonin levels in obsessive compulsive patients (Marazziti et al., 1999). **Neurotrophins**, including nerve growth factor, may mediate anxiety and emotional or behavioural responses (Alleva and Santucci, 2001). Nerve growth factor levels are higher in those in the early stages of a romantic relationship than those that are not in a relationship or in the later stages of a long-term relationship. In addition, the intensity of the romantic love is positively correlated with levels of nerve growth factor (Emanuele et al., 2006).

Love and loss

The loss of love through the dissolution of a relationship or bereavement is a common experience. Though this loss is stressful and distressing (Stoessel et al., 2011) most men and women successfully adapt to the loss (Bonanno et al., 2002). A minority of individuals experiencing bereavement experience complicated grief, characterised by recurrent painful emotions and preoccupation with the deceased. It is suggested that while those experiencing (normal or complicated) grief experience pain in response to loss-relevant stimuli, for those with complicated grief, reward centres are also activated (O'Connor et al., 2008). Though the activation of these reward centres is not necessarily satisfying, the reward promotes a form of craving and addiction that hinders adaptation to the loss.

Maternal love

Maternal love is a powerful motivator of maternal behaviour and essential for the appropriate development of the mother–infant attachment relationship. The brain regions activated by maternal love overlap with those activated by romantic love (Bartels and Zeki, 2004). These typically centre on the reward areas of the brain and contain a high concentration of oxytocin and vasopressin receptors. Research indicates that oxytocin encourages maternal responsiveness, and oxytocin antagonists reduce maternal behaviour (Holman and Goy, 1995; Pedersen, 1997). Though it acts more slowly than oxytocin, vasopressin also influences maternal behaviour. The regions deactivated during romantic love (associated with negative emotions and judgement) are also deactivated during maternal love (Bartels and Zeki, 2004). Maternal love may also activate a number of regions (e.g. periaqueductal grey matter) that are not activated during romantic love (Bartels and Zeki, 2004) and specific maternal brain responses for their own infant's distress have also been identified (Noriuchi et al., 2008).

Jealousy

Jealousy is a complex emotion that is experienced in response to a real or imagined threat to a valued relationship. It is frequently a source of relationship conflict (Daly and Wilson, 1988) and as a result is often conceptualised as a 'dark' or negative emotion. Jealousy does, however, serve an important adaptive function. It alerts men and women to potential relationship threats and may prompt a person to engage in a number of behaviours intended to maintain their current relationship, often referred to as 'mate retention' behaviours (Buss, 1988a). These include a range of strategies such as monitoring partners (e.g. checking whether they have started to change the way they dress or whether they spend more time out of the home) and potential rivals (e.g. checking whether they are flirting with your partner or trying to impress them). These mate retention behaviours increase the likelihood of relationship maintenance and increase overall reproductive success (Buss, 2000).

Both men and women react jealously to sexual (e.g. having sex with another person) and emotional (e.g. sharing deep thoughts and feelings) infidelity. There are important sex differences, however, as men are more likely to respond jealously to sexual infidelity, and women are more likely to respond jealously to emotional infidelity (Buss et al., 1992). These reactions reflect the challenges faced by men and women over evolutionary history and the potential relationship threats experienced by each sex. As for most species, men cannot be sure (because of internal female fertilisation) that they are the biological parent of a woman's child. In evolutionary terms men that unknowingly raise another man's child (referred to as 'cuckoldry') waste both important resources (e.g. time, money, effort) and the opportunity to produce their own offspring. This represents a considerable threat to men. Though estimates vary, approximately 10 per cent of children are raised by men who mistakenly believe that they are the biological father (Platek and Shackelford, 2006). Men can, of course, reduce this threat by monitoring their partner (particularly when she is most likely to become pregnant) and 'guarding' her from other men. This explains why men are most sensitive to sexual infidelity.

For most species, including humans, females make a greater investment in any offspring than males (Trivers, 1972). For women, to produce one child there is an energy-intensive nine-month pregnancy followed by breast feeding and care, so while women do not face the threat of cuckoldry, the support that they receive from men is important. The dissolution of a romantic relationship or diversion of resources (such as time and money) to another woman results in a loss of support and protection. In evolutionary terms, this reduces the chances that she or her child will survive the harsh environment. As a result, women focus on signs that her partner is emotionally attached to another women rather than sexual infidelity. The specific reproductive challenges faced by each sex have therefore influenced the development of sex-specific jealousy mechanisms.

Studies consistently demonstrate that men are more distressed by sexual infidelity and women are more distressed by emotional infidelity (Sagarin et al., 2012). A number of critics have suggested that these findings reflect the methodological design adopted by researchers rather than actual sex differences (Harris, 2002). In particular, many studies employ hypothetical forced-choice scenarios in which participants are instructed to imagine that their partner has been emotionally (but not sexually) unfaithful or sexually (but not emotionally) unfaithful and report which form of infidelity is most distressing. This could be problematic as it may be difficult (or upsetting) for people to imagine these scenarios. In addition, men may believe that a woman would not have a sexual relationship without an emotional connection to a man. He therefore assumes that a woman described as having a sexual affair is also emotionally connected to her lover. Similarly a woman may report that emotional infidelity is most upsetting because she assumes that a man would not have a close emotional relationship with a woman if he were not also in a sexual relationship with her.

Sex differences are not restricted to these forms of forced-choice test, however. Differences between men and women have also been identified by researchers using continuous rather than forced-choice measures (Sagarin et al., 2012) and physiological rather than self-report measures (Buss et al., 1992; Pietrzak et al., 2002). Furthermore, sex-specific responses extend beyond hypothetical scenarios to actual infidelity. When questioning partners about an extra-pair relationship (i.e. affair), men are more likely to focus on the sexual aspects of the relationship, whereas women focus on emotional aspects of the infidelity (Kuhle et al., 2009; Schutzwohl, 2006). The interrogations allow men and women to assess the threat posed by the extra-pair relationship and decide whether to continue, alter or terminate their romantic relationship. Similarly, those accused of infidelity display sex-specific responses. Men are more likely to deny an emotional attachment to an extra-pair partner, and women are more likely to deny a sexual relationship (Kuhle et al., 2009). The responses allow the unfaithful partner to reduce the threat of relationship dissolution or retaliation. This is particularly important as men are more likely to dissolve relationships after sexual infidelity, and women are less likely to forgive an emotional affair (Shackelford et al., 2002).

People with morbid jealousy have hypersensitive jealousy mechanisms and display jealous cognitions, emotions and behaviours at a lower threshold than others. The sex differences outlined above are also apparent for those diagnosed with morbid or chronic jealousy (Easton et al., 2007). Though few studies have considered the biological basis of jealousy, men and women have specific neuropsychological responses to emotional and sexual infidelity, and this is a promising area of future research (Takahashi et al., 2006). It has also been suggested that organic brain pathology may contribute to morbid jealousy (Kuruppuarachchi and Seneviratne, 2011). A substantial minority of those with morbid jealousy demonstrate an organic psychosyndrome (Mullen and Maack, 1985) and a range of pathologies including degenerative disorders and infections have been related to morbid jealousy (Cobb, 1979).

Similarly, few studies have investigated the hormonal correlates of jealousy. For women, the use of hormonal contraceptives, menstrual cycle stage and **estradiol** levels are associated with higher self-reported jealousy and more intense jealousy (Cobey et al., 2011; Cobey et al., 2012; Geary et al., 2001). Furthermore, estradiol levels are associated with the greater use of mate retention behaviours intended to maintain the current relationship (Welling et al., 2012), indicating that the influence of hormone levels extends beyond feelings or emotions to specific behaviour. It is unclear, however, whether these hormonal variations in jealous responses have an adaptive function or are a consequence of other cyclical processes such as changes in partner preference.

The expression and recognition of emotional expressions

Emotions are expressed through a variety of facial expressions, bodily postures and non-verbal signals, suggesting that the communication of these emotions is also adaptive. The current section outlines the evolutionary benefits and biological processes associated with the expression and recognition of emotions.

Innate display and adaptive function

Emotional expressions are displayed by a number of species (Fox, 1970; Langford et al., 2010) and can be conceptualised as innate, species-typical, unlearned responses (Darwin, 1872). In humans a complex array of superficial facial muscles enables the display of facial expressions, and the cerebral cortex activates the facial nucleus both directly and indirectly. A number of emotions exist cross-culturally, each with an associated facial expression (Eibl-Eibesfeldt, 1970; Ekman and Friesen, 1975). As shown in Figure 5.1 (a) to (g), these universal emotions include anger, fear, surprise, sadness, disgust and happiness (Ekman, 1973). Facial expressions automatically capture our attention (Vuilleumier, 2002) and have an important role in human communication (Ekman, 1992). The person producing the expression transmits important information about their emotional state and may influence the behaviour of others. For example, smiling may encourage trust and cooperation, and sadness may lead to additional social support (Scharlemann et al., 2001). Therefore, the accurate production of facial expressions and ability to modify emotional displays are associated with peer acceptance and social status (Fabes et al., 1999; Field and Walden, 1982). Those observing emotions obtain valuable information from others. For example, observing disgust may promote avoidance of a food source.

The expression of emotion may be reflexive – for example, a spontaneous expression of fear in response to danger. The similarity of body postures, facial expressions and non-verbal signals displayed by blind and sighted people, and the emotional expressions displayed by infants and non-human animals suggest that emotional expressions are innate rather than learned behavioural patterns (Steiner et al., 2001). Though innate, facial displays are to an extent modifiable and under conscious control. People may produce a facial expression to exaggerate an emotional state or provide false information about an emotional state (Ekman and Friesen, 1975).

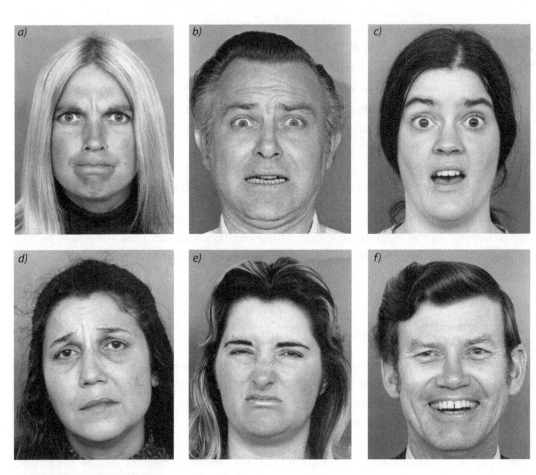

Figure 5.1: *Universal emotions*
a) Anger
b) Fear
c) Surprise
d) Sadness
e) Disgust
f) Happiness
g) Contempt

*Source: From Ekman, 1973, with the permission of
Paul Ekman PhD/Paul Ekman Group, LLC.*

For example, we may choose to suppress our sadness in the presence of some people or exaggerate an expression to demonstrate that we empathise with another person. Social context therefore influences the expression of emotional responses (Wagner and Lee, 1999) and 'display rules' may identify the appropriate context in which emotions should or should not be expressed.

There are, however, important differences between posed and spontaneous facial expressions. For example, posed expressions are more symmetrical than spontaneous expressions (Weddell et al., 1990) and, reflecting these differences, people are able to distinguish between genuine and false facial expressions (Ekman, 1992).

Emotion recognition

Humans accurately recognise emotional expressions (Huang et al., 2012), and human infants can distinguish between happiness, sadness and surprise within the first few days of life (Field et al., 1982). There are, of course, some important exceptions, and as illustrated in Figure 5.2, the emotions of schizophrenic patients are typically less accurately identified than controls. This perception and recognition of emotions forms a fundamental part of social interaction and survival (Darwin, 1872; Ekman, 1992). For example, the expression of fear may alert others to potential danger, and the expression of sadness may encourage others to offer valuable support. Though much of the research in this area focuses on the importance of visual stimuli, a range of information is used to inform emotion recognition. Emotions are categorised more quickly when individuals are presented with both audio and visual information rather than audio or visual information only (Collignon et al., 2008). In addition, the consistency of audio and visual emotional information facilitates appropriate behavioural responses to the stimuli (Dolan et al., 2001). When presented with inconsistent audio and visual emotional information, however, participants favour the visual information, suggesting a visual dominance in the processing of emotional information (Collignon et al., 2008). If a person is presented with unreliable visual information, the auditory information is preferred (Collignon et al., 2008), indicating an evaluation of the quality of information presented.

Figure 5.2: *Percentage of emotions displayed by controls and schizophrenic patients accurately identified: posed and evoked emotional displays are displayed on the left and right of the figure*

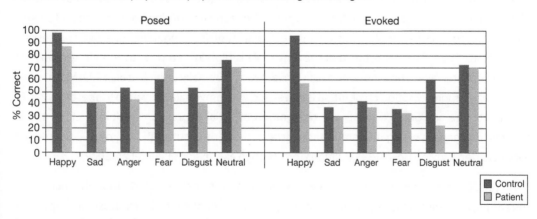

Source: Reproduced from Healey et al., 2010.

A number of individual differences (Fox et al., 2008) and psychiatric conditions (Kohler et al., 2004) influence the ability to recognise and respond to emotional expressions. **Alexithymia** refers to the inability to consciously experience emotion (Lane et al., 1996) and exists on a continuum from normal to pathological (Parker et al., 2008). It is characterised by difficulty processing (Sifneos, 1973), recognising (Parker et al., 2005) and expressing (McDonald and Prkachin, 1990) emotions, and lower empathy (Guttman and Laporte, 2002). In particular, alexithymia is associated with difficulties detecting emotion and with perceiving emotions as less intense (Prkachin et al., 2009). Reflecting the importance of emotional expressions in human interaction, the relationships of alexithymics contain higher levels of hostility and conflict and are less satisfying (Gutman, 2007; Humphreys et al., 2009). Consequently, alexithymia is associated with discomfort with closeness (Montebarocci et al., 2004), attachment difficulties (Mallinckrodt and Wei, 2005) and social isolation (Kokkonen et al., 2001). A number of previous studies have investigated the biological mechanisms related to alexithymia, though a range of methodological issues such as inconsistent measurement of alexithymia have hindered progress (see Larsen et al., 2003 for a review).

Processing and biological mechanisms

A number of cortical and sub-cortical structures form the neural basis for emotional face processing (Adolphs, 2002a). The processing of facial expressions involves: a) the core visual analysis of facial features; and b) attributing emotional significance to those traits (Adolphs, 2002a). The analysis of facial traits involves a number of brain areas, including the lower occipital gyrus and fusiform gyrus (Haxby et al., 2000; Said et al., 2011). The attribution of emotional significance includes areas such as the striate cortex, fusiform face area, superior temporal gyrus and orbito frontal cortex (Bruce and Young, 1986; Haxby et al., 2000). The limbic system and amygdala, in particular, are important for the relation of facial expressions to personal identity and emotions (Guyer et al., 2008).

The amygdala has an important role in the processing of emotional expressions (Adolphs, 2002b) and especially the processing of negative facial expressions (e.g. Adolphs et al., 1999; Calder et al., 1996) such as fear (Adolphs et al., 1994). The amygdala is activated during both implicit and explicit processing of emotional facial expressions, though activation is stronger during explicit processing (Habel et al., 2007). The importance of the amygdala is highlighted by activation in response to emotional avatar faces and emotional faces presented subliminally (Morris et al., 1999; Moser et al., 2007). Furthermore, emotion recognition is correlated with amygdala activation (Habel et al., 2007). Damage to the amygdala disrupts the recognition of facial expressions (Adolphs et al., 1994). Accurate recognition of negative emotions may be particularly problematic as amygdala-damaged patients often provide positive evaluations for negative expressions (Sato et al., 2002).

During social interactions, the faces we observe are dynamic rather than static, though much of the current psychological research focuses on the processing of static facial expressions. Important differences appear to exist between the processing of dynamic and static faces. There is greater recognition accuracy for dynamic compared to static facial expressions (Ambadar et al., 2005), and those unable to process static facial expressions may be able to accurately recognise dynamic facial expressions (Adolphs et al., 2003). The enhanced ability to recognise dynamic expressions may reflect greater responses to dynamic stimuli in those regions involved in the processing of facial expressions (Kilts et al., 2003) and a wider network of brain activity in response to dynamic expressions (Trautmann et al., 2009). The processing of dynamic faces forms an interesting area of future research.

Critical thinking activity

The importance of tears

Critical thinking focus: critical and creative thinking

Key question: Why do we cry when we feel sad?

Read the following article: Balsters, MJH, Krahmer, EJ, Swerts, MGJ and Vingerhoets, AJJM (2013) Emotional tears facilitate the recognition of sadness and the perceived need for social support. *Evolutionary Psychology*. Available online at www.ep journal.net/wp-content/uploads/EP111148158.pdf.

The article outlines the importance of tears as a visual cue that encourages other people to recognise sadness and offer support. Focus on the studies conducted by the researchers. Can you think of any factors that may have influenced the results? For example, many of the studies conducted by psychologists (including this one) depend on students based in Western countries such as the UK and USA because these men and women form a convenient sample. Do you think that other people would respond differently to tears? Try to identify other factors that may have influenced the findings.

Critical thinking review

This activity asks you to read a journal article and consider the way in which researchers design, conduct and report their research studies. There are a number of factors that influence the outcomes of our research. While researchers may try to control some of these factors, such as ensuring that participants taking part in a fear study do or do not have a phobia, some factors are difficult or impossible to control. For this reason, researchers focus on building a solid foundation of research findings rather than claiming that one individual study 'proves' a hypothesis.

In this study, the researchers suggest that tears act as a visual signal that encourages other people to offer social support. Can you think of any other signals that we use to signal our emotions and prompt other people to behave in a particular way? These signals may be consciously or unconsciously used to influence the perceptions and actions of other people.

Skill builder activity

Measuring emotions

Transferable skill focus: understanding and using data

Key question: *How do researchers actually assess emotions?*

Researchers often use questionnaires to measure specific emotions such as fear, disgust and jealousy. View the jealousy instrument (Buss et al., 1999) available online at http://homepage.psy.utexas.edu/homepage/group/busslab/measures.htm and imagine how you would feel completing this as a research participant.

Would it be easy for you to imagine yourself in these scenarios and answer honestly about your feelings? Are there any important aspects of jealousy not covered by the questionnaire? Do you think that people from different cultural backgrounds would interpret the questions differently? If you were asked to create a questionnaire to assess emotions, what would you need to consider and how would you start to design it?

Skill builder review

This task asks you to think about the process of data collection and how the questions that we ask can influence our results. When selecting research materials such as questionnaires, it is important to consider issues such as the reliability (i.e. the consistency of the questionnaire) and validity (i.e. whether the questionnaire actually assesses the concept that it claims to address) of the measure. Think about how these issues can affect the results of a study and search the internet for alternative jealousy questionnaires to see how these compare.

Assignments

1. To what extent do emotions impact on human survival? Consider both positive and negative consequences in your answer.

2. Discuss the biological and psychological factors influencing disgust sensitivity.

3. Outline the biological mechanisms influencing the recognition of emotional expressions. To what extent is the recognition of emotions an essential human ability?

Summary: what you have learned

Now you have finished studying this chapter you should:

- understand the James-Lange and Cannon-Bard theories of emotion;

- be able to discuss the adaptive benefits of key emotions, including anger, disgust, fear and love;

- recognise sex differences and individual variation in emotional responses, including evolutionary explanations for these differences;

- be able to identify the brain regions and hormones associated with specific emotions;

- understand the biological mechanisms associated with the recognition and processing of emotional expressions;

- have developed your skills relating to the ability to synthesise and evaluate written information;

- understand the importance of research measures and design.

Further reading

Archer, J (2009) The nature of human aggression. *International Journal of Law and Psychiatry*, 32, 202–208.

A detailed account of human aggression.

Armfield, JM (2006) Cognitive vulnerability: a model of the etiology of fear. *Clinical Psychology Review*, 26, 746–768.

A review of fear-related research.

Darwin, C (1872) *The expression of the emotions in man and animals.* London: John Murray.

Darwin's seminal work on human and non-human emotion.

Sagarin, BJ, Martin, AL, Coutinho, SA, Edlund, JE, Patel, L, Skowronski, JJ and Zengel, B (2012) Sex differences in jealousy: a meta-analytic examination. *Evolution and Human Behavior*, 33, 595–614.

A review of sex-related differences in jealousy.

Stevenson, RJ, Case, TI and Oaten, MJ (2009) Frequency and recency of infection and their relationship with disgust and contamination sensitivity. *Evolution and Human Behavior*, 30, 363–368.

A detailed account of the relationship between infection experience and disgust.

Chapter 6

Memory

Learning outcomes

By the end of this chapter you should:

- *be aware of areas of the brain that govern the formation and retention of different memory processes;*
- *understand the influence of evolution and genetics on human memory;*
- *recognise the impact of hormones on memory functioning;*
- *have a critical understanding of the research methodologies used to explore memory processes;*
- *be aware of future directions in memory research;*
- *have developed your critical thinking skills.*

Introduction

Luis Buñuel, the Spanish film-maker, once said *Life without memory is no life at all . . . Our memory is a coherence, our reason, our feeling, even our action. Without it, we are nothing.* Psychologists also note that memory is critical to human functioning, with the study of memory placed at the heart of many psychology courses. Cognitive psychologists have developed complex computational models of memory processing as a result of over a hundred years of experimentation. However, our understanding of the biological systems that support memory is still in its infancy. The aim of this chapter is to outline current knowledge regarding the locations of key memory functions within the cortex. We will also explore the impact of genes, hormones and drug use on memory.

Although substantial progress has been made in exploring the biology of human memory, the field is limited by the research methods available. Early research depended on the use of case studies, such as the case of HM who, after brain surgery, developed an inability to lay down new memories. Although case studies have been important in helping us to gain insight into the areas of brain responsible for memory, they also have serious limitations. More recent memory research has made use of new methods such as transcranial magnetic stimulation (TMS) and brain imaging; for example, brain imaging studies have highlighted differences in the brain structure of taxi drivers who have memorised the extensive road networks of London. However, even the most modern research methods used to unravel the mysteries of human memory are still open to criticism. The current chapter will therefore critically evaluate the methodologies used in memory research and consider the limitations of various approaches.

Finally in this chapter, we will consider future directions in memory research. Understanding of the biology of memory is critical to evaluating the safety of cognitive enhancer drugs that can improve memory. Understanding the biology of memory can also improve treatments for medical disorders such as post-traumatic stress disorder (PTSD). Without knowing how and where emotional memories are formed it is difficult to develop treatments that can rid sufferers of the painful and intrusive memories that occur in PTSD.

Types of memory

Memory can be simply described as our ability to retrieve information that is no longer present in our environment. However, there are many different types of memory, and psychologists use various classifications. One classification system is based around how long the memory has been held for and forms the basis for the Atkinson and Shiffrin (1968) **multi-store model of memory**.

- *Sensory memory* This type of memory refers to memories that are very short-lived, lasting only up to a few seconds. Sensory memories related to the visual system are known as iconic memories and are captured via the retina and the visual cortex. Echoic memories are similar to iconic memories but are sound-based and encoded via the cochlea and the temporal lobe.

- *Short-term memory* Short-term memories are those memories that are currently in our consciousness. These memories may be in our short-term store because they have just occurred and are in the process of being encoded into our long-term memory store or because they have been retrieved from our long-term memory store ready for use. The conceptualisation of short-term memory was refined in 1974 with the development of the **working memory model** by Alan Baddeley and Graham Hitch.

- *Long-term memory* These are memories that are not currently in our consciousness. Instead, long-term memories such as the address of a friend or the date of a relative's birthday are stored away so they can be retrieved when needed.

The classification of memories can also be based on the type of information that is being retained. Two main types of information are thought to be stored: explicit and implicit memory. Within explicit and implicit memory there are many further classifications as illustrated below.

Explicit memory refers to knowledge and skills that we overtly and consciously know. Below are some examples of explicit memory.

- *Eidetic memory* This type of memory refers to occasions when people claim to be able to recall a very detailed visual image for a long period of time. This type of memory is commonly known as photographic memory and is very rare (with some researchers claiming that eidetic memories do not exist at all).

- *Prospective memory* This refers to our ability to remember to complete an action in the future. An example of a prospective memory is remembering to pick up a pint of milk in the supermarket on your way home or to post a card in time for your friend's birthday.

- *Semantic memory* This type of memory is also known as declarative memory and refers to our ability to store and recall factual information. An example of a semantic memory is remembering all the capital cities in Europe or the key dates in American history.

- *Autobiographical memory* This type is similar to semantic/declarative memory but specifically relates to our ability to recall information about our personal past. Autobiographical memories could include memories of your first day at school or your favourite family holiday.

Implicit memory refers to memories that are not held consciously.

- *Procedural memory* This refers to our ability to remember how to complete complex motor actions without the need for conscious input. For example, when we start to learn to drive a car we need to consciously remember each action, such as when to change gear or to put our seat belt on when we get into the car. However, after training, these actions become implicit, requiring no conscious attention.

Memory stages

Memory processes can be broken down into three main elements: input (encoding), storage and retrieval (Figure 6.1). However, this is a very simplistic view of how memory functions and more resembles a computer than a human. Memory processes in humans have a tendency to go wrong. For example, has a friend ever said a phone number to you so quickly that you have forgotten it before you have had chance to write it down? Or when taking part in a quiz have you ever been sure that you know the answer to a question but been unable recall the information at that moment? Both these examples illustrate how fragile human memory can be. Researchers today are only now starting to understand the factors that can influence memory at the encoding, storage and retrieval stages.

Evolutionary processes in human memory

Evolutionary psychology suggests that the way the modern brain functions and is structured is the result of adaptations to environmental pressures in our past. Evolutionary psychologists James Nairne and Josefa Pandeirada (2008) therefore suggest that when examining human memory it is important to consider why the ability to store and retrieve memories may have developed. For

Figure 6.1: A model to represent the three distinct stages of memory processing

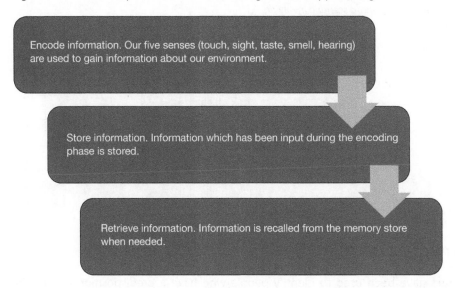

Encode information. Our five senses (touch, sight, taste, smell, hearing) are used to gain information about our environment.

Store information. Information which has been input during the encoding phase is stored.

Retrieve information. Information is recalled from the memory store when needed.

example, it is important to consider what function memory served for Stone Age people. Once evolutionary pressures are identified then, it is claimed, we can look for their 'footprints' in the way in which memory works in the modern human.

The concept of adaptive memory – the idea that human memory developed to help us cope with environmental pressures such as identifying threats or remembering the location of food – was examined by Nairne et al. 2007. Adaptive memory theory would suggest that we are more likely to remember information important to survival than other types of information. Using an experimental design, Nairne and Pandeirada completed a study to test this hypothesis. In the study participants were asked to look at a list of words and make a judgement. In one condition participants were asked to imagine that they were stranded in the grassland of a foreign land and to decide whether the items on the list would be useful. In the second condition participants were asked to look at the same list of equipment but this time they had to make a judgement as to whether the equipment listed would be useful when moving to a new home. In the control condition, participants were simply asked to rate the pleasantness of each word. All participants were then given a surprise recall task for the words in the list. The results in Figure 6.2 show that participants who were asked to judge the items in the list in a survival context had significantly better recall than participants in the other two conditions.

The results of Nairne et al.'s (2007) study suggest that evolutionary pressures still impact on how memory functions today, with information related to survival being more likely to be encoded and recalled than other information. It would appear that memory is not simply a tool to remember past events; memory has evolved to safeguard us from threats and help us with behaviours that enhance survival.

Figure 6.2: *Proportion of correct recall for words rated for their relevance to a survival scenario, a scenario involving moving or for pleasantness*

Source: Nairne et al., 2007.

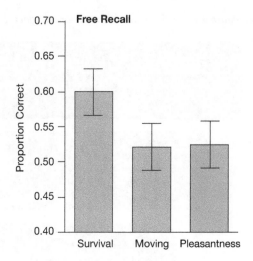

Genetic markers for memory

Genetic markers have been used to identify people who have a predisposition for certain diseases. For example, women who have the faulty BRCA1 and BRCA2 gene have been shown to have a higher genetically based predisposition to develop breast cancer. Identification of genetic markers for diseases is helpful for both the diagnosis and treatment of many illnesses. However, recently researchers have become interested in whether certain gene expressions can explain the normal variation in certain characteristics within the normal population. For example, our genes govern basic characteristics such as hair colour and height. It is therefore possible that certain genes may also have an important influence on how good our memories are. Environmental factors such as diet and education explain some of the variation seen in memory functioning within the population. However, the high heritability of memory abilities suggests that memory has a genetic element. For example research suggests that around 50 per cent of the between-person variation in episodic memory performance is heritable (Papassotiropoulos et al., 2006). Studies that have tried to identify memory-related genetic variation have suggested that the Kibra (kidney and brain expressed protein) gene is associated with memory performance. However, other studies have not been able to show that the Kibra gene influences memory abilities (Need et al., 2008).

The location of memory within the cortex

In 1904 the German biologist Richard Semon suggested that experiences may leave a physical trace (an engram) within the brain. Since then researchers have been trying to identify the specific location of memory functions within the cortex. However, finding exactly where memories are located has turned out to be very challenging. Evidence as to where various memory functions reside comes from a diverse range of sources. Sources of information include case studies of patients with memory problems, brain imaging studies and even studies that involve the direct stimulation of the cortex. Researchers then face the very difficult challenge of putting all this information together in order to establish where memory processes are located and what factors modulate memory encoding, storage and retrieval.

In the future it may be possible to identify the specific brain location of a specific memory. For example, in the future it may be possible to locate all your memories associated with your tenth birthday party or the layout of your local supermarket. Case studies of patients with cortical lesions suggest that related memories are located in specific cortical areas. For example, Gabrieli (1998) found that some patients lost very specific memories – such as the names of fruits and vegetables or manufactured items – as a result of a brain injury. However, current research can give us only a general guide as to which regions of the brain are associated with certain memory processes.

- *Semantic (declarative) memory* This is located in the medial-temporal regions (such as the hippocampus and parahippocampus) and the diencephalic (hypothalamus and the thalamus) brain regions (Hu et al., 2009).

- *Emotional memories* Brain imaging studies show activation of the amygdala when **emotional stimuli** are encoded, suggesting that the amygdala plays an important role in encoding emotional memories (Canli et al., 2000).

- *Working (short-term) memory* The prefrontal cortex has been shown to become activated during both verbal and spatial working memory tasks (D'Esposito et al., 1995). However, the exact location of the specific elements of working memory is not yet known.

- *Procedural memory* Evidence of the importance of the basal ganglia for procedural memory comes from patients with Parkinson's disease (a progressive neurodegenerative disease that causes problems with movement such as tremor). Parkinson's patients show impairments in motor skill learning while having normal declarative memory. Further evidence from brain imaging studies suggests that the basal ganglia become activated during the learning phase of a procedural task (Packard and Knowlton, 2002).

Although the areas of the brain listed above have been identified as being critically important to each of the associated memory processes, the exact mechanisms that govern how these memories are encoded, stored and retrieved are not yet fully understood.

The role of hormones in memory formation

Aristotle used the metaphor *carvings on a wax tablet* to describe how memories are imprinted in the mind. Over the past thirty years biological psychologists have attempted to uncover how these 'carvings' occur – that is to say, researchers have worked to uncover the precise neurochemical mechanisms that cause memories to become encoded in the brain. Many environmental factors can enhance **memory consolidation**. For example, a longer encoding time and having a more elaborate encoding method have both been shown to increase memory retention. Recent research suggests that hormonal changes can both enhance and impair memory processing.

- *Adrenaline* is released when the body faces a threat and is designed to improve our chances of survival. Studies have shown that increased levels of circulating **adrenaline** leads to enhanced encoding of long-term memories, with higher levels of adrenaline being associated with better memory performance (Cahill and McGaugh, 1998).

- *Cortisol* is released following activation of the hypothalamic–pituitary–adrenal (HPA) axis during stressful events. It is thought that **cortisol** can cross the blood–brain barrier and acts on areas of the brain important to memory functioning. These areas include the prefrontal cortex, the amygdala and the hippocampus. Research has found that when people are under high levels of stress the increase in cortisol leads to impairments in declarative (Tops et al., 2004) and autobiographical memory recall (Buss et al., 2004), and causes deficits in working memory (Kirschbaum et al., 1996). Further evidence for the negative effect of cortisol on memory processes comes from Cushing's disease patients. In Cushing's disease, tumours in the **adrenal glands** cause excess secretion of cortisol. Patients with Cushing's disease have been found to have atrophy of the hippocampus and associated memory problems.

- *Estradiol* is a **sex hormone** that is found in both men and women. In women estradiol governs the development and functioning of the reproductive system, as well as the growth of certain bones. Estradiol has been found to be associated with working memory performance with women with higher levels of circulating estradiol performing better on a working memory task (Hampson and Morley, 2013).

- *Progesterone* is a female sex hormone that peaks during the luteal phase of the menstrual cycle. Researchers have found that elevated progesterone is associated with enhanced memory performance. For example, Ertman et al. (2011) found that higher levels of progesterone correlated with better recall of emotional stimuli.

- *Testosterone* is considered to be a male sex hormone but is actually found in both men and women. **Testosterone** production is highest during early puberty and helps develop the characteristics associated with the adult body. Testosterone supply reduces in the elderly, and supplementation has been found to help memory functioning in elderly men suffering from memory problems (Cherrier et al., 2005).

Methodologies used for memory research

In order to expand our understanding of memory functioning biological psychologists use an extensive number of methodological approaches. Each method has the potential to increase our understanding of the biology underpinning memory systems. The section outlines how different research methods can enhance our understanding of memory. However, each method also has a number of limitations, which are also explored.

Case studies

One of the most straightforward ways to investigate which areas of the brain are associated with certain memory processes would be to create a lesion in the area of interest and see what memory impairments occur. However, this approach is highly unethical as it would lead to irreversible brain damage. Biological psychologists therefore have to study people who have cortical lesions due to brain traumas caused by sporting or traffic accidents, strokes, tumours, disease or surgery.

One of the most famous case studies within memory research is the case of Henry Molaison. Henry Molaison (known only as HM in journal papers until his death in 2008) underwent brain surgery that removed the hippocampus from both sides of his temporal lobes. The aim of the operation was to reduce the frequency of HM's debilitating epileptic seizures, and in this regard the operation was a success. However, shortly after the surgery a serious side effect of the operation came to light. HM was suffering from profound anterograde amnesia – that is to say, HM could no longer lay down any new memories. Interestingly, HM's declarative memory prior to the operation was preserved and he was able to recall events from his past. HM commented on his condition that *Every day is alone in itself, whatever enjoyment I've had, and whatever sorrow I've had* (Milner et al., 1968, p217). However, although HM was unable to lay down new declarative memories, he was able to learn new procedural skills. For example, HM's procedural memory appeared to be intact as he showed improvement on a mirror drawing task. However, HM's declarative memory was so impaired that he did not lay down any memories about the training session and could not even recall having completed the mirror drawing task before (Corkin, 1984). The case study of HM has therefore helped biological psychologists to locate declarative memory within the medial-temporal regions. Further, the fact that HM's procedural memory was preserved suggests that procedural memory is not located in the hippocampal regions.

Critical thinking activity

Evaluating the use of case studies in memory research

Critical thinking focus: use of case studies

Key question: *What can the case studies in Scoville and Milner's (1957) paper tell us about where memory functions are located in the brain?*

Read the following article: Scoville, WB and Milner, B (1957) Loss of recent memory after bilateral hippocampal lesions. *Journal of Neurology, Neurosurgery, and*

Psychiatry, 20 (1), 11–21. The paper can be downloaded for free at www.ncbi.nlm. nih.gov/pmc/articles/PMC497229/pdf/jnnpsyc00285–0015.pdf.

Scoville and Milner describe the case of HM and other patients who underwent operations to remove all or part of their hippocampal structures and the resulting memory problems experienced. The paper concludes that operations that remove brain matter from both sides of the medial temporal lobe can lead to permanent impairment in recent memory encoding.

- What evidence suggests that hippocampal lesions are the cause of the memory problems experienced by the patients described in the paper?

- What other reasons could account for some of the cognitive difficulties experienced by patients in the study?

- What are the limitations of making generalisations from case study research?

- Are there any other methodologies that could have been used to find the same results?

Critical thinking review

Case studies have an important role to play in our understanding of where memory is located in the brain. The work of Scoville and Milner (1957) was groundbreaking and helped to pinpoint the encoding and storage of declarative memories within the hippocampal structures. Of the ten patients described in the paper three patients underwent radical bilateral medial temporal lobe resections. The observations made in the paper suggest that patients who had the most invasive surgery had the most pronounced memory deficits. However, no matter how extensive the surgery, all patients showed some degree of memory impairment. The results of these ten case studies highlight the importance of the hippocampal structures in encoding new declarative memories.

As with most case study research, a number of key limitations should be kept in mind. First, case study research rarely has details of pre-morbid (before the brain injury) functioning. It is therefore difficult to say with absolute certainty that the impairments Scoville and Milner's patients experienced post-surgery were not there prior to the operation. Second, as the patients in the study also suffered from conditions such as schizophrenia and epilepsy, it is possible that their memory was compromised prior to surgery. Pre-existing memory problems could have been caused either by their medical condition or by the drugs used to control their condition. For example, HM is reported to be taking *heavy and varied* **anticonvulsant** *medication* (Scoville and

Milner, 1957, p16). Third, the results of each of the case studies reported in the paper are not directly comparable. For example, the operations undertaken on each of the patients were slightly different, with people apparently having had the same operation actually having slightly different amounts of their hippocampi removed. Fourth, following trauma the brain can reorganise brain functions in order to compensate for impairments. This means that if a brain injury is a few years old, memory processes may be relocated to undamaged areas of the brain. All these factors mean that interpreting the results of case study analysis is complex and that conclusions should be treated with some caution.

Given the limitations of case studies, is it possible to gain insight into the location of memory processes using any other means? The answer is yes. It may be possible to gain information about the role of the hippocampus in memory processing using other methodologies. For example, researchers could monitor the **cerebral blood flow** to the hippocampus while people learn new declarative information. However, alternative methodologies also have limitations that are discussed below. Furthermore, now the risks associated with operations that remove sections of the temporal lobe are better understood, it is unlikely the type of operation that HM experienced will ever be repeated.

Electronic stimulation

In the 1940s and 1950s the Canadian neurosurgeon Wilder Penfield completed groundbreaking work using electrical probes to stimulate parts of the brain. The primary aim of Penfield's research was to explore the causes of epilepsy. However, Penfield observed that by electrically stimulating the temporal lobes with a mild electric current he could cause patients to summon up past memories. For example, one patient undergoing the procedure exclaimed: *Yes, Doctor, yes, Doctor! Now I hear people laughing – my friends in South Africa . . . Yes, they are my two cousins, Bessie and Ann Wheliaw* (Penfield, 1968, p834).

In the 1970s, studies using electrical stimulation continued, with the majority of the research being carried out on epileptic patients undergoing neurosurgery. For example, the careful and systematic work of Paul Fedio and John Van Buren (1974) led to the identification of a number of key locations for memory functioning within the brain. For example, Fedio and Van Buren reported that electrical stimulations of the left posterior temporo-parietal cortex led to problems with the retrieval of stored information, whereas stimulation of the anterior temporal neocortex led to anterograde memory loss. More recent studies have explored memory phenomena such as feelings of déjà vu. For example, Fabrice Bartolomei and colleagues (2004) found that feelings of déjà vu could be induced via direct stimulation of the sub-hippocampal structures.

However, the use of direct electrical stimulation of the cortex does have a number of limitations. First, the technique is very invasive. Although the technique does not normally result in permanent damage to the participant's brain, direct contact with the cortex is required. As operations to expose the brain are not without risk, this means that the technique can be used only on people who are undergoing brain surgery for other reasons. In the majority of studies that use direct stimulation of the cortex, the participants are undergoing treatment for epilepsy. This means that research has only a small pool of potential participants, as only a limited number of epileptic patients will need neurosurgery. Further, it is possible that people with epilepsy have differences in their memory processing as a result of their condition or because of the medication they are taking. This means that generalisations for the participants in electrical stimulation studies to the general population should be undertaken with caution.

Transcranial magnetic stimulation (TMS)

Transcranial magnetic stimulation (TMS) is a relatively new technique that allows non-invasive stimulation of the brain. TMS, unlike previous electrical stimulation techniques, does not require the probe to touch the cortex directly. Instead, TMS is a non-invasive technique where a powerful rapidly changing current is delivered via a small coil of wire placed directly on the participant's scalp. The technique is painless, and although it can temporarily lead to cognitive impairments, no lasting damage has been recorded. The technique can be used to cause a 'virtual brain lesion', so researchers can explore which behaviours are compromised when certain brain areas are impaired (Mottaghy et al., 2000). For example, TMS studies that have carried out repetitive TMS of the dorsolateral prefrontal cortex have reported impairments in verbal working memory tasks. These results suggest that the dorsolateral prefrontal cortex has an important role to play in working memory processes.

The advantage of using TMS is that cognitively 'normal' participants are more able to take part compared to traditional electrical stimulation techniques that require more invasive procedures. Results from participants who are more representative of the normal population also mean that the research is more generalisable. However, some problems have been reported with the use of TMS. One problem is that the coil delivering the current can get very hot, and care must be taken to cool the coil if extensive periods of testing are to be undertaken. A second, potentially more serious, problem is that TMS has been reported to trigger seizures. However, seizures do appear to be very rare following TMS and have usually occurred in participants with pre-existing medical conditions that make seizures more likely.

Drugs and hormones

Certain drugs and hormones can cross the blood–brain barrier and act on areas of the brain that are known to be involved in memory functioning. Researchers have explored the effects of a large number of drugs and hormones on memory by administering these substances to participants and then observing the effects. For example, Romuald Brunner and colleagues (2006) wanted to examine the impact of **glucocorticoids** (stress hormones) on memory processes. In their study they examined how well different types of memory functions were carried out in people who were taking high levels of glucocorticoids for a range of neurological conditions. Their study found that all the patients taking high doses of glucocorticoids had marked impairments in their long-term memory but not in their short-term memory. The researchers therefore concluded that gluco-corticoids can affect the areas of the brain that govern long-term memory.

The second way in which the effects of drugs and hormones can be explored in humans is by changing a person's environment in order to induce an **endogenous** release of the substance the researchers wish to examine. For example, in a study by Sabrina Kuhlmann and colleagues (2005), levels of the glucocorticoid cortisol were increased via exposure to a laboratory stressor, Trier Social Stress Test (TSST). The TSST involves participants preparing for and undertaking a simulated job interview. The mock job interview is then followed by a maths task that involves counting backwards in threes from a given four-digit number. Kuhlmann et al. (2005) found that cortisol levels were significantly elevated after exposure to the stressor and that participants also showed an impairment in their long-term memory.

Although studies that examine the impact of drugs and hormones on memory are useful, they do have a number of problems. When researchers are using environmental stimuli in order to generate the release of hormones such as cortisol, they have to be very careful that the stimuli are interpreted the same way by all their participants. For example, some people may have a very large cortisol response after completing a public-speaking task as they are not used to public speaking. However, other participants may be more confident and more practised in public speaking and therefore not generate the same level of cortisol post-task. A further problem is that drugs and hormones may not have the same effect on all populations. For example, in the case of cortisol administration different effects have been found dependent on the age and the gender of the participant.

Animal studies

Animals have been used in studies of biological systems for centuries and have led to major advancements in our knowledge of memory systems. Animal experiments allow the systematic exploration of factors that affect memory, and allow studies to be carried out in controlled environments. For example, Diamond et al. (1999) investigated the effects of stress on the ability of rats to learn the layout of a water maze. The rats explored a maze layout to look for the hidden platform either in their home cage or in a cage near a cat. The results indicated the presence of the cat (the stressor) caused the rats to show impairment in their ability to learn spatial information. The results of this study in conjunction with other animal and human studies have helped to explain the impact of stress on memory processes – in this case, learning.

Putting aside the moral debate about whether animal experimentation should be used, there are a number of methodological considerations that may limit the usefulness of animal memory research.

- Different animal species and breeds may have different reactions to different drugs used in research.

- Differences between human and animal brain structures may mean that memory systems are not directly comparable.

- Outcome measures between human and animal studies may reduce the ability to compare the results between species. For example, is a rat learning a route around a water maze the same as a human learning the geographical locations of London tourist attractions?

Brain imaging

In the early 1900s a technique known as pneumoencephalography was used in order to gain clear X-rays of the brain. For this technique to work the cerebrospinal fluid from around the brain was drained and replaced with air. The resulting change in the relative density of the brain to its surroundings meant that cortical areas could be seen on an X-ray. Not only was the technique painful but it was also dangerous for participants, and it was not until the 1970s that safe, non-invasive brain imaging techniques started to be developed that could give detailed images of the brain.

- Computerised axial tomography (CAT) scans can provide researchers with structural images of the brain. The technique uses X-rays and is based around the premise that bone, tissue and blood absorb X-rays to varying degrees. An image can therefore be created based on the differences in X-ray absorption between the different elements of the brain. Although the images produced are not very detailed, they are good enough to be used for the diagnosis of brain abnormalities such as the damage caused by tumours or strokes. CAT scans are therefore useful to memory researchers who wish to identify which areas of the brain have been damaged in patients presenting with memory impairments.

- Magnetic resonance imaging (MRI) uses powerful magnets and radio waves to create a three-dimensional image of the brain. Like the CAT scan, the MRI is generally used to generate structural images of the brain. However, the MRI images are much more detailed than can be gained from the CAT scan. Further, as the MRI does not use radiation, the technique can be used with a wider range of participants, including groups such as pregnant women.

- Functional magnetic resonance imaging (fMRI) is a more recent refinement of MRI. Using similar technology to the MRI scanner, fMRI works using magnets to detect changes in blood flow and oxygenation levels. When a particular area of the cortex is activated in order to complete a cognitive task, then more oxygen is needed in that area. In order to increase the supply of oxygen to the activated brain region, cerebral blood flow in that region is increased. Researchers can therefore use fMRI to pinpoint the location in the cortex that has been activated when a certain cognitive task is undertaken by examining where increases in blood flow have occurred. From a research point of view the fMRI has many advantages, producing high-quality detailed images of blood flow within the cortex. However, although the procedure is painless, people with pacemakers should be aware that the scanner may cause their device to fail, and people with claustrophobia may not be able to stay in the scanner as they might feel too enclosed. Figure 6.3 shows a brain scan of an adult completed using an fMRI scanner.

- Electroencephalography (EEG) is a non-invasive and relatively cheap form of brain imaging. Participants have a number of electrodes placed directly on their scalp. The electrodes then detect changes in electrical activity. One advantage of using EEG is the high temporal resolution. That is to say, EEG can detect changes in electrical activity in the brain very quickly. A further advantage is that it is relatively cheap to use.

- Positron emission tomography (PET) uses trace amounts of short-lived radioactive material that are injected directly into the participant's bloodstream. When the radioactive material starts to decay, a positron is emitted that is picked up by the scanner. When brain areas become activated due to the demands of a cognitive task, the blood containing the radioactive material will flow to this area. Areas of high radioactivity are therefore associated with more brain activity.

Overall, brain imaging gives us a useful window into the functioning of the brain. However, most of the brain imaging techniques discussed in this section require the participant to lie down on their backs and then be placed in a cramped scanner. The types of memory tasks that can be

Figure 6.3: *Top-down and cross-sectional views of a human brain completed using an fMRI scanner*

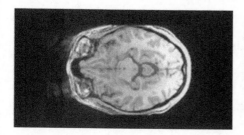 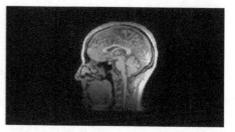

observed under these conditions are limited. For example, we may be able to ask participants in a fMRI scanner to learn and recall a word list. However, we would not be able to carry out brain scans of people carrying out memory tasks underwater or at high altitude. A further limitation is the cost involved in carrying out brain imaging studies. The cost of the scanner and the number of highly trained staff needed to operate the equipment mean that running studies using fMRI or PET scans is expensive.

Skill builder activity

The Knowledge – London taxi drivers and advanced memory feats

Transferable skill focus: Evaluating written text

Key question: *What are the similarities and differences in the methodological approaches taken in the papers by Maguire et al. (1997) and Maguire et al. (2006)?*

Eleanor Maguire and colleagues have undertaken a number of studies that have explored the brain regions that are involved in the recall of spatial information. The studies have focused on London taxi drivers who undergo 2–4 years of training to learn the layout of all the streets in the city of London. Their knowledge is then assessed before they can be granted a taxi licence to operate in the city. In a series of studies using brain imaging, Maguire et al. have explored the structural differences in the hippocampus and the parahippocampal gyrus of the London taxi drivers.

Your task is to compare and contrast two papers. First read the paper Maguire, EA, Frackowiak, RS and Frith, CD (1997) Recalling routes around London: activation of the right hippocampus in taxi drivers. *The Journal of Neuroscience*, 17 (18), 7103–7110. The paper is available from www.jneurosci.org/content/17/18/7103.full.

Next read the paper Maguire, EA, Woollett, K and Spiers, HJ (2006) London taxi drivers and bus drivers: a structural MRI and neuropsychological analysis. *Hippocampus*, 16 (12), 1091–1101. The paper can be accessed at http://193.62.66.20/Maguire/Maguire2006.pdf.

Now answer the following review questions.

What type of brain imaging technique is employed in each of the two studies?

What conclusions regarding the structures that support memory for spatial locations can be drawn from the two papers?

Skill builder review

The two papers illustrate how two different brain imaging technologies can be used to investigate memory. In the 1997 paper Maguire et al. use PET to explore the areas of the brain that are used when topographical memories are retrieved. For example, the taxi drivers were asked to recall a complex route around London. The brain images showed activation of a network of brain regions, including the right hippocampus. When participants were asked to recall non-topographical semantic memories a different pattern of activation was observed. These observations led Maguire and colleagues to conclude that the right hippocampus is important when people need to navigate large-scale spatial environments.

In the 2006 paper Maguire and colleagues used structural MRI scans to investigate the areas of the brain responsible for spatial knowledge. Previous studies had shown that London taxi drivers have higher levels of grey matter volume in the hippocampus than controls. However, critics had suggested that grey matter in the hippocampus could be modulated by the levels of stress that taxi drivers experienced. The 2006 study therefore included a control group who experienced the same level of driving strain but did not have the same level of spatial knowledge – London bus drivers. The results of the study suggested that taxi drivers but not bus drivers had more grey matter in their mid-posterior hippocampi and less in anterior hippocampi. These results help to identify the areas of the cortex that specifically support the recall of topographical information. Together the results of the two studies further our understanding of the areas of the cortex involved in the storage and recall of geographical locations. However, the two studies also illustrate the large amount of work and careful research that is needed in order to explore just a small element of human memory.

Future directions

Our understanding of the biology of memory is increasing at a rapid pace. New technologies such as brain imaging techniques are allowing us to undertake studies that would not have been possible 30–40 years ago. One of the main drives for enhancing our understanding of memory is to treat disorders that can impair memory functioning, such as the intrusive memories associated with post-traumatic stress disorder (PTSD). Another interesting area of research is looking at how memory functioning may be improved, not only in people suffering from **dementia** but also in the general public who may want to improve their memory to help with job performance or academic study.

Erasing unwanted memories

In the future it may be possible to pop a pill and forget a specific memory. This could be useful if a therapist needs to remove a **traumatic memory** from a client. However, today our ability to remove unwanted memories is limited. One of the main barriers is that we are currently unable to locate specific memories within the cortex. Further, our understanding of how memories are encoded and retrieved is also limited. We can reduce the impact of traumatic memories, but the side effects of such treatments are significant. However, for patients with PTSD, who often report upsetting intrusive memories, the benefits of removing such memories would be considerable.

Research has started to explore the possibility of memory reconsolidation (changing a past memory), and propranolol (a drug commonly used to treat hypertension and anxiety) has shown promising results. It is thought that propranolol blocks off the effects of adrenaline on areas of the brain associated with memory. One area that is affected by propranolol is the amygdala, which governs emotional memories. This may explain why propranolol appears to diminish the emotional impact of traumatic memory without reducing the memories themselves. Other treatments for PTSD that appear to reduce the impact of traumatic memories include EMDR (eye movement desensitisation and reprocessing) and hypnosis. However, it is not clear how treatments such as EMDR and hypnosis modulate the storage and retrieval of memories at a biological level.

Drug enhancers for memory performance

Over the past decade there has been a rise in the number of people taking drugs that they believed to enhance their memory performance. As we learn more about the psychobiology of memory our ability to enhance memory functioning increases. The possibility that we can enhance memory using cognitive enhancing drugs has led to some interesting debates, not only about drug safety but also about the moral dimension of such drug use. Henry Greely and colleagues (2008) note the increase in prescription drugs being used by **non-clinical populations** to improve memory. Drugs such as Ritalin (methylphenidate) used in the treatment of attention deficit disorders have been used to increase working memory performance via their actions on the catecholamine system. Other drugs, such as Aricept (donepezil) used by Alzheimer's disease sufferers, have been shown to improve memory by raising levels of **acetylcholine** in the brain in healthy individuals.

Critical thinking activity

The use of cognitive enhancer drugs in everyday life

Critical thinking focus: considering ethical issues

Key question: *Should the use of cognitive enhancer drugs be compulsory in some situations?*

Read the following paper: Greely, H, Sahakian, B, Harris, J, Kessler, RC, Gazzaniga, M, Campbell, P and Farah, MJ (2008) Towards responsible use of cognitive-enhancing drugs by the healthy. *Nature*, 456 (7223), 702–705. It can be found at the following URL: www.geneticsandsociety.org/downloads/brain%20enhancing%20drugs.pdf.

Greely and colleagues (p. 703) pose the question: *Should surgeons be made to take an extremely safe cognitive enhancer drug to improve performance when they are carrying out risky operations?*

Develop a detailed argument for and against the use of cognitive enhancer drugs.

Critical thinking review

The simple answer would be that it is wrong to make people take a drug that they do not wish to take. However, with moral debates it is very rare that the answer to the question is simple. Table 6.1 highlights some of the arguments for and against the use of cognitive enhancers.

Table 6.1: Arguments for and against the use of cognitive enhancer drugs in students

Against	For
Unequal availability due to lack of supply/ finance make the use of cognitive enhancer drugs unfair.	Many resources, such as adequate nutrition and good schooling are not equally shared.
It is not natural to use cognitive enhancer drugs every day.	Most of our lives are 'unnatural', such as wearing synthetic clothes and heating food up in a microwave.
The dangers of both short-term and long-term use are unknown.	Safety trials could be undertaken to establish that the drugs are safe.
True competency is unknown if students use enhancer drugs during assessments.	Cognitive enhancer drugs such as caffeine are used by people every day.
Drugs deemed safe for use in a clinical population may not always be safe in a healthy population.	People could be given the information regarding the risks so they can use their own judgement.

It is important to remember that certain legal cognitive enhancers are used on a daily basis and are useful to boost cognition in some situation. For example, coffee (containing the stimulant caffeine) is often suggested to boost driving performance when people are tired. We might therefore go as far as to advise drivers of the benefit of stopping for a coffee when they are undertaking long motorway trips. It becomes a more interesting moral question when we consider whether we should make a driver drink a double espresso so that they are more alert when driving with their young family in the car.

Studies that have looked at the benefits of using cognitive enhancing drugs in stressful situations have found real benefits. For example, Yesavage and colleagues (2002) found that commercial pilots who took the drug donepezil for 30 days were able to deal with flight emergencies in a simulator better than those who had taken a placebo. So does this mean that we should get all airplane pilots to take donepezil? The answer is again difficult. Although many cognitive enhancer drugs are deemed safe and are licensed for use with children, any drug can still have an element of risk associated with its use. Further, cognitive enhancer drugs may lead to a trade-off in cognitive abilities. For example, the drug Ritalin has been reported to increase concentration but to reduce creativity. Further, any element of compulsion in the use of cognitive enhancer drugs does raise important ethical questions. Can we make someone take a drug they do not want to, even if it saves lives? On the other hand, it could be argued that chemical cognitive enhancers are just another step in human progress. For example, the development of the light bulb allowed workers to work through the night. The light bulb was not banned due to the negative effect that it might have on workers and we would insist that surgeons carried out operations with the lights on.

One conclusion that could be drawn is that although cognitive enhancer drugs may lead to improved memory function, compelling surgeons to use them is not desirable. Issues such as drug safety or possible cognitive trade-offs mean that the choice should be down to the individual. In the world today we do not demand that other cognitive enhancing interventions are carried out, such as a good night's sleep or adequate nutrition. Therefore it could be argued that the choice to use safe and legal cognitive enhancing drugs should be down to the individual. However, this might not be the same conclusion that you have arrived at. Within many moral debates there are no clear-cut answers and so it is important that you can explain clearly how you have arrived at your personal viewpoint. The key point is that you should be able to back up your conclusion with well thought-out thorough arguments.

Skill builder activity

Location of memory processes within the cortex

Transferable skill focus: IT and independent learning

Key question: *How do researchers locate and evaluate new research findings?*

Using a database such as Google Scholar, carry out a search for a paper that attempts to locate a memory process within the brain. Then complete the table below in order start thinking critically about the paper that you have chosen. You can use the information in this chapter to help with the evaluation of the paper.

Title	Author	Year	Methodology used	Key conclusions	Evaluation

One of the major problems of completing a literature review is the large number of papers that are available to you. If we put the word 'memory' into the Google Scholar search box, then over 4 million results appear. It is therefore important that you make a more selective search. In this case you will need to include the type of memory that you are interested in. For example, you could enter the term 'working memory' or 'declarative memory' in order to narrow down the search. In addition, you could include the words 'location' and 'brain' or you could include a particular brain imaging technology or research methodology. You could also reduce the number of references returned by using the more advanced search options and adding a date range. By doing this you can focus on more up-to-date research and remove older papers from your literature search. Generally, adding more search parameters will allow you to gain more relevant results.

Skill builder review

One of the main problems of using a database to complete a literature search is that you do not always get access to the complete paper. To view many psychology journal papers you need to have a subscription to that journal. If you are studying at university, then it is possible that your university subscribes to the journal and you can access the journal for free. Another way to access the full text version of a journal paper is to check the author's home page or website as many academics have versions of their work that you can download for free. Further, increasingly some journals are making some papers 'open access', which means you do not need to subscribe to the journal to download them. One important point to make here is that you should not base your understanding of a paper solely on the abstract. The abstract contains only a very brief summary of research, and although it is useful when deciding if the topic area of the paper is of interest, you need to read the whole paper to get a full understanding of the research.

The following is a worked example. By entering the words 'working', 'memory', 'location' and 'brain', and limiting the year range to 2005–current, Google Scholar returned over 128,000 results. The first page was scanned and the most relevant sounding titles selected. If the full version of the paper was available, the abstract was reviewed to see if the paper would be of interest. The first paper selected for review was Finn, AS, Sheridan, MA, Kam, CLH, Hinshaw, S, and D'Esposito, M (2010) Longitudinal evidence for functional specialization of the neural circuit supporting working memory in the human brain. *The Journal of Neuroscience*, 30 (33), 11062–11067, and the table was completed. The full text of the paper is downloadable for free from www.jneurosci.org/content/30/33/11062.long.

Title	Author	Year	Methodology used	Key conclusions	Evaluation
Longitudinal evidence for functional specialisation of the neural circuit supporting working memory in the human brain	Finn, Sheridan, Kam, Hinshaw and D'Esposito	2010	Ten female adolescents underwent two functional MRI scans. The first scan was at 15 years of age and the second at 18 years of age.	During the working memory task adolescents used the pre-frontal cortex. However, when the participants were younger they also used the hippocampus. This suggests that different areas of the brain support working memory at different ages.	This is an interesting paper as this research is the first to show that the areas of the brain responsible for working memory can change with age. However, the sample size is very small (n=10) and only female participants were used. As sex hormones have been shown to affect WM it is not possible to generalise these findings to males.

Assignments

1. Discuss why it is important to consider the evolutionary pressures on memory when investigating memory functioning.

2. Critically evaluate the use of case studies as a method of locating memory functions within the cortex.

3. Critically discuss the reasons for and against the use of memory-enhancing drugs for people in high-risk occupations such as surgeons.

Summary: what you have learned

Now you have finished studying this chapter you should:

- understand the areas of the brain that have been identified as being involved with memory processes;

- be able to evaluate the different methodologies used within memory research;

- be able to discuss critically the future research that needs to be completed in memory research;

- critically understand the issues surrounding the use of cognitive enhancement drugs;

- have developed your critical understanding of brain imaging techniques;

- have developed your critical thinking as well as your IT and independent learning skills.

Further reading

Brunner, R, Schaefer, D, Hess, K, Parzer, P, Resch, F and Schwab, S (2006) Effect of high-dose cortisol on memory functions. *Annals of the New York Academy of Sciences*, 1071 (1), 434–437.

The impact of elevated cortisol on memory functioning is considered in this paper.

Corkin, S (1984) Lasting consequences of bilateral medial temporal lobectomy: clinical course and experimental findings in HM. *Seminars in Neurology*, 4 (2): 249–259.

This paper outlines the research findings of one of the some important case studies in memory research.

Greely, H, Sahakian, B, Harris, J, Kessler, RC, Gazzaniga, M, Campbell, P and Farah, MJ (2008) Towards responsible use of cognitive-enhancing drugs by the healthy. *Nature*, 456 (7223), 702–705.

In this paper the ethical considerations relating to the use of cognitive-enhancing drugs are discussed.

Nairne, JS and Pandeirada, JN (2008) Adaptive memory: remembering with a Stone Age brain. *Current Directions in Psychological Science*, 17 (4), 239–243.

This paper considers the evolutionary importance of memory and the impact on current memory performance.

Chapter 7

Motivation

Learning outcomes

By the end of this chapter you should:

- understand the evolutionary importance of motivation;

- recognise biological mechanisms influencing pleasure and reward;

- be able to identify the biological and psychological mechanisms influencing eating;

- understand the biological mechanisms influencing sexual differentiation and sexual behaviour;

- understand the biological mechanisms associated with the development and maintenance of addiction;

- have developed the ability to process and evaluate written information.

Introduction

Motivation fulfils an important evolutionary function. It is the internal state that stimulates the actions required to achieve a particular adaptive goal, such as the drive to find and ingest food and water. This process includes the experience of pleasure, i.e. 'liking', followed by the drive to obtain the reward, i.e. 'wanting', and reward-based learning (Berridge and Kringelbach, 2013). The current chapter outlines the biological mechanisms associated with two motivated behaviours – sexual behaviour and eating – emphasising the specific reward circuitry that regulates the motivation (Breiter and Rosen, 1999). In our own species, this circuitry is often manipulated through the use of substances such as alcohol and cocaine, so the chapter also considers the biological mechanisms that influence the development and maintenance of addiction.

Pleasure and reward

Early research studies demonstrated that rats will work to receive electrical stimulation targeted at specific brain regions close to the hypothalamus (Olds and Milner, 1954). In fact, when provided with a choice, the rats preferred the brain stimulation to food. These findings contributed to the notion of a reward system within the brain that serves to reinforce behaviour and encourage repetition. The reward system involves a wide range of cortical and subcortical regions including the hypothalamus, septum, nucleus accumbens, amygdala and orbitofrontal cortex (e.g. Baxter and Murray, 2002; Berridge and Kringelbach, 2008; Rolls, 2000). For example, activity in one region (the putamen) is related to the expectation of reward (Knutson et al., 2003), predictability of reward (McClure et al., 2003a) and size of reward (Cromwell and Schultz, 2003). This activity has been produced in response to a range of motivation types, including academic achievement and financial motivation (Mizuno et al., 2008).

Dopamine (a neurotransmitter) may have an important role in the reward system, as there are high concentrations of dopamine in the reward system. Dopamine pathways extend from: a) the ventral tegmental area to limbic structures such as the nucleus accumbens; b) the ventral tegmental area to the frontal cortex; and c) the substantia nigra to the striatum. It is argued that the dopamine systems may mediate the salience of rewards (Berridge and Robinson, 1998) and that sex differences in the regulation of dopamine activity in the ascending mesolimbic projects are responsible for sex differences in motivation (Becker, 2009). Though much of the research in this area focuses on dopamine systems, serotonin (another neurotransmitter) also has an important role in the representation and processing of rewards (Kranz et al., 2010; Nakamura et al., 2008). The serotonergic system includes neurons that project to areas associated with reward, and serotonergic action appears to regulate dopamine transmission and activity in reward regions (Muschamp et al., 2007). Furthermore, serotonin activity is related to reward value.

Eating

For all species, achieving a balance between acquiring (i.e. selecting and eating food) and utilising energy (e.g. moving) is essential for survival. Locating and eating foods rich in energy and nutrients are therefore core activities. While this type of consumption has been important during our own evolutionary history, the range of inexpensive sugary and fatty foods available in Western countries, often referred to as an **obesogenic environment** (Hill and Peters, 1998), has created other threats to our well-being and survival. In particular, the number of overweight and obese people has increased in recent years, and the weight of those who were already overweight has increased the most (Flegal and Troiano, 2000). This section outlines the biological and psychological mechanisms that influence our eating attitudes and behaviour.

Hunger

For optimum health, the foods that we consume should contain a range of amino acids, vitamins, minerals, carbohydrates and fats. Of course, desirable foods may not be available, and food supplies are often unreliable, so our bodies store short-term and long-term energy. Short-term energy is stored in the liver and muscles in the form of **glycogen** while adipose tissue (fat stored below the skin) stores long-term energy in the form of glycerol and fatty acids. In this context, hunger can provide the motivation to source and consume food. There is surprisingly little clarity or consensus within the research literature regarding the causes of hunger. Though early studies related hunger to the contractions experienced when the stomach is empty (Cannon and Washburn, 1912), the biological mechanisms underpinning hunger are much more complex. In fact, it is still possible to feel hungry when the stomach has been removed (Ingelfinger, 1944). Furthermore, it may be important to separate areas involved in hunger from those influencing related mechanisms such as weight control.

It has been argued that the ventromedial hypothalamus and lateral hypothalamus control satiety and hunger respectively (Stellar, 1954), largely based on studies demonstrating that lesions to these areas lead to excessive eating (ventromedial hypothalamus, Hetherington and Ranson, 1940) or the cessation of eating (lateral hypothalamus, Anand and Brobeck, 1951). While these areas are clearly associated with hunger and eating, the notion that they represent satiety and hunger centres may be too simplistic. For example, the ventromedial hypothalamus may be associated with the adoption of a higher 'set target weight', leading to initial overeating followed by a more natural eating pattern. More recent accounts therefore regard these areas as important components of a larger hunger and eating system (Rolls, 1994).

A range of brain areas are associated with the representation and integration of food-relevant information. These include the amygdala, thalamus, insula and orbitofrontal cortex. The amygdala and insula are associated with satiety (Wang et al., 2008), and the insula also has an important role in the integration of sensory information (e.g. taste, smell) and perception of flavour. Lesion or damage to the insula may therefore impact on taste (Mak et al., 2005).

Stress and sensitivity to food cues

Whether it is finishing a meal to please the host or being tempted by the dessert menu, we are all familiar with the fact that eating behaviours are not determined by hunger alone. A number of factors, such as our emotions (Macht, 2008), learning (Tylka et al., 2013) and the presentation of food (Choplin and Motyka Joss, 2012), each influence the type and amount of food that we consume.

Stress can increase or decrease food consumption (Greeno and Wing, 1994; Wilson et al., 2008) and induce binge eating (Boggiano et al., 2005) in a range of species. In particular, exposure to stress and perceptions of stress are associated with an increased drive to eat and a reduced ability to restrain eating (Groesz et al., 2012). Unhealthy, i.e. non-nutritious, highly palatable foods, are typically sought during stressful periods, which may provide relief from discomfort and pleasure in the short term (Dallman et al., 2005) and calm the **hypothalamic–pituitary–adrenal (HPA) axis** stress response (Warne, 2009). The increased food intake when stressed is particularly evident in women (Wansink et al., 2003) and those with a greater reaction to the stressor (Newman et al., 2007).

Exposure to food or food-related cues increase interest in food and eating (Nederkoorn et al., 2000). The impact of these can be investigated through attentional biases that involve selective attention to personally relevant stimuli (Smeets et al., 2009). With regard to eating, attentional biases for unhealthy (e.g. sweet) food are related to hunger and body weight (Gearhardt et al., 2012). Sensitivity to food cues does, of course, vary. Those who are more sensitive to reward detect the presence of reward stimuli more effectively. Sensitivity to reward is related to overeating and obesity (Guerrieri et al., 2008; Nederkoorn et al., 2006) though this may depend on levels of hunger (Guerrieri et al., 2012).

A number of studies indicate that overweight men and women are more responsive to food-relevant cues (Jansen et al., 2003) and are more likely to select large amounts of food following exposure to these cues (Tetley et al., 2009). The focus on food-related stimuli (e.g. eye fixation) displayed by obese people compared to their normal-weight peers occurs when not hungry (Castellanos et al., 2009), which may reflect the fact that compared to those of normal weight, obese people focus more attention on food-relevant stimuli at early automatic stages of information processing (Nijs et al., 2010).

Craving and binge eating

Food cravings are related to the inability to restrain eating (Meule et al., 2011), binge eating (Meule et al., 2012) and consequently body weight (Franken and Muris, 2005). Brain areas associated with food craving include the insula (Pelchat et al., 2004). While those with addictive eating patterns experience increased cravings for food, they do not, however, experience greater positive reinforcement (i.e. pleasure) from the eating that results (Meule and Kubler, 2012).

Binge eating involves consuming large quantities of food in a short period of time. Both eating disorder patients (bulimia nervosa) and non-patients (e.g. obese men and women or emotional eaters) may engage in binge eating. Unhealthy foods (e.g. those high in fat or sugar) are typically the focus of binge eating episodes, which can occur regardless of whether the individual is hungry or sated (Marcus and Kalarchian, 2003). Compared to other eating behaviours, little research has investigated binge eating, but it has been shown that in other species binge eating leads to dopamine release in the nucleus accumbens (Avena et al., 2008).

Food-related disorders

Body weight is an important and distressing issue for many people, and researchers use the term 'normative discontent' to describe the dissatisfaction that most women feel with their body weight. Consequently some men and women use a range of harmful techniques to lower, increase or control body weight. These techniques include restriction of diet, laxatives, steroids and diet pills (Tylka and Subich, 2002). For a minority of men and women, these body- and food-related concerns can lead to eating disorders such as anorexia nervosa and bulimia nervosa.

Anorexia nervosa is characterised by a refusal to eat, distorted body image and fear of weight gain. Adolescent girls and women are most likely to suffer from anorexia nervosa, and the weight loss that occurs may disrupt the menstrual cycle. Though **bulimia nervosa** patients also display a fear of weight gain and distorted body image, they also binge eat (typically unhealthy 'junk food') then vomit or take laxatives to purge their bodies of this food. These disorders are associated with distorted perceptions of food and biased processing of eating-relevant stimuli (Fairburn et al., 1999). Serotonin is associated with eating disorders (Kaye et al., 2009), and acute tryptophan depletion – which lowers serotonin – further increases the interference caused by food-relevant stimuli (Pringle et al., 2012).

Anorexia nervosa and bulimia nervosa are not the only eating-related disorders that exist. **Prader-Willi syndrome** is a neurodevelopmental disorder characterised by preoccupation with food and constant attempts to find and consume food. Specific symptoms may include hoarding food, stealing food and eating food such as food thrown away by others that is generally believed to be unappealing (Ogura et al., 2008). The syndrome is genetically determined, and a range of studies have investigated the biological mechanisms associated with the disorder. In particular, studies employing functional magnetic resonance imaging (fMRI) indicate that activation of the hypothalamus, nucleus accumbens, orbitofrontal cortex and insula (Shapira et al., 2005) may be associated with Prader-Willi syndrome. Studies further demonstrate that in Prader-Willi syndrome patients these areas are activated in response to food cues (Dimitropoulos and Schultz, 2008), and regional blood flow is related to the level of eating symptomology (Ogura et al., 2013).

Sex

Beyond the satisfaction of our primary needs, such as hunger and safety, there may be few more salient motivators than sex. Both male and female rats are willing to cross an electrified area to copulate (Warner, 1927), while in our own species much of our behaviour is targeted (consciously or unconsciously) at members of the opposite sex. The current section outlines the benefits of sexual (as opposed to asexual) reproduction and the biological mechanisms that influence sexual differentiation (i.e. development as male or female) and sexual behaviour.

The benefits of sexual reproduction

All mammals (including humans) reproduce sexually, and most vertebrates reproduce exclusively through sexual reproduction. This form of reproduction involves the fusion of two gametes, which ensures that the offspring contains genetic material from both parents. The sex-producing larger (ova or eggs) and smaller (sperm) gametes are referred to as female and male respectively. At first glance, it may seem more beneficial to reproduce asexually, ensuring that each offspring carries all our genetic material, rather than allowing another individual to benefit from the investment that we make in the development and rearing of the offspring, so it is reasonable to assume that there must be an adaptive benefit to sexual reproduction. It has been suggested that sexual reproduction may reduce the impact of harmful genetic mutations (Paland and Lynch, 2006). Sexual reproduction may also produce novel combinations of genetic material that are particularly adaptive in stressful environments (Goddard et al., 2005).

In mammals, females make a much greater investment in each offspring than males. Fertilisation takes place within the female, and the female is also responsible for gestation and the production of milk (lactation) for the offspring. Female mammals (including women) are therefore more sexually cautious than males, and males are most likely to compete for the attention of willing sexual partners. This investment also impacts on the number of offspring produced by each sex. Females are limited by the time it takes to raise each offspring, and in humans women are further limited by the menopause, which reduces the age at which she is fertile. In comparison, males are limited primarily by their access to fertile females. Consequently, females are unlikely to produce vast quantities of offspring, but male competition for female attention makes it likely that she will have some offspring. In contrast, males are capable of producing large numbers of offspring, though only a minority of (high quality) males will achieve this, and a greater proportion of males will have no offspring.

Male and female development

Chromosomes determine human sex, with males and females possessing XY and XX chromosomes respectively. When abnormalities occur (such as for Klinefelter Syndrome, whereby individuals possess one Y chromosome and two or more X chromosomes), embryos that have a Y chromosome will develop as a male. The specific gene that determines sex is named the SRY gene (i.e. *Sex-determining Region of the Y* chromosome). This gene leads the genital ridges in the embryo to develop into testis. In females, the ridges develop into ovaries. In addition to sexual differentiation of the internal and external genitalia, organising hormones (which cause permanent change during development) influence the organisation of the brain (Cohen-Bendahan et al., 2005), therefore male and female brains, though similar, demonstrate important sex differences (see Ngun et al., 2011 for a review). These include differences in the basal ganglia, hippocampus and amygdala, and in the size of the brain – the male brain is larger (Witelson et al., 2006). Evidence also indicates different patterns of brain activation in men and women. For example, while men encode emotional memories with the right amygdala, women use the left amygdala (Canli et al., 2002), suggesting that different strategies may be employed to perform the same activity (Lenroot and Giedd, 2010). Secondary sexual characteristics, including wider female hips and deeper male voice, emerge at puberty. This phase begins when the hypothalamus secretes gonadotropin-releasing hormones

(GnRH), which stimulate the development and release of follicle-simulating and luteinising hormones by the anterior pituitary gland. Sex steroids are then secreted, which influence a range of physical changes such as breast development. A range of factors such as body weight and nutrition may also impact on the age at which a child begins puberty (Foster and Nagatani, 1999).

The sexual pleasure cycle

Though many of the findings in this area stem from animal research, there are important differences between the sexual behaviour of humans and the behaviour of other species. In particular, the sexual responses and abilities of humans are influenced by a range of emotions and cognitions. For example, it is argued that a lack of sexual interest is often related to difficulties within the relationship and withdrawal of sexual intimacy may be an adaptive response to an unstable or unsatisfying relationship (Bancroft, 2002). Similarly, women are aware of their own menstrual cycle stage and fertility (Small, 1996) and may modify their sexual activity in response to the likelihood of pregnancy. The context in which sexual behaviour occurs is also important. Unlike non-primates, humans and other primates mate during the non-fertile phase (Wallen, 2001) and during pregnancy (Pazol, 2003), while sexual behaviour rarely occurs in public due to moral and legal guidelines. Research in this field has, of course, been hindered by a range of ethical and methodological issues.

Sexually mature adults are not constantly sexually motivated, and a suitable stimulus such as an attractive mate is typically required. Therefore the first phase of the sexual pleasure cycle (also referred to as the sexual response cycle) is the development of sexual desire. In motivation terms this is consistent with the concept of wanting (Berridge, 1996). A range of sexual stimuli may increase desire, and the recognition and processing of these stimuli are associated with specific areas of brain activation. For example, pheromones are associated with activity in the occipitotemporal cortex, orbitofrontal cortex and hypothalamus (Zhou and Chen, 2008).

The majority of research studies investigating the impact on sexual stimuli focus on visual material, which activates areas such as the anterior cingulate cortex, amygdala and hypothalamus and clearly attracts attention (van Lankveld and Smulders, 2008). For men, sexual arousal in response to sexual stimuli is category specific, i.e. heterosexual men are aroused by images of women and homosexual men are aroused by images of men. In contrast, heterosexual and homosexual women are both aroused by images of men and women (Chivers et al., 2004). There are, of course, also individual differences: controls demonstrate deactivation in the media orbitofrontal cortex (an area associated with the control of motivations) in response to sexual images, whereas activity in this area remains in men with hypoactive sexual desire disorder. Furthermore, sexual images are associated with deactivation or unchanged activity in the secondary somatosensory cortex, anterior cingulate cortex and frontal lobes of men with hypoactive sexual desire disorder but associated with activation in controls (Stoleru et al., 2003).

Arousal during sexual activity may differ (and be associated with different brain activation patterns) from sexual desire. For example, while the amygdala is activated by viewing erotic stimuli (Gizewski et al., 2006), activation is reduced during sexual activity. The reduced activation may reduce vigilance or caution and encourage intimacy. Indeed, during arousal and sexual behaviour, we are less likely to be distracted by external stimuli (Koukounas and McCabe, 2001). Other regions associated with sexual arousal include the anterior cingulate cortex and hypothalamus (Komisaruk et al., 2004).

The orgasm experience involves a loss of control, feeling of release, high arousal and involuntary muscular contractions (Mah and Binik, 2005). Orgasm is associated with activity in the prefrontal cortex and orbitofrontal cortex (Georgiadis et al., 2006). This is consistent with evidence suggesting that the orbitofrontal cortex is activated when experiencing other pleasures such as eating chocolate (Small et al., 2001). The importance of motor areas is highlighted by the fact that poor motor control is related to premature ejaculation (Rosenbaum, 2007). Important differences occur between women as while men typically experience orgasm during sexual intercourse, it is more likely to occur in women through clitoral stimulation than penetrative sex alone (Brewer and Hendrie, 2011; Lloyd, 2005). It is also more difficult to judge whether women experience orgasm, and researchers are reliant on women's subjective accounts.

The satiety or post-orgasmic refractory period is the final phase of the sexual response cycle during which the individual is less responsive to sexual stimuli. Research indicates activity for men within areas such as the amygdala, parahippocampal gyrus and anterior cingulate cortex during this time (Georgiadis et al., 2010). Preliminary research also indicates an anterior cingulate–hypothalamus pathway that may be involved in this phase of the cycle (Georgiadis and Kringelbach, 2012). There are considerable differences between individuals, and between men and women in particular during this phase, highlighting the need for additional research in this area. See Figure 7.1 for the adult sexual pleasure cycle.

Figure 7.1: *The adult sexual pleasure cycle*

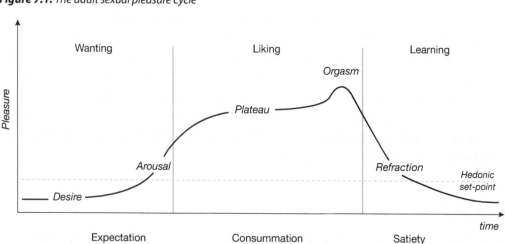

Source: Georgiadis and Kringelbach (2012).

Sex hormones

Hormones are secreted into the bloodstream by the endocrine glands. The sex steroid hormones (androgens, oestrogens and progestins) are most closely associated with sexual behaviour and physiology, though non-steroidal sex hormones which include prostaglandins and monoamines are also influential. It is important to note that while testosterone (an androgen) and oestrogen are often thought to be 'male' and 'female' hormones respectively, testosterone and oestrogen exist in both men and women (in different levels) and impact on their sexual development and behaviour. For example, estradiol influences sperm development (Hess et al., 1997).

Hormone therapies therefore offer potential treatments for sexual disorders. Oestrogen treatments increase sexual behaviour, and progesterone exaggerates these effects (Mong and Pfaff, 2003). The loss of sexual desire experienced by menopausal women is reversed by hormone therapy (Sherwin et al., 1985). This further illustrates that while the majority of research studies that investigate the impact of sex hormones on women's brain activity focus on variation across the menstrual cycle in adult premenopausal women, women's brains may be influenced by sex hormones across the lifespan. Those administering hormone treatments for other conditions should therefore consider the influence this may have on patient sexual behaviour. For example, dopaminergic treatment for Parkinson's disease may influence sexual behaviour, increasing the likelihood of hypersexuality and paraphilia (Berger et al., 2003; Cannas et al., 2006; Kanovsky et al., 2002).

Learning

Though much of the research literature focuses on biological mechanisms only, sexual behaviour is influenced by both biological mechanisms and learning experience (Woodson, 2002). In a variety of species, learning has been shown to influence a wide range of sexual behaviours including the selection of an appropriate mate, approach and ability to achieve penetration (e.g. Crawford and Domjan, 1993; Galef and White, 2000). Acknowledging the range of motivational and performance factors influenced by experience and the environment, Woodson (2002, p70) defines sexual learning as *a lasting change in a species-specific appetitive or consummatory sexual behavior following any social or sexual experience during development or in adulthood*. In practical terms, however, it is often difficult to separate the impact of early experience on motivation and ability. In other species, learning (and conditioning, in particular) has been shown to influence sperm production (Domjan et al., 1998) and offspring number (Hollis et al., 1997), clearly highlighting the evolutionary benefits of adaptation to the environment and behavioural plasticity.

The menstrual cycle

Sexually mature pre-menopausal women experience regular hormonal fluctuations across the reproductive or 'menstrual' cycle. The length of the menstrual cycle varies considerably between women and between cycles, though most last between 26 and 35 days and the average cycle lasts for 28 days (Mihm et al., 2011). This section outlines the physiological, cognitive and behavioural changes that occur across the menstrual cycle.

Menstrual bleeding is the most observable stage of the human reproductive cycle, although the external loss of blood occurs in relatively few species (Martin, 2007). During the menstrual phase the endometrium (inner lining of the uterus) breaks down and is discarded, although the deepest layer is retained and aids later regeneration. For most women this phase lasts three to six days. The next stage is referred to as the follicular stage. During this phase, the hypothalamus secretes gonadotropin-releasing hormone, causing the pituitary gland to secrete luteinising and follicle-stimulating hormones. These hormones stimulate the growth of ovarian follicles, which mature within the ovary. The secretion of estradiol by the follicle leads to a gradual thickening of the endometrium and increased secretion of cervical mucus.

The fertile phase of the cycle consists of the day of ovulation (the release of an ovum from an ovary) and the five previous days (Wilcox et al., 1995). If sperm are present, the ovum may be fertilised. If fertilisation does not occur, the ovum dies after a short time (12–24 hours) in the oviduct. Following release of the ovum, the ovarian follicle becomes the corpus luteum, responsible for the secretion of progesterone and to a lesser extent oestrogen. The progesterone encourages the body to establish an environment suitable for pregnancy – for example, thickening the endometrium, inhibiting the production of another follicle. The stage between ovulation and menstruation is referred to as the luteal or postovulatory phase. If fertilisation does not occur, the corpus luteum ceases to produce estradiol and progesterone, leading to the breakdown and shedding of the endometrium, which characterises the menstrual phase.

Behaviour

Women's behaviour varies across the menstrual cycle. As shown in Figure 7.2, women dress more provocatively and place a greater emphasis on their appearance when most fertile (Roder et al., 2009; Schwarz and Hassebrauck, 2008). These cyclical variations do not simply reflect a greater sexual interest during the fertile phase as women are particularly likely to attend situations such as parties during the fertile phase *without* their partner (Grammer et al., 1997). Women are also more likely to engage in imagined or real sexual relationships with men other than their partner (Baker and Bellis, 1995; Gangestad et al., 2002).

Partner preferences also demonstrate cyclical shifts. The preference for physical traits including faces (DeBruine et al., 2005), voices (Feinberg et al., 2006), body shape (Little et al., 2007), height (Pawlowski and Jasienska, 2005) and odour (Havlicek et al., 2005) associated with masculinity vary across the cycle. Preferences for non-physical traits such as social status (Havlicek et al., 2005) and dominance (Senior et al., 2007) also increase during the fertile phase. Together, these findings indicate that women place a greater emphasis on physical quality and are more accepting of short-

Figure 7.2: *Women's self-perception and behaviour on low fertile and fertile cycle days*

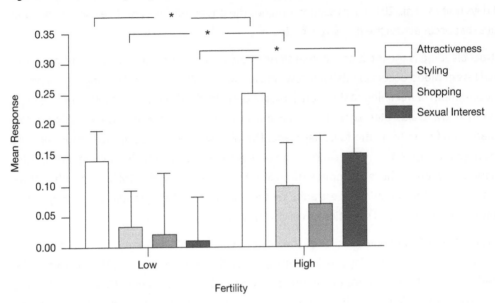

Source: Roder et al., 2009.

term sexual relationships during the fertile phase compared to the non-fertile phase. This may reflect a dual strategy whereby women obtain long-term support from one partner but (during the fertile phase) engage in sexual intercourse with the most high-quality men, who are often unwilling to provide women with long-term investment.

Concealed ovulation

In a number of non-human primates, exaggerated sexual swellings provide a clear visual signal of ovulatory status (Deschner et al., 2004). While women do not signal ovulation to the same extent, a number of visual changes do occur. For example, breast size is related to menstrual cycle phase (Milligan et al., 1975) and women's voices and body odour are rated as more attractive during the fertile phase (Pipitone and Gallup, 2008; Thornhill et al., 2003). In addition, asymmetry, a signal of developmental instability and environmental stress, is highest during the non-fertile phase and lowest during the fertile phase (Manning et al., 1996). In evolutionary terms, these subtle changes may allow long-term partners to monitor their mates during the most fertile phase, thus reducing the likelihood that their partner will become pregnant with another man's child (see the section on jealousy in Chapter 5).

Of course, though research consistently demonstrates a shift in sexual desire and behaviours across the menstrual cycle, there are a number of methodological issues that impact on research in this area. Self-reported cycle length is subject to measurement error (Small et al., 2007). These errors may be exacerbated by irregular cycles (Golden and Carlson, 2008) and socio-economic and regional variation in the length of each menstrual cycle phase (Harlow, 2000).

Addiction: the dark side of motivation

Addiction is characterised by preoccupation with an addictive substance or behaviour (e.g. drugs or gambling) and poor impulse control, despite the negative consequences of this on their own lives and on the lives of others (Hyman and Malenka, 2001). It is argued that there is an addiction cycle involving three interacting stages (Koob and LeMoal, 1997). The first stage involves preoccupation and anticipation; the second features binging and intoxication; the final stage is characterised by withdrawal and negative affect, with addicts experiencing a range of psychological and physical withdrawal symptoms (Goodman, 2008). While addiction may increase pleasure and reward initially, therefore, progression through these stages is associated with a change from motivation through positive reinforcement and reward to motivation through negative reinforcement and the removal of painful side effects (Koob, 2004). A number of factors, including substance type and dosage, may impact on the addiction cycle. See Figure 7.3 for an illustration of the progression of alcohol dependence.

Figure 7.3: *The progression of alcohol dependence over time*

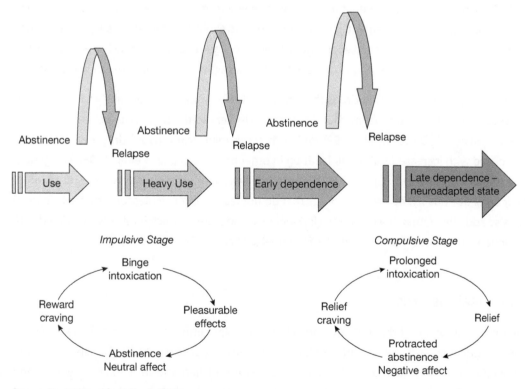

Source: Reproduced from Koob, 2009.

Substance abuse is typically associated with high relapse rates (Goodman, 2008; Piasecki, 2006), and the treatment options available demonstrate limited success (O'Brien, 2008). Heightened memories for experiences related to substance abuse and sensitivity to drug-related stimuli may contribute to the development of addiction and likelihood of relapse (Hyman et al., 2006). For example, exposure to drug-relevant visual cues leads to greater activation in the visual areas among addicts compared to non-addicts, and these activations are related to cravings and severity of dependence (Smolka et al., 2006). These findings suggest that drug-related cues are more likely to attract the attention of addicts and lead to increased brain activation. The majority of research focuses on drug abuse, but substance-based addictions and other addictions such as gambling share a number of characteristics, including negative consequences, tolerance, the subjective experience (e.g. craving and preoccupation) and withdrawal (Goodman, 2008), so the biological mechanisms influencing addiction and motivation are thought to be similar.

Factors influencing vulnerability to addiction

Addictions often begin in adolescence or early adulthood (Goodman, 2008), which may in part reflect the faster development of brain regions associated with promoting motivation compared to those associated with behavioural control (Rutherford et al., 2010). Reported sex differences include men's greater engagement in addictive behaviours for pleasure (positive reinforcement) and women's greater engagement in these behaviours to avoid negative affect such as depression (negative reinforcement) (Blanco et al., 2006). In addition, genetic factors may increase the risk of developing an addiction (Tsuang et al., 1998) and are an area of increasing research interest.

A range of studies indicate that drugs that reach the brain rapidly are more likely to be addictive (Gossop et al., 1992). It has been argued that rapid delivery to the brain is associated with more intense pleasure (Comer et al., 1999) and so is more reinforcing. Rapid drug delivery is also associated with increased self-administration in other primates (Panlilio et al., 1998). The greater pleasure often afforded by drugs that are rapidly delivered to the brain may not fully account for their addictive quality, however, as drugs that do not lead to intense pleasure (such as nicotine) are also addictive. Other environmental influences include stress, which is reliably associated with addiction and relapse (Dewart et al., 2006; Ouimette et al., 2007).

Biological systems

Overall it is argued that the addictive process involves impairments in the motivation–reward, affect regulation and behavioural inhibition systems (Goodman, 2008). Disruption to the motivation–reward system leads the addict to feel unsatisfied and in a state of tension and irritability, while disruption to the affect regulation system leads to emotional instability and distress. Disruption to the behavioural inhibition system leads to a greater emphasis on short-term as opposed to long-term consequences (Goodman, 2008).

A number of brain regions demonstrate heighted activity in response to addiction cues. For example, addicts display increased activation in the orbitofrontal cortex, right nucleus accumbens, bilateral anterior cingulate and medial frontal cortex, dorsolateral prefrontal cortex and caudate nucleus in response to addiction relevant stimuli (Ko et al., 2009). In addition, brain activity in response to these cues is associated with the strength of cravings, severity of dependence, behavioural reactions, treatment effectiveness and risk of relapse (Ko et al., 2009; Kosten et al., 2006; Yalachkov et al., 2010). There are some inconsistencies between findings, however, as some brain areas identified as important for the development and continuation of addiction are not activated in all studies (Wilson (SJ) et al., 2004). Furthermore, a number of substances may influence brain structure and function (Beveridge et al., 2008).

The importance of these areas for motivation, reward and behavioural inhibition is clear. The orbitofrontal cortex develops expectations of reward (Bonson et al., 2002) and is associated with goal-directed behaviour and the assessment of motivationally relevant stimuli (Rolls, 2000). The nucleus accumbens is a key component of the brain reward circuitry, and activation of the nucleus accumbens represents the expected reward (Taneka et al., 2004). The dorsolateral prefrontal cortex relates present experiences to former experiences and develops goal-directed action (Goldman-Rakic and Leung, 2002). The caudate nucleus is associated with the development of automatic stimulus–response behaviours (Vanderschuren and Everitt, 2005) relevant for a range of addictive behaviours such as reaching for a cigarette at the end of a meal.

The role of dopamine

The dopaminergic system, including the ventral tegmental area and nucleus accumbens, has been the focus of much of the addiction research. In particular, increased levels of dopamine in the nucleus accumbens is associated with a range of addictive behaviours, including eating (Avena et al., 2006), gambling (Bergh et al., 1997), smoking (Brody et al., 2004) and alcohol consumption (Yoshimoto et al., 1991). These effects may vary according to addiction type. Adaptations within the mesocorticolimbic reward circuitry that result in altered dopaminergic activity (Kauer and Malenka, 2007) may influence continued drug seeking (despite negative consequences of the abuse) and frequency of relapse (Everitt et al., 2008). In part, these consequences may reflect the role of dopamine in retrieving memories of salient events and identifying the salience of rewards (McClure et al., 2003b). For a review of the role of dopamine receptors in drug addiction, see Heidbreder et al., 2005).

Critical thinking activity

Survival and substance use

Critical thinking focus: critical and creative thinking

Key question: *How do evolutionary psychologists explain substance abuse?*

Read the following article.

> Richardson, GB (2012) Immediate survival focus: synthesizing life history theory and dual process models to explain substance use. *Evolutionary Psychology*, 10, 731–749. Available online at www.epjournal.net/wp-content/uploads/EP107 31749.pdf

The authors of the article use life history theory and dual process models to explain substance use. Referring back to the previous material, try to think about whether this account explains all aspects of substance use, particularly addiction. Should researchers focus on theoretical explanations of human behaviour, or is it more important to focus on the practical applications of these findings? Does this particular explanation offer practitioners and those supporting addicts any practical guidance? As a researcher, how would you start to test some of the predictions of this account of substance use? Are there any ethical or practical difficulties when adopting this methodological approach?

Critical thinking review

This activity asks you to read a journal article and consider the way in which researchers can provide evolutionary explanations for particular behaviours. In this article, the researchers focus on a theoretical account of the behaviour rather than the generation of new raw data. When reading these theoretical articles, try to decide if there are any alternative explanations that the author has not considered. Also assess whether the authors recognise the limitations of their argument and whether they support their claims with the findings of other researchers. Evaluating the ideas of other researchers can be difficult, but it is a valuable academic skill, so try to read these articles with a 'critical eye'. Finally, try to think of other **maladaptive behaviours** that evolutionary theory could explain. Can you think of any ethical or practical consequences (positive or negative) of these explanations?

Skill builder activity

Searching for journal articles

Transferable skill focus: information technology and independent learning

Key question: *How do students and researchers find information on their chosen subject?*

Online search engines provide access to a wealth of interesting research articles, including recently published findings. Google Scholar (available at http://scholar.google.co.uk) does not require a password or registration. Simply type in the area of interest (such as 'eating motivation') to view a range of articles in the area of interest. You can then choose to focus on the most relevant or recently published research. Now use the search engine to find articles in an area of interest or an area of motivation that is not covered by this chapter (such as thirst and drinking). If you find a particularly useful article, clicking on 'related articles' will generate similar responses.

Skill builder review

This task asks you to source new research articles. This is a valuable academic skill that provides access to recently published research and a wide range of subjects. Google Scholar is a search engine that is available to everyone (and no passwords or registration are needed). Each university will also have access to specific academic search engines such as PsychInfo. Try to find which search engines you can access and spend some time searching for new research studies. This is a great way to source information for assignments and helps provide access to a wide range of material. The more information that you read, the more deeply you will understand the subject area – and be able to think about alternative explanations for research findings.

Assignments

1. To what extent does motivation impact on human survival? Consider both positive and negative consequences in your answer.

2. Discuss the biological and psychological factors influencing the consumption of food.

3. Outline the sexual response cycle and discuss the role of both biological (e.g. hormone) and environmental (e.g. learning) factors in sexual behaviour.

Summary: what you have learned

Now you have finished studying this chapter you should:

- understand the evolutionary importance of motivation and the impact of motivation on human survival;

- recognise biological mechanisms influencing pleasure and reward, including the role of dopamine and serotonin;

- be able to identify the biological and psychological mechanisms influencing eating, including hunger, stress, exposure to food cues, binge eating and food disorders;

- understand the biological mechanisms influencing sexual differentiation and sexual behaviour, including the sexual pleasure and menstrual cycles;

- understand the biological mechanisms associated with the development and maintenance of addiction and factors influencing vulnerability to addiction;

- have developed your skills relating to the ability to synthesise and evaluate written information;

- understand the importance of research measures and design.

Further reading

Groesz, LM, McCoy, S, Carl, J, Saslow, L, Stewart, J, Adler, N, Laraia, B and Epel, E (2012) What is eating you? Stress and the drive to eat. *Appetite*, 58, 717–721.

A review of stress and eating behaviour.

Ko, C-H, Liu, G-C, Hsiao, S, Yen, J-Y, Yang, M-J, Lin, W-C, Yen, C-F and Chen S-S (2009) Brain activities associated with gaming urge of online gaming addiction. *Journal of Psychiatric Research*, 43, 739–747.

An outline of the neurobiological mechanisms associated with addiction.

Mihm, M, Gangooly, S and Muttukrishna, S (2011) The normal menstrual cycle in women. *Animal Reproductive Science*, 124, 229–236.

Paper detailing the menstrual cycle.

Ngun, TC, Ghahramani, N, Sanchez, FJ, Blocklandt, S and Vilain, E (2011) The genetics of sex differences in brain and behavior. *Frontiers in Neuroendocrinology*, 32, 227–246.

A review of sex differences.

Chapter 8

Language

Learning outcomes

By the end of this chapter you should:

- have an understanding of the differences between proximate and ultimate explanations for biology of language;

- know how language differs from non-human animal communication;

- be able to evaluate different evolutionary theories for language;

- be able to discuss the role that proximate biological factors (such as genes, brain and neurotransmitters) have in producing language.

Introduction

Communication is an integral part of existence for most species, especially for those who live in complex social worlds (Frith and Frith, 2010). Communication happens in many different ways – through scent-marking and odours (in rodents, for example), through vocalisations and through non-verbal gestures and facial expressions. Humans are unique in that we are the only species that have evolved an open-ended, flexible, grammatical, spoken language (Pinker, 2010). Whereas most non-human animal communication consists of alarm calls and signals identifying the present state of the individual, human language can convey an almost infinite number of meanings, referring to the past, present and future. Interestingly, human children acquire this complex system of communication without any conscious effort, suggesting that language is an innate, evolved capacity. Language in humans has a close relationship to **social cognition**, and has co-evolved together with our cognitive capacities.

In this chapter, we will review evidence for multiple proximate (biological) and ultimate (evolu-tionary) influences on human language. As you will remember from the introductory chapter, proximate causations refer to biological causes that are active during the lifetime of an individual, often within the body of an individual. Proximate, biological causes are such things as genetics, brain structures, neurons and hormones, and they explain *how* language works. Ultimate, evolu-tionary causations explain *why* language evolved in the first place, explaining what benefits language capacity had for our ancestors. There are several competing ultimate theories, and we will be reviewing some of them in this chapter. Of course, you have to bear in mind that these proximate and ultimate biological influences are not isolated from culture and upbringing, but there is not enough space to discuss the complex interactions here. If you are interested in this, there is plenty of research papers and books that you can have a look at.

What is language?

In order to understand how language differs from other forms of communication, we need first to define what we mean by the word language. There are many definitions (see, for example, design features by Charles Hockett and Stuart Altman, 1968). Essentially, language is a system of communication that consists of many different features. **Syntax**, for instance, is about the rules of organising language into grammatical sentences, **semantics** is about how we interpret the meaning of words, and **phonology** and **phonetics** are about the physical mechanisms and patterns of the sounds in the speech. Human language may be a unique form of communication in that we can put together an infinite number of sounds to form meaningful words and sentences. Further, language capacity is not restricted to spoken language. The complexity of communication extends to non-verbal language as well, as **sign languages** are as rich in form and structure as spoken languages are. It is important to note that language is closely linked to thought and cognition, and that language and cognition (especially social cognition) have evolved together, supporting each other (Fitch et al., 2010).

Researchers have tried to define the differences between human and animal communication. One of the things that might set language apart from other forms of communication is **recursive grammar**, where we can embed clauses within sentences in order to communicate increasingly complex amount of information (Hauser et al., 2002). For example, consider the sentence 'Alice knew that the cat ate the mouse'. By embedding this sentence within a new sentence, we can add a new meaning, such as 'Fiona thought that Alice knew that the cat ate the mouse'. We could carry on building on this embedded structure – for example, 'Fiona thought that Alice knew that the cat ate the mouse that belonged to Fiona's little brother', giving the sentence a completely new meaning by embedding new clauses within the structure. Michael Corballis (2007) has suggested that recursive grammar is closely linked to human ability for recursive thought, and might have a close relationship with **theory of mind**, mental time travel and concept of self. We will return back to animal and human differences later on in this chapter.

Another feature of human spoken language is the way that the **larynx** (also called the 'voice box') is structured. The larynx is an anatomical structure found in the neck region of all mammals, amphibians and reptiles, and it has a function in aiding breathing and controlling the pitch and volume of sound. In very small infants, as well as in most non-human animal species, the larynx is situated high, just behind the tongue. This makes breathing and eating easier, but does not allow the production of speech sounds. In humans only, the larynx and the **hyoid bone** (also called the 'lingual bone') have descended much lower, allowing the formulation of phonemes typical to different languages. This comes with a great cost, as in adult humans the respiratory and the digestive tracks are no longer separated, resulting in a risk of choking while eating.

Task — You can easily find your larynx by placing your fingers on the front of your throat, just under the chin. When you swallow, you can feel the larynx moving up and down. In men, the larynx can be found where the Adam's apple is. In most other species (and newborn babies), the larynx is positioned just behind the tongue, and allows swallowing and breathing through the nose at the same time.

Biological (proximate) explanations

Genetics

There is now convincing evidence to suggest that our ability to acquire spoken language has got a genetic base (Deriziotis and Fisher, 2013; Fisher and Marcus, 2006; Marcus and Fisher, 2003). Of course, the picture is far from simple, as there are likely to be several genes interacting with the environment in producing language. One way that researchers can investigate the existence of language-specific genes is by looking at genes that are active in human neurodevelopmental disorders (such as specific language impairment; Newbury et al., 2010). Another method is to look at genetic differences between humans and our closest relatives, the great apes, in order to identify differences in communication-related behaviours (Fisher and Marcus, 2006).

In the 1990s, researchers identified an extended British family of Pakistani origins (named in the literature as the KE family), half of whose members suffered from **severe language impairment** (SLI). This condition affects the control of movements of the lower part of the face, making speech utterances difficult. As well as speech difficulties, the condition is characterised by impairments in written expression of the language, without any other intellectual impairments. The KE family members who are affected have mutations in a Forkhead-domain gene, **FOXP2**. This gene is active in different parts of the brain, and is involved in brain maturation and in language and speech development (Spiteri et al., 2007). Further, there is some evidence that FOXP2 is more active in the brains of girls than in those of boys (Bowers et al., 2013), which could partially explain why girls often excel over boys in linguistic capacity. Interestingly, the same gene is active in songbirds that learn to imitate new sounds, and could be important for neural plasticity required in learning (Chen et al., 2013). The gene is different in humans and apes only by few **amino acids**, but could give interesting cues about what makes human communication different from other species.

Task — Read the following link:

http://genome.wellcome.ac.uk/doc_WTD020797.html

Think about what the discovery of the gene means to our understanding of language evolution.

Brain functioning

Perhaps some of the most convincing support for the argument that language is an evolutionary adaptation is provided by our specialised neural circuitry, facilitating production and comprehension of language. Famous examples are **Broca's area**, associated with the production of speech and syntax, and the comprehension of grammar, and **Wernicke's area**, associated with the comprehension of language. In a way, Wernicke's area deals with formulating an action plan of what we are going to say, and Broca's area implements the action plan. Broca's area is located in the left frontal cortex, and Wernicke's area in the left temporal lobe. Both of these areas are connected by a neural loop called the **lateral sulcus** (or **Sylvian fissure**). In this loop, Broca's area and Wernicke's area are connected by a bundle of nerves called the **arcuate fasciculus**, where language-related information is rapidly transferred between the areas.

More recently, a third important brain area for language has been discovered, located behind Wernicke's area in the **inferior parietal lobule** (Catani and Jones, 2005). This area has also been named as the **Geschwind's territory** after an American neurologist who discovered the area in the 1960s. The inferior parietal lobule is another connection (i.e. in addition to the arcuate fasciculus) between Broca's and Wernicke's areas, and is an area that is the last one to develop during childhood as it develops between the ages of 5 and 7 years old. This area is connected to both Broca's and Wernicke's areas by a large bundle of nerve fibres, and plays an important role in relaying information between the two language areas. It is believed that this area plays a major role in language development during childhood, culminating in the ability to read and write, and is also a key to understanding the evolution of language in humans.

Task — Check the location of the language areas by following this link:

http://thebrain.mcgill.ca/flash/i/i_10/i_10_cr/i_10_cr_lan/i_10_cr_lan.html

You can find here illustrations and more information of the localisation of language in the brain.

Broca's aphasia (or expressive aphasia) is a condition that results from damage to Broca's area, and is characterised by slow, simple, halted sentences. Patients with this condition have difficulties in expressing themselves, but can usually make themselves understood, and have no problems with comprehension of language. In Wernicke's aphasia (or fluent aphasia), patients have no trouble in producing language, but the words that they use often make no sense. Further, patients are often unaware of their nonsensical speech, and become angry because others cannot understand them.

Task — Read this transcript from two patients (one with Broca's aphasia and the other with Wernicke's aphasia) recalling the children's story Cinderella:

www.departments.bucknell.edu/linguistics/lectures/aphasia.html

What differences do you note in their speech?

The human brain is strongly lateralised, and most language functions are concentrated on the left side of the cerebral hemisphere. Over 90 per cent of right-handed individuals and 67–85 per cent of left-handed individuals have lateralisation of language skills in the left side of the brain. However, brain imaging studies have shown that there is individual variation on how lateralised language is, and not all of us use the left side of our brain. For example, some people use both sides equally, which also improves the speed of recovery after a stroke (Knecht et al., 2002).

Is human language unique?

There is a lot of research interest in investigating whether human language is unique, probably because language is often paraded as one of the hallmarks of humanity, setting us apart from other species of animals. Of course, it is important to note that all species are interesting and important in their own rights, rather than because they may have similarities with humans. Different species have evolved different forms of communication (e.g. the waggle dance in bees or echolocation in bats) because of different environmental and social pressures during their evolutionary history. Nevertheless, looking at other species can give us important information about human language. When investigating uniqueness of human language, researchers have looked at songbirds and how they learn to sign, and primates – especially apes – and the mental structures that could be precursors for human language. There has also been great interest in studying communication in dolphins (Janik, 2013) as these sea mammals have both the capacity for vocal learning, and the mental structures for complex, intentional communication.

Vocal learning

Songbirds (such as the starlings you might be able to see or hear in the park) have similar neural and genetic substrates for language to those of humans, and the developmental trajectories of baby babbling and bird song are surprisingly similar (Bolhuis et al., 2010; Lipkind et al., 2013). Both birds and babies learn vocal communication from their conspecifics via imitation of sounds coupled with genetic predisposition for the learning. This means that both birds and infants have the capacity to learn an infinite number of sound combinations, which is also the basis for the human ability to learn several different languages. In both songbirds and humans, learning to produce specific sound combinations is not purely genetic; it is reliant on cultural learning from others. This flexibility in learning can lead to the existence of slightly different vocal cultures in songbirds, in the same way as different languages emerge in human cultures (Fehér et al., 2009; Peters et al., 2012). Learning of vocal communication is produced by a combination of genes and social learning, and is an example of **convergent evolution** in humans and songbirds.

Researchers have found several genetic substrates (for example, FOXP2) producing circuits in the brain that allow bird singing and human speech. In both songbirds and humans, deficits in the

FOXP2 gene produce deficits in vocalisations (Teramitsu and White, 2006). It is interesting that this gene has a very similar function in songbirds and humans, and it could evolve separately in species for which flexible learning of sounds is important. However, despite the similarities in the neural and social substrates of vocal learning in humans and birds, there are crucial differences in how the vocalisations are used. For example, one important difference between birdsong and human speech is the lack of semantics in birds. Although birds can produce an endless amount of combination of syllables, there is no meaning attached to these sounds, and their main functions are to attract mates and defend territory. The function of language and bird vocalisations are therefore very different.

Another form of vocal communication found in many primates is **lip smacking**, the fast pressing of lips together to produce syllables. Recent research has shown that the gelada baboon – a species of primates that lives in remote mountains in Ethiopia – produces sounds resembling human speech by smacking its lips together (Bergman, 2013). Thore Bergman, a primatologist who studies gelada baboons, repeatedly mistook the gelada sounds for other humans calling him, and decided to study their communication in more detail. He found that geladas use lip smacking in a similar way to how humans use small talk – to bond with each other. In fact, there are some researchers who claim that human speech originated from lip-smacking sounds produced while eating (MacNeilage, 1998), an idea that the gelada research seems to support.

Task — Listen to the gelada talk by following this link:

http://vimeo.com/63663133

Teaching other species to talk?

There have been several attempts to try to teach chimpanzees human language, but the anatomy of chimpanzee vocal tract prevents them from learning to communicate in spoken words. This was demonstrated back in the 1950s, when Catherine and Keith Hayes, a scientist couple, adopted a chimpanzee called Vicki. After years of training, she was only able to produce four words: mama, papa, cup and up. However, she gained a great understanding of human words despite the inability to communicate in spoken words herself (Hayes and Hayes, 1952). More recent research has fruitfully used non-verbal language (for example, sign language) to discover the linguistic abilities of non-human primates. It is possible that the great apes have evolved a mental ability to produce language, but lack the speech apparatus that is needed for spoken language.

Interestingly, species of birds (for example, parrots) seem to have both the vocal cords and the mental ability to use human spoken language in communication. A famous example is Irene Pepperberg's Alex, an African grey parrot, who prematurely passed away in 2007 after 30 years of laboratory training. Alex's capacity to use language has revealed fascinating aspects about bird cognition and emotions, including showing that parrots (also called feathered primates because of their cognitive skills) have the mental capacity of a 5-year old child (Pepperberg, 2012). Some critics have suggested that Alex learned skills (such as abstract reasoning, numbers and shapes) by operant conditioning and route learning. However, Pepperberg's experiments were scientifically rigorous, and it is possible that Alex really did grasp complex concepts and use language and grammar in a meaningful and flexible manner. As humans and parrots are separated by some 280 million years of evolution, it is interesting to see what kind of evolutionary pressures might have led to the convergence of the vocal and brain structures needed for meaningful communication with syntax.

Task — Type 'Alex the parrot' into an academic search engine (such as www.scholar. google.com). There should be thousands of academic references to the late celebrity parrot. Read some of the abstracts of the articles to get an idea of what Alex taught us about the mental capacity of parrots. Now repeat the search by adding the word 'language'. You will be able to see articles that tell us what experiments with Alex have revealed us about language in birds. If you wish, you may also try to find online video clips to see Alex in action.

Mental capacity for language

Other primates, especially the great apes, have been of great interest in trying to find cognitive precursors for human language. Researchers have investigated whether the great apes have the mental ability for human communication, teaching chimpanzees, bonobos, gorillas and orang-utans to communicate via sign language or a board containing symbols. One famous case of a language-trained ape is Kanzi, a bonobo chimpanzee, who was taught to communicate via pointing at a board containing symbols. These symbols are used to signify different words, and can be put in a sequence to produce grammatical language. One of the interesting things about Kanzi is that he learned the language while observing the researchers teaching language to his adoptive mother, Matata. Sue Savage-Rumbaugh, one of the researchers responsible for training the pygmy chimpanzees, has reported that Kanzi uses the language to express emotions (Lyn and Savage-Rumbaugh, 2012), to deceive others and to communicate events in the past and in the future. Kanzi has a vocabulary of about 500 words, and comprehension of over 3,000 words, having a linguistic capacity similar to a 2–3 year old child. Savage-Rumbaugh has suggested that teaching the apes to communicate in human language could change the cognitive ability of the species, making them more similar to humans than apes in the wild are.

There has been recent interest in domestication, and how this may affect the cognitive ability of species such as dogs (Hare and Tomasello, 2005; Miklósi et al., 2004). Research suggests that when breeding dogs, humans have been artificially selecting for genes that are related to social competence and communicative abilities (Miklósi and Topál, 2013). Dogs can learn up to 1,000 words for different objects and actions (Pilley and Reid, 2011), having the ability to develop very large *receptive* vocabularies (words that an individual can understand). However, *productive* vocabularies (producing sounds that have a meaning) are much smaller in dogs, and it is an evolutionary puzzle why humans have evolved the capacity for both understanding and producing a large number of words. Domestication is important for understanding how social cognition relates to communicative abilities, and can be useful when asking questions about human language and social cognition.

Dolphins have been shown to have the capacity to communicate in a flexible, open-ended way (Janik, 2013). Bottlenose dolphins learn to produce their own signature whistles by copying sounds into a unique combination that nobody else uses. These whistles carry information about the identity of individuals, and are based on a similar process of vocal learning found in humans and songbirds. More amazingly, other dolphins can recognise these whistles even when they are produced by a computer, and the whistles can be copied by others who can then use them in directing their communication towards the right individual (King and Janik, 2013). These whistles seem to be used in a similar way to how humans use names, which would indicate that dolphins have the semantics (i.e. meaning) in their communication that the songbird vocalisations are lacking. Experiments in captive dolphins have revealed that they have the capacity to produce and understand syntax, and researchers have also begun to unravel the complex communication of dolphins in the wild.

The communication skills of dolphins are based on complex social cognition. For example, dolphins have an incredible social long-term memory, and they can remember their former friends and mates even after 20 years of separation (Bruck, 2013). This complexity has evolved in the context of a *fission-fusion* social system, which is characterised by a fluid, changing composition of social groups.

The animal language research is not without its critics. Noam Chomsky, a prominent linguist, has argued that humans are genetically hardwired for language, and that other species cannot truly learn to communicate in the same way as humans. Steve Pinker, an evolutionary psychologist, claims that the apparent linguistic abilities of apes are no more than learning to press buttons in order to receive a reward, and that they lack a true understanding of language (Pinker, 1994). See this link if you are interested in Noam Chomsky's arguments against the idea that apes can be taught human language: www.chomsky.info.

Evolutionary (ultimate) theories

Why do only humans have language? How and when did it evolve? Did language emerge all of a sudden, or can we see a slow build-up over time? Did language evolve from vocalisations or from gestural communication? These are some of the pressing questions for scholars studying the evolution of language. In fact, there are many controversies and little agreement about why, how and when language evolved (Christiansen and Kirby, 2003). Indeed, studying the origins of language was deemed so controversial that the Linguistic Society of Paris famously banned any discussions in 1866, as did the London Philological Society in 1872. It was not until some 100 years later that the evolutionary origins of language became an acceptable field of investigation again.

Interestingly, eminent evolutionary biologists Maynard Smith and Szathmary (1997) noted that the evolution of language is one of the eight major transitions in the evolution of life, affecting radically the course of evolution. Language is an important evolutionary force because it allows information to be transferred from one generation to another via cultural means.

One of the difficulties of studying the evolutionary origins of language is that language does not leave any direct fossil evidence for us to investigate. Thus we have to infer the evolution indirectly from several different sources. This can be done, for example, by looking at: (a) archaeological evidence for symbolic capacity; (b) fossilised skulls and the presence of language-specific brain areas; (c) fossil evidence for anatomical features related to speech; (d) cognitive capacities of other species; (e) specialised brain circuitry and genetic make-up for language; (f) inferring past from the present, for example, by investigating what the uses of modern language are. Investigating language evolution is a truly inter-disciplinary pursuit, requiring expertise from several different fields (see Uomini and Meyer, 2013, for an example of collaboration between experimental neuroscientist and an archaeologist). It is not a wonder that there are a lot of arguments surrounding evolutionary explanations and theories. When you read the literature, keep in mind that for every piece of evidence there is also an argument against the evidence.

Functional explanations

Currently, there are many adaptationist and by-product theories for the evolution of language. The by-product theories of language assert that language did not evolve because it was beneficial for our ancestors but that it was rather a by-product of another feature that was adaptive. For example, Gould (1997) claims that as the human brain expanded in size, language accidentally emerged from the structure of the brain. However, language seems to meet the hallmarks of an evolutionary adaptation. Hauser and Fitch (2003) suggest that language has special design features that are typical of evolutionary adaptations, such as: (a) universality among all normally developing humans; (b) specialised neural circuitry and brain areas; and (c) a typical pattern of development. Thus it is safe to make the claim that human language is an evolutionary adaptation rather than a by-product of something else.

One of the most convincing evolutionary theories for language is that it evolved to facilitate social bonding (Dunbar, 1998). Modern primates spend a lot of their daily activity budgets on grooming (moving ectoparasites from skin), which also works as an effective form of social bonding. Grooming communicates information about social ranks and cliques as these grooming patterns are far from being random. Grooming also bonds individuals together by releasing endorphins. When group sizes started to increase in early hominids (possibly due to environmental pressures), maintaining the grooming cliques became increasingly difficult. According to Robin Dunbar, language in humans evolved to replace grooming in maintaining social bonds and gaining fitness-relevant information about other group members. Complex vocal communication emerged as a type of vocal grooming, allowing one individual to communicate to multiple partners at the same time. Further, language allows us to know about the reputation of other people, something that is crucial for our **evolutionary fitness** when choosing who to associate with. Indeed, humans spend a lot of time talking about other people, and this social gossiping is an excellent tool for spreading valuable information about the trustworthiness of others.

Solving the **free-rider** problem is an important evolutionary puzzle. Free-riders (or individuals who try to benefit from others) should have advantage over others in terms of evolutionary fitness (i.e. reproducing and transferring their genes to the next generation). Cooperative individuals are in danger of being exploited by free-riders, which can lead to reduced evolutionary fitness (i.e. less chance of reproducing and transferring genes to the next generation). Further evidence for the evolutionary origins of language as a tool for deterring free-riders comes from research looking at different accents within a language.

Accents are often related to geographical boundaries, and people who have similar accents live relatively close to each other. Thus, when choosing who to cooperate with, selecting a partner with a similar accent makes sense, as you are more likely to interact with them repeatedly due to living close to each other. People with very different accents can live quite far from you, and may not reciprocate a favour that you give to them. There is plenty of evidence to suggest that: (a) we trust people with similar accents more; (b) we are more likely to do a favour to a person with a similar rather than a dissimilar accent; and (c) this preference emerges quite early during the development, and is often present by the age of 4–5. Accents can function as a 'tag', identifying who is a safe person to cooperate with (Cohen and Haun, 2013). The research on accents and cooperation provide more evidence for the idea that language evolved as a tool for enhancing cooperation and deterring free-riders.

Phylogenetic explanations

One of the bones of contention in language evolution is the idea of continuity versus discontinuity. To put it simply, continuity theories assume that language did not appear suddenly from nowhere but rather evolved gradually from cognitive structures possessed by our primate ancestors, and these structures should be seen in other extant species, too. The discontinuity theory proposes that language emerged from a genetic mutation in a single individual, rapidly spreading through the whole species. Most researchers and theorists support the continuity theory, although there are some (such as the eminent linguist Noam Chomsky) who vehemently defend the discontinuity idea. Rather than language appearing suddenly out of nowhere, it is much more likely that it is a product of accumulation of genetic and cultural changes that have slowly led to the evolution of language as we know it today (Dediu and Levinson, 2013).

The continuity theorists are divided even further into those who believe that language gradually evolved from vocal utterances of our ancestors and those who think that language in humans has origins in gestural communications (Sterelny, 2012). According to the gestural origins theory, language first emerged through sophisticated gestures, and was only later accompanied by speech. Further, there are many who believe that language co-evolved together with tool use in the hominid lineage, and started off as a complex gestural system rather than vocalisations. There is, in fact, a whole issue of the prestigious scientific journal *Philosophical Transactions of the Royal Society B: Biological Sciences* dedicated to research investigating links between gestures, tool use and language evolution (Steele et al., 2012). There is evidence that stone tool production and language recruit the same areas of the brain as language, pushing the origins of language back to at least 1.8 million years ago, when the Acheulean stone tool culture of Homo erectus emerged (Uomini and Meyer, 2013).

The idea for gestural origins of language is supported by the communication system of the great apes, our closest relatives, who shared a last common ancestor with humans some 14 million years ago (Hill and Ward, 1988). Apes use gestures in a flexible way, and they may learn the gestural communication via cultural learning, showing regional variation (a bit like different languages) between different populations. For example, although vocalisations are fairly similar between the two species of chimpanzees, they are very different in their gestural communication (Pollick and de Waal, 2007). Chimpanzees may have some of the cognitive prerequisites for language, such as the ability to understand another person's attention (MacLean and Hare, 2012). Joint attention is an important building block for understanding that the other individual has a mind and intentions, and is essential for developing language.

Further, there is evidence that sign languages can emerge quite spontaneously, not only in deaf communities but also among Australian aborigines avoiding speech taboos associated with some ceremonies and Native Americans who used it as lingua franca, allowing fluent communication among different tribes coming together (see Corballis, 2010, for more examples). In infants, gestures come before the spoken words, and are probably important for the development of spoken language (Iverson and Golding-Meadow, 2005). We use a lot of gestures while we speak, and gestures and speech are used mutually in aiding understanding of what we are trying to say (Kelly et al., 2010). Indeed, trying *not* to gesture while you talk is extremely difficult, as gesture and speech complement each other in such a natural way. Co-speech gestures are gestures that would be meaningless unless they were complementing speech (such as showing others the size of the fish that you caught), and they are produced subconsciously, without any effort. In fact, language, gestures and action are represented in the same areas of the brain (Willems and Hagoort, 2007), suggesting that there is a close evolutionary relationship between speech, gestures and action.

Other evidence for gestural origins of language comes from studies that link the neural substrates of manual actions and spoken language. For example, in monkeys, the F5 area of the pre-motor cortex is functionally analogous to Broca's area in humans. You will remember that Broca's area is an area in the brain that is responsible for the production of language (both spoken and sign language) and the comprehension of grammar, as well as complex motor movements. In monkeys, brain cells in this brain area are active when the individuals are both grasping an object and watching someone else grasping an object. In the same way, when we are listening to a speech sound, the same neurons in the brain are active as when we are producing the sound ourselves. These neurons are located in the primary and pre-motor cortex, the same locations where perceiving and executing a motor action are represented (Wilson et al., 2004). Further, reading action words (such as licking, kicking and picking) out loud activate the same pre-motor cortex areas that are activated when these actions are produced (Hauk et al., 2004). This **mirror neuron system** may provide a precursor for understanding the action of others, and learning by imitation, both of which are important in the development of human language. Moreover, research has shown that mirror neurons may help us to attach meaning to words and sentences, and an improved mirror neuron system could account for the evolution of language.

Although there is convincing evidence for gestural origins of language, there is also research that suggests that language originated in the form of vocalisations. For example, a recent brain imaging study on chimpanzees found that our closest relative shows activation of Broca's area when engaging in vocalisations rather than during gestural communication (Taglialatela et al., 2011).

It is possible to look at the evolutionary trajectory in hominids to see when human vocal language emerged. One of the earliest human ancestors, *Australopithecines*, did not have the descended larynx that is required for the formulation of words. If we look at the position of the voice box as an indicator for language, the evidence suggests that spoken language emerged quite late during human evolution.

Critical thinking activity

Evidence for and against Neanderthal language

Critical thinking focus: analysing and evaluating

Key question: *Did Neanderthals have language?*

There has been a great deal of academic debate surrounding the cognitive and linguistic abilities of Neanderthal people (*Homo sapiens neanderthalis*). Neanderthals were a sub-species of humans who diverged with the modern human lineage about half a million years ago, and inhabited Europe and Eurasia during the last Ice Age. Although Neanderthals were distinctively human, they had very robust bodies, and neuroanatomy that was quite different from us. Proponents of Neanderthal language argue that language and the capacity for symbolic thought were present as early as 500,000 years ago. If it can be demonstrated that Neanderthal people had language, it probably was there when the Neanderthal and human ancestors split into different lineages (Dediu and Levinson, 2013). There are others who fiercely contest the idea of early language evolution, and argue that language emerged late, perhaps only 50,000 years ago, as a result of a single genetic mutation (Bickerton, 1990). Evidence for language can be gleaned from fossilised skulls and activities suggesting a symbolic capacity. For this critical thinking activity, you should read the following article reviewing evidence for Neanderthal language:

Dediu, D and Levinson, SC (2013) On the antiquity of language: the reinterpretation of Neandertal linguistic capacities and its consequences. *Frontiers in Psychology*, 4, 397. http://pubman.mpdl.mpg.de/pubman/item/escidoc:1760 092:4/component/escidoc:1760372/Dediu_Front_Psy_2013.pdf

While you read the article, make a note on what evidence the authors present for Neanderthal language.

Then, read the criticism for the article:

Berwick, RC, Hauser, M and Tattersall, I (2013) Neanderthal language? Just-so stories take center stage. *Frontiers in Psychology*, 4, 671. www.frontiersin. org/Language_Sciences/10.3389/fpsyg.2013.00671/full

While you read the article, make a note of the evidence the authors have against Neanderthal language.

After you have read both of the articles, try to form your opinion on whether Neanderthals had language or not.

Critical thinking review

This activity should help you to read academic arguments and counter-arguments, and try to reach an informed, evidence-based conclusion on a contentious topic. For every claim, there is a counter-claim arguing against that piece of evidence. Here are some of the points that both of the articles raised for and against Neanderthal language:

For: Despite earlier claims that humans and Neanderthals were genetically very different, more recent research has found that there was a significant amount of genetic overlap, suggesting interbreeding between these species. Further, there is evidence of the FOXP2 gene in Neanderthals.

Against: FOXP2 gene is just one of the many genes that are active in language production and comprehension, and should not be taken as evidence for full-blown human language.

For: An enlarged thorassic vertebral canal found in fossils points at a voluntary control of breathing, which is one of the prerequisites for speech production. There is also fossil evidence that modern-type auditory capacity was present in ancestors pre-dating humans and Neanderthals. As speech production has co-evolved with speech comprehension, it is interesting to see that during human evolution, the tuning of the ear canal into the range of human speech happened quite early.

Against: Anatomical capacity for speech should not be taken as evidence for the connection between these structures and the brain.

For: The material culture of Neanderthals points at symbolic capacity, which is essential for the semantics of language (i.e. attaching meaning to an arbitrary word). Neanderthals lived successfully in hostile, arctic conditions. They had mastered the use of fire, used clothing and buried their dead, which could indicate a belief in the after-life.

Against: Cultural products not as impressive as in humans.

Skill builder activity

Grooming, gossip and evolution of language

Transferable skill focus: understanding and using data

Key question: *By practising observational skills, address the question, 'Did language evolve as a tool to control free-riders via social gossip?'*

Robin Dunbar (1998) has suggested that humans evolved language as a form of social control, allowing individuals to keep track of others and their trustworthiness by practising social gossip. Dunbar and his research team eavesdropped on conversations in public places and discovered that most of the time people gossip about other people. Dunbar's idea is that during human evolution, when group sizes grew bigger, people had to have means to find information about other people in order to know how reliable and worthy social partners they are.

We would like you to read the following article:

Dunbar, RI, Marriott, A and Duncan, ND (1997) Human conversational behavior. *Human Nature*, 8, 231–246

This can be found via an academic search engine such as www.scholar.google.com. Pay attention especially to the methods and results sections of the article.

For one day (choose a day when you are active), make a note of people's conversations in public places. Try to choose people who know each other. Divide the conversation topics into broad categories. For example, Dunbar and colleagues used categories such as social (anything to do with social activities, personal relationships, personal likes or dislikes), politics, music and culture, and technical. When you listen to the conversations, devise a check-sheet for noting down (a) the sex of the person who is talking and (b) which category the topic of the conversation falls into. You should note down the topic of conversations at 30-second intervals.

Have a look at the differences in different categories. Are the sexes similar in their conversation topics? What topics were most common? Do your results correspond with Dunbar et al's (1997) results? If not, what do you think the reasons are? What do your results tell you about the evolution of language?

Skill builder review

This activity should have helped you to get familiar with the observational method and data collection, including thinking about how to collect the results, as well as how to interpret the data. Further, it should have helped you to develop skills in reading research articles, especially in terms of understanding the methods and results section of the article.

Assignments

1. Do non-human animals have the capacity for language? Review evidence for and against animal language.

2. Is language lateralised?

3. Do sex differences in language exist? What could be proximate (biological) and ultimate (evolutionary) reasons for sex differences?

Summary: what you have learned

Now you have finished studying this chapter you should:

- be able to explain what human language is, and how it differs from non-human animal communication;

- understand how proximate (e.g. genes, brain functioning) differ from the ultimate (evolutionary) explanations for language;

- discuss the proximate, biological (e.g. brain circuitry and lateralisation, genes) influences on language;

- have knowledge of some of the cognitive prerequisites for language, and whether other species possess these;

- be able to discuss the evolutionary origins of language;

- know how the theories for gestural versus vocal origins of language differ from each other.

Further reading

Dediu, D and Levinson, SC (2013) On the antiquity of language: the reinterpretation of Neandertal linguistic capacities and its consequences. *Frontiers in Psychology*, 4, 397.

Dunbar, RIM (2004) Gossip in evolutionary perspective. *Review of General Psychology*, 8, 100–110.

Some good papers explaining the functional and phylogenetic aspects of language.

Gillespie-Lynch, K, Greenfield, PM, Feng, Y, Savage-Rumbaugh, S and Lyn, H (2013) A cross-species study of gesture and its role in symbolic development: implications for the gestural theory of language evolution. *Frontiers in Psychology*, 4.

A paper that reviews the use of gesture in non-human species, and discusses the implications for human language.

Fitch, W, Huber, L and Bugnyar, T (2010) Social cognition and the evolution of language: constructing cognitive phylogenies. *Neuron*, 65, 795–814.

Hillix, WA and Rumbaugh, D (eds) (2004) *Animal bodies, human minds: ape, dolphin, and parrot language skills*. New York: Springer.

Good book and a journal article linking social cognition and mind to the evolution of language.

Groen, MA, Whitehouse, AJ, Badcock, NA and Bishop, DV (2013) Associations between handedness and cerebral lateralisation for language: a comparison of three measures in children. *PloS one*, 8, e64876.

Interesting research on the relationship between language and handedness.

Chapter 9

Consciousness

Learning outcomes

By the end of this chapter you should:

- *understand what is meant by primary and extended consciousness;*

- *be able to discuss some of the neurobiological bases of consciousness;*

- *be able to describe a number of disorders of consciousness;*

- *have gained an understanding of what disorders of consciousness mean to under-standing the biology of consciousness;*

- *know the basic evolutionary (phylogenetic and functional) theories of conscious-ness.*

Introduction

The biology of consciousness has become a popular topic of investigation in recent years, primarily because advances in neuroscience allow us to use scientific methods in studying experiences that previously were thought to be purely subjective (Baars et al., 2003a). This raises some fascinating questions, such as: 'Can we locate consciousness in specific parts of the brain?'; 'Are newborn babies conscious?'; 'Are species other than humans conscious?'; and even 'Could a machine ever become conscious?' Our view of the relationship between biology and conscious experience has profound philosophical and ethical implications, especially in relation to issues such as euthanasia, abortion and animal welfare. Furthermore, consciousness provides an interesting topic for evolutionary scientists who are investigating the **phylogeny** (evolutionary history) and **function** (the reason why it evolved) of awareness.

Consciousness is a complex topic, partly because there are many definitions for what it means. In fact, what makes studying consciousness difficult is that every field of study uses the words 'conscious' and 'unconscious' in different ways (Solms and Panksepp, 2012). For instance, consciousness can be analysed in terms of (a) the level and (b) the content of awareness (Majerus et al., 2005). The level of consciousness is about alertness and wakefulness – how awake, attentive and aroused an individual is. The content of consciousness is about the perception of self and the environment, the quality of the awareness. William James suggested as early as 1904 that consciousness consists of interactions with the brain, the body and the environment, rather than something that resides solely in the brain.

Consciousness has been divided further into affective and cognitive components (Solms and Panksepp, 2012). Affective, or emotional, consciousness relies on simpler, more ancient brain structures, (Panksepp, 2005), whereas cognitive consciousness (which can be divided further into visual, memory, etc.) is reliant on higher-order cognitive processes, and requires the cerebral cortex. Some theorists think that the complexity of the cerebral cortex also correlates to the richness of conscious experience, implying that humans, with an extremely convoluted 'thinking' part of the brain, would have more intricate conscious experience than other species with less developed cerebral hemispheres. Linking the primary and extended consciousness together is also another type of consciousness, **interoceptive awareness** (or body consciousness), which is about how our brain represents our internal states of the body. We will talk about these concepts in more detail later on in the chapter, after we have looked at how researchers are able to study the subjective nature of consciousness using objective scientific measures.

Consciousness and science

For long periods during the twentieth century, consciousness was not considered a topic that was worthy of scientific investigation. This was mainly due to the prevalence of the behaviourist school of psychology, where only overt, measurable behaviour could be studied. In contrast, conscious experience is inherently internal and subjective, and based on 'qualia' (Latin for 'what sort' or 'what kind'). **Qualia** is the subjective quality of how we experience the world, or 'the way things seem to us' (Dennett, 1988). There seems to be a fundamental difficulty or even contradiction in attempting to study something that is subjective using the reductionist, objective methods of science (e.g. Chalmers, 1995). This has been (and still is) an important topic of debate for philosophers and scientists, and it is important to realise that questions regarding the place of consciousness in the material world have not been conclusively resolved. The current scientific importance of the topic of consciousness was reflected in the creation, in the 1990s, of several specialist journals such as the *Journal of Consciousness Studies* and *Consciousness and Cognition* for the dissemination of research studies into consciousness. Despite the challenging philosophical issues surrounding this topic, researchers have been able to make progress in studying consciousness from a scientific perspective, by adopting the view that conscious subjective experiences are fundamentally related to biological processes (such as neural functioning), and can be inferred from the behaviour, brain activity and subjective reports of an individual.

Task — For a few minutes, think about your own definitions for consciousness. What do you think it means to be conscious? Does an individual need to be awake and attentive in order to be conscious? Are there different levels of consciousness?

Primary and extended consciousness

Most researchers would agree that being awake and attentive constitutes very necessary, basic ingredients of consciousness (Parvizi and Damasio, 2001). When an individual is in a state of coma, they would not be classified as being conscious. Some other states, such as sleep, could be classified as altered states of consciousness. Consciousness is interesting in that it is a changeable, dynamic process, consisting of stages that each have neurobiological base. For example, coma, one of the clearest disturbances of awareness, is induced when the brainstem is damaged. Consciousness seems to depend on the interaction between widely distributed neural networks, including the **thalamocortical system** as well as the brainstem area (Edelman, 2003).

Most scientists divide consciousness into two basic components: primary (or core) and extended consciousness. Primary consciousness links to the more primitive affective consciousness, whereas extended consciousness is more cognitive in nature. Primary consciousness is a fairly simple process of being able to be aware of external and internal events, store them in the memory and use this information in directing behaviour appropriately. For example, an organism might identify feelings of hunger and direct behaviour to satisfy the need to eat. This type of consciousness is also known as 'sensory consciousness' as it is about feeling internal sensations such as pain and hunger, but the feelings are fleeting and temporary and not necessarily stored in the long-term memory. Organisms that are aware sense that the content of their thoughts belong to themselves, and can act on the content of their thoughts without the use of language or great memory capacity. Primary consciousness probably emerged very early during pre-history, and would have been adaptive in terms of directing focus to pleasurable stimuli (e.g. food, mates) and avoiding unpleasant stimuli (e.g. predators). Individuals who were able to seek food and to run away from danger would have had an advantage over individuals who could not discriminate between pleasurable and dangerous stimuli.

Higher-order consciousness is a more complicated process than primary consciousness, and entails being conscious about being conscious. Extended consciousness allows an organism to have an autobiographical memory (sense of self), which is placed within the past, present and expected future of the organism. This often depends on the linguistic ability of the organism, and might only be possible in humans (although this is debated). In the present chapter, we will be concentrating mostly on the biological base for basic, primary consciousness. If you are interested in the biology of higher-order consciousness, you may want to look at some of the suggested reading at the end of the chapter. It should be noted that humans do not really experience primary conscious states without using the extended consciousness as well in trying to explain the world. Only in states such as meditation, where we are absorbed fully in our internal states, are humans tuned in with the sources of primary conscious experiences only.

Interoceptive awareness

We are introducing the idea of conscious body awareness (also called 'interoceptive' or 'visceral awareness') in more detail as the body–mind relationship is important for emotions, consciousness and behaviour, and can be understood in terms of biological processes. The idea that our bodily sensations (such as heartbeat, blood pressure, respiration and satiety) can give rise to subjective awareness of emotion dates back to the James-Lange theory of emotion, which is explained in more detail in Chapter 5. For example, perceiving a fear-eliciting stimulus (such as a grizzly bear while walking in the woods) gives rise to autonomic bodily reactions (such as racing heart and sweaty palms). The emotion fear is evoked *because* we feel the racing of our heart. Bodily sensations are important in directing our behaviour and creating conscious feelings, but we are often unaware of these influences.

There is interesting research on bodily changes in temperature and how this affects the way we feel about other people and the world. For example, in experiments it has been shown that when participants were holding a cup with a hot drink in it rather than a cold drink, they felt closer to other people (IJzerman and Semin, 2009) and perceived a stranger as having a warm personality (Williams and Bargh, 2008). The connection between feeling warmth and perceiving others as warm is a good example of how bodily sensations affect our evaluations of others. There is, in fact, a constant neuronal, chemical feedback loop between the body and the brain, and the brain is interpreting the bodily signals without us being aware of the influences. These interpretations can translate into affective experiences, the way we feel about the world and other people. Some individuals are better than others at consciously detecting the states of their internal body, which could also be related to increased self-awareness, or the knowledge of what constitutes the 'material me' (Craig, 2002).

Task ⎤ Try to feel your heartbeat without feeling your pulse. Next, try to feel your intestines and how they work without touching your stomach with your hands. This task is easier for some people than for others, and is related to higher awareness and intensity of emotions.

Visceral awareness can be measured by looking at the accuracy of detecting the timing of one's heartbeat, detection of the functioning of intestines, and respiratory resistance threshold detection tasks (see, for example, Critchley et al., 2004). Interestingly, research has found that there is a link between our body awareness and brain areas that are dealing with emotions and awareness of other people.

Body awareness is largely dependent on the **anterior insular cortex** (AI). The AI is also known as the 'viscerosensory cortex' as it is active in perceiving bodily sensations such as body temperature, muscle tension and gut activity. Recently, it has been suggested that AI plays a fundamental part in the formation of conscious, subjective experience (Craig, 2009), and could be an essential neural prerequisite for formulating 'qualia'. Research has found that individuals who have thicker AI are better at recognising their own bodily states (Critchley et al., 2004) and, interestingly, that practices that increase body awareness (such as meditation) relate to increased thickness of the AI (Lazar et al., 2005). Further, AI is active in social emotions and understanding other people's minds (Lamm and Singer, 2010), suggesting that consciousness of one's own body is also linked to how well we understand and empathise with other people. Perhaps there is a biological link between the compassion of Buddhist meditators, their bodily awareness and the thickness of the AI (Grant et al., 2010). Interoceptive awareness is an exciting area of investigation when studying the neural bases of consciousness, and provides interesting links between higher- and lower-order conscious processing.

States and disorders of consciousness

In order to better understand what consciousness is, it is useful to look at different states of consciousness found in humans and many other species, and also at what happens when normal consciousness is disturbed. One of the differences between states of consciousness is *arousal* and *awareness*. Arousal (or 'wakefulness') can be measured as the ability to open the eyes and having basic reflexes such as coughing and swallowing. Arousal is supported by several brainstem cells that are in contact with the thalamus and cortical areas. Awareness involves slightly more complicated actions of communicating, following instructions, remembering and planning. Awareness is dependent on how well the cerebral cortex is integrated with the subcortical areas such as the thalamus. Different states of consciousness can, in principle, be measured by different levels of arousal and awareness. In reality, accurate measurement of consciousness is challenging, as there are no objective measuring tools at the moment (Majerus et al., 2005).

Table 9.1 shows the differences in awareness and arousal in different states. In wakeful, *normal conscious state*, for example, an individual is highly aware of themselves and their surroundings, and is highly aroused and responsive to stimulus. In *deep sleep, coma, or under anaesthesia*, an individual loses awareness of surroundings and themselves, and has low responsiveness and arousability. *Vegetative state* (or 'wakeful unawareness') is characterised by high arousal where an individual may be able to open the eyes and have basic reflexes such as coughing, gagging, moaning and yawning, but is not conscious of what is happening around them and has low self-awareness. Vegetative state is a disturbance of normal consciousness as a result of a brain injury, where an individual is seemingly awake and responsive, but not aware of their surroundings. *Minimally conscious state* is characterised by some – although fleeting – signs of awareness. *Locked-in syndrome* is often mistaken for vegetative state, as although an individual is aware and aroused, inability to move or communicate prevents the patient from signalling awareness. Patients can often communicate only through blinking or moving their eyes. Awareness is therefore often tested by asking the patient to blink as an answer to questions. In clinical settings, levels of

Table 9.1: *Arousal and awareness in different states of consciousness*

	High awareness	*Low awareness*
High arousal	Normal consciousness, Locked-in syndrome	Vegetative state
Low arousal	Minimally conscious state (fluctuating arousal)	Coma, Sleep, Anaesthesia, Epileptic seizures

consciousness can be measured with diagnostic tools such as the Glasgow Coma Scale, which is based on visible activities such as opening of eyes, motor response and communication ability.

Absence seizures (or absence attacks) are a type of epileptic seizure typically occurring in children, with an onset between the ages of 4 and 12. The condition is characterised by loss of consciousness for short, 5–10-second periods at a time, often several times a day. During the seizures, the child becomes unresponsive, and appears to be in a trance-like state, as if they are daydreaming. In school settings, the attacks are often mistaken for inability to concentrate rather than correctly identified as an epileptic seizure. Absence seizures are scientifically interesting, as they can reveal how the brain works during unconscious states, and highlight the brain areas and activity that are needed for primary consciousness to exist (Laufs et al., 2006).

Altered states of consciousness

Throughout history, humans have used a variety of methods to cause specific changes to their internal conscious experience. From a scientific point of view, the study of such 'altered' states of consciousness can provide a window for researchers to investigate the structure and function of consciousness. One of the most widely studied methods for achieving changes to the structure of conscious experience is meditation. While meditation has traditionally been used as a form of religious practice, more recently scientists have been able to distil the essential psychological aspects of meditation, and, in the form of 'mindfulness', meditation is currently used as a technique for stress reduction and psychological well-being (Kabat-Zinn, 1996). Meditation practice has been shown to have beneficial effects on biological processes such as the immune system as well as causing functional changes in the brain related to positive emotions (Davidson et al., 2003) and structural changes such as increased grey matter density in the brainstem (Vestergaard-Poulsen et al., 2009).

A second method for altering consciousness is through the use of drugs that have a direct effect on the central nervous system. Research into the effects of these drugs can provide important information about the neural basis of conscious experience and how alterations in neurotransmitter activity modulate conscious awareness. There are a wide variety of such consciousness-inducing drugs and they are often associated with very different subjective effects. One class of drugs that has a profound effect on the nervous system and on subjective conscious experience are called 'psychedelic' drugs (literally 'mind-manifesting'). After taking a psychedelic drug, users often report a subjective 'expansion' of consciousness, and commonly experience perceptual distortions (e.g. Dubois and VanRullen, 2012). Animal models suggest that the effects of the drug are related to its action on global excitatory and inhibitory neurotransmitter circuits, in particular serotonin (Nichols, 2004). Although research on the effects of psychedelic drugs on the biological systems of humans is relatively scarce (partly due to these drugs being illegal in many countries), nevertheless this research sheds new light on the complex interplay between chemical processes in the brain and subjective consciousness.

The role of the brain in creating consciousness

Measuring brain activity is an important source for determining whether an individual is conscious. There are thought to be several neurobiological underpinnings of consciousness, rather than just one location in the brain responsible for this. In this section, we will be discussing some of the brain regions, connections between the regions, and patterns of activity in creating conscious experience.

There are three ways in which the neurological correlates of consciousness can be investigated (Seth and Baars, 2005). First, scientists can measure brain waves to determine whether an individual is conscious. Consciousness is related to low amplitude, irregular brain activity whereas unconscious states (such as deep sleep, coma, anaesthesia and epileptic states) are characterised by high amplitude, regular, slow-wave brain activity (Baars et al., 2003b). Second, scientists can investigate what role different parts of the brain (such as the brainstem, thalamus and cortex) play in consciousness. For instance, it has been found that damage to the brainstem and thalamus can abolish consciousness altogether, whereas damage to the cerebral cortex can disturb certain features of consciousness (such as colour vision or facial recognition) but will not result in a complete loss of consciousness. Third, conscious experience is widely distributed in different cortical regions, spreading from the sensory cortex to other cortical areas. This pattern of the spreading of activity is not found when people perform automatic, rehearsed activities that do not involve conscious effort, nor is it present when consciousness is lost due to coma or anaesthesia.

Brainstem

At the very basic level, the **reticular formation** – a network of nerve fibres and cells in the brainstem extending to other regions of the brain – is responsible for maintaining functions such as the sleep–wake cycle, motor control and pain modulation, and conscious experiences. The reticular formation is also important in *habituation*, which occurs when the brain filters out unimportant stimuli, such as repetitive, continuous background noise. For example, an individual who lives in a busy city area may be able to sleep through the noise of the traffic, but will be woken up if there are other noises (for example, a crying baby) that are not continuous, and may be important.

The reticular formation is one of the most phylogenetically (evolutionarily) old structures, and it has been related to the evolution of general arousal (Pfaff et al., 2012). The reticular formation allows an organism to concentrate on relevant features of the environment by filtering out irrelevant stimuli before they reach the cortical areas. When the brainstem is damaged, connections between the cortex and the brainstem are destroyed, resulting in a permanent loss of consciousness. The reticular formation of the brainstem activates the thalamus and the cerebral cortex, areas that are more responsible for active, conscious experiences. Although the function of the reticular formation in producing conscious experience is obvious, this system itself is still quite poorly understood.

Thalamus

The thalamus is a walnut-shaped structure, part of the limbic system, located near the centre of the brain, at the top of the brainstem. The thalamus has a major role in distributing motor and sensory signals to the cerebral cortex, and regulates our conscious states of sleep and alertness. In a way, the thalamus is like a gateway that directs messages from the subcortical areas to the correct locations in the cortex. The thalamus has been branded as the main candidate for controlling conscious states, and damage to this brain structure has been related to disorders of consciousness (Schiff and Plum, 2000). For example, unilateral (one-sided) damage of the thalamus can cause altered states of consciousness similar to mania and delirium. Bilateral (two-sided) damage can cause total loss of consciousness, and result in a coma. However, a coma caused by thalamus damage is still characterised by some cyclic activity of arousal and alertness, suggesting that the thalamus cannot be solely responsible for conscious states (Schiff, 2008).

Cortex

The cerebral cortex (the upper, 'intelligent' layer of the brain) relates to many components of conscious experience, and different parts of the cortex are associated with different types of awareness. Further, conscious experience seems to spread all around the cortex, involving multiple cortical areas (Crick and Koch, 2003). In fact, according to one model of consciousness, the dynamic core hypothesis, conscious experience is based on a widely spread network of neural structures involving the thalamus and a large constellation of cortical areas (Edelman, 2003). The experience of qualia can be explained by neural networks that are specific to each individual and is shaped by both genetics and life experiences. It is difficult to pinpoint exactly which areas of the cerebral cortex are the most important, as all the lobes seem equally active in creating awareness.

One example of a specific cortical structure is the *right anterior insular cortex*, a structure that lies deep in the fissure that separates the temporal lobe from the parietal and frontal lobes. This structure is active in creating interoceptive awareness, consciousness of bodily functions (for example, the ability to feel the heartbeat accurately enough to time it). The insular cortex seems to have an important role in tracking subconscious internal states of an organism that are transformed into conscious, cognitive experiences. The right anterior insula is also active in producing individual differences in awareness of pain (how intensively we feel a painful stimulus), and how we perceive skin sensations such as temperature. The *visual cortex* is the main brain area for producing subjective, visual experiences, and brain imaging studies have linked the brain activity in the visual cortex to subjective experiences of seeing (Kamitani and Tong, 2005). The *frontal cortex* (especially areas in the prefrontal cortex) creates a subjective awareness of the self, and is also important in how we perceive other individuals as intentional creatures. Interestingly, other cortical areas, such as the *parietal cortex,* are indirectly related to processing aspects of different forms of consciousness. For example, when we see an object (such as a teacup), the visual cortex is active in translating the experience into being conscious of the object. Parietal areas are active in visual tasks, too, although the parietal cortex has got no function in recognising objects. It has been suggested that the parietal cortex plays an important part in shaping our first-person perspective of things, and makes us see the world from our own perspectives (Baars et al., 2003b). Interestingly, when the right parietal cortex is damaged, patients often neglect things that are on their left visual field. For example, when eating food from a plate, they often leave the left side of the plate untouched, as they claim that they cannot see the left side of the plate. It is possible that the concept of 'observing self' is crucial in creating conscious experience, and is largely reliant on cortical areas such as the parietal and the prefrontal cortex.

The 'corticocentric' view of consciousness has been challenged in recent research, as it has become clear that consciousness can exist even if the cerebral cortex has been destroyed (Merker, 2007). In a rare condition called hydranencephaly, the cerebral cortex is absent to varying degrees and has been replaced by cerebrospinal fluid. Hydranencephaly normally forms in the second tri-semester of pregnancy, and is probably caused by a viral infection, toxoplasmosis bacteria, or substance abuse (Kurtz and Johnson, 1999). Although many of these infants die soon after birth, some of them may linger a bit longer, and can survive up to their teenage years. Although the condition may entail blindness, deafness and intellectual impairments, these children are capable of conscious, goal-directed behaviour, and have emotional experiences like any other children. Thus we can safely assume that primary consciousness, or simple awareness, can exist without the cerebral cortex. However, as Morin (2007) has pointed out, there is no evidence that hydranencephaly-children have the ability for a full-blown consciousness, and they most likely are not able to reflect on their awareness. Thus, for full, higher-order conscious experience of the type that humans typically experience, the cerebral cortex is probably essential. However, while the above research indicates that the cortex is essentially related to different *types* of consciousness awareness, scientists are still uncertain about the exact brain mechanisms that give rise to consciousness.

Brain waves

An exciting avenue of research into the relationship between the brain and consciousness is the investigation into brain rhythmic activity. According to theories in this area, consciousness is not considered to be caused so much by a specific *part* of the brain, but rather by a specific *type of activity* of groups of neurons. Brain rhythms ('oscillations'), which are observable using EEG or MEG, are known to be related to the 'binding together' of distributed information in the brain (for a review, see Buzsaki, 2006). For example, if you see a red car driving on the road, different areas of the visual cortex are representing each of the different features that constitute the object (i.e. the colour, the shape, the motion etc.) However, your consciousness experience is of one unified object, i.e. of a red car, not of a group of separate features. It is thought that the coordination of the different features is related to the separate brain areas temporarily sharing the same rhythmic behaviour, i.e. oscillating at a similar frequency (at around 40 times per second). It is hypothesised that neuronal activity at around this frequency may relate to conscious experience, given that one of the main hallmarks of our conscious experience is its unified, whole nature (Singer, 2001). Moreover, the short-term (i.e. on the level of tenths of a second) coordination of different brain areas by rhythmic synchrony mirrors another main feature of conscious experience – its constantly changing nature. The intriguing parallels between the dynamic activity of the brain expressed by oscillatory behaviour and key features of our conscious experience have made this one of the most exciting areas of research in biological psychology and cognitive neuroscience, but much further research is needed to fully understand the causal link between the brain and consciousness.

Evolution of consciousness

Task — For a few minutes think about *why* it would be of advantage for an organism to be conscious.

In 2006, *The Washington Post* told the story of Shania the octopus, that lived in the National Aquarium in Washington. In order to combat the boredom associated with captive living, the keepers gave her a Mr Potato Head toy to play with. The keepers had to come up with innovative entertainment to keep the octopus busy, because otherwise (and probably out of boredom), she would find her way out of her tank, and crawl into the tank of other creatures, and eat them for supper. Shania seemed to take great pleasure in playing with and snuggling her toys, in a very similar way that a human child would do. Octopuses, invertebrate sea creatures in the family of Cephalopods, are remarkable in their apparent complex intelligence. Despite their odd-looking mollusc appearance, they possess many cognitive, affective and behavioural traits that were thought to be typical only to mammals. It was previously thought that invertebrate sea creatures are simple-brained, evolutionarily lower animals, that could not possibly have conscious awareness. Octopuses most likely possess primary consciousness and, evolutionarily speaking, are an example of *convergent evolution* with mammals (where species with very different ancestors become more similar). You can read Shania's story by following this link:

www.washingtonpost.com/wp-dyn/content/article/2006/08/15/AR2006081500916.html

There are two main evolutionary questions that we can ask when talking about the evolution of consciousness. The first is about the evolutionary history (phylogeny) of awareness. When did it emerge? If the behaviour of Shania the octopus shows signs of consciousness, the phylogeny of awareness could prove to be very ancient indeed, as the family Cephalopods evolved over 400 million years ago. The other question is about the evolutionary function of consciousness. If consciousness was selected for because it was advantageous for the animal to have, what were the selection pressures that led to the evolution? We will discuss some of the theories and evidence for both of these evolutionary questions in turn.

Many researchers think that the adaptive feature of consciousness lies in the emotional experience – individuals are seeking pleasurable experiences and avoiding experiences that are noxious (Cabanac et al., 2009; Panksepp, 2005). It is easy to see how an individual capable of discriminating between self and others in the world of predators and prey would have had a survival advantage. Jaak Panksepp (2005) talks about *affective consciousness*, shared at least by all mammalian species, as a variant of consciousness that should be relatively easy to investigate.

According to Damasio (1998), consciousness was probably reliant on the evolution of brain structures, and most certainly is present in mammalian species with relatively complex cortical structures and connections between these structures. According to Damasio, *core consciousness was born once the presence of certain neuroanatomical devices permitted a description, by one part of the brain of what other parts of the brain were doing* (Damasio, 1998, p1882). It is easy to see why awareness would have resulted in better survival and reproduction once it initially evolved.

In order to trace the existence of primary consciousness in other animals, scientists have started to investigate the brain structures and activity of non-human species, coupled with behavioural reports of conscious, goal-directed activity. If a species possesses brain structures that are related to consciousness in humans, it is plausible that these animals also have conscious experiences. This most likely holds true to mammalian species that have similar cortical and subcortical structures to humans, including the thalamocortical circuitry. Thus it is safe to say that at least your pet dog, cat or a rat is a conscious creature.

Animal consciousness can also be tested by using some of the same research methods that have been used in humans. For example, researchers have investigated *binocular rivalry*, or changes in perception, to test brain activity in conscious visual experiences in humans. In this paradigm, a different stimulus is presented to each eye (for example, vertical lines to the right eye, and horizontal lines to the left eye). This results in an alternating vision of vertical and horizontal lines, as the brain does not allow the visual system to see both lines simultaneously. When brain activity is measured in an fMRI scan, it is possible to reveal which brain areas are active when the vision is consciously changed between the stimuli. Researchers have found that visual perception is controlled by the parietal cortex (Zaretskaya et al., 2010) and the primary visual cortex (Rees, 2007), and this applies to humans as well as to many other species of primates.

Another method for measuring non-human consciousness is to investigate the brain wave patterns during sleep and wakefulness. Researchers studying insects have claimed that remote roots of consciousness might be found in species as far removed from humans as fruit flies (Swinderen, 2005). Fruit flies have been shown to exhibit brain activity typical of stages of sleep and awakeness in humans, and also to possibly have much higher connectivity between different areas than had been thought previously. Thus, rather than being a recent evolutionary development, the roots of consciousness may have emerged hundreds of million years ago. Although the existence of consciousness is debated in non-mammalian (as well as non-vertebrate) species that have quite different brain structures to mammals, at least birds and cephalopods (octopi) are very likely to have primary consciousness. Birds from the Corvid family (for example, crows, jays and magpies) exhibit complex, innovative behaviours that must rely on past experience and conscious applications of that experience to the present task. This implies that these species must be capable of conscious thoughts, and exhibit some form of awareness.

Task — Do fish feel pain? Locate the following article (on Google Scholar, for example):

Chandroo, KP, Duncan, IJ and Moccia, RD (2004) Can fish suffer? Perspectives on sentience, pain, fear and stress. *Applied Animal Behaviour Science*, 86, 225–250.

The capacity to have a subjective experience of pain has been used as a marker for consciousness – if an individual is not conscious, they cannot possibly feel pain. Read the article, and make note of the evidence for fish having the capacity for pain. What does this mean for consciousness? What kind of ethical and welfare implications does this have?

Skill builder activity

Coma and brain activity

Transferable skill focus: independent learning

Key question: *What does coma tell us about the biological bases for consciousness?*

Karen Ann Quinlan is an important figure in the right to die controversy. In 1975, as a 21-year-old young woman, she came back from a party where she had consumed alcohol, opioids and valium. She subsequently had a heart attack, lost consciousness and stopped breathing twice for a period of 15 minutes. This led to irreversible brain damage, and she lapsed into a vegetative coma. After several months, her parents requested that she be taken off the ventilators and be allowed to die. After a legal battle the parents won the case, and Karen was removed from active care. She continued to exist in a vegetative state for nearly ten years until she died of pneumonia at the age of 31 years. Karen's case had a significant impact on the ethics of health care, and resulted in the establishment of ethics committees in care settings. After Karen died in 1986, her brain and the spinal cord were studied extensively.

Your task is to read one of the reports on Karen's brain, in order to evaluate the relative importance of different brain parts in producing consciousness. You should locate the following article:

> Kinney, HC, Korein, J, Panigrahy, A, Dikkes, P and Goode, R (1994) Neuropathological findings in the brain of Karen Ann Quinlan: the role of the thalamus in the persistent vegetative state. *New England Journal of Medicine*, 330, 1469–1475.

You should be able to get a full PDF version on www.scholar.google.com or through an institutional online journal database. While you read the article, write down answers to the following questions.

1. Why did the doctors think Karen was in a vegetative coma rather than in a coma or a locked in-state?

2. What areas of the brain were damaged?

3. What areas were left undamaged?

4. What does Karen's brain tell us about the nature of human consciousness?

Skill builder review

In a vegetative state, there is evidence of arousal (for example, motor activity, reflexes such as coughing, moaning, yawning) without awareness (loss of speech, planned behaviour, memory). Karen did sustain motor activity and reflexes that are not present in locked-in syndrome or in a coma. Further, the EEG measures showed some variation in the brain activity, and evidence of sleep–wake cycles, which are absent in a coma.

The most extensive damage in Karen's brain was observed in the thalamus – the structure that relays neuronal messages between the brainstem and the cortical areas. Although there was some damage to the cortical areas, this alone would not have been sufficient for causing vegetative coma.

Although there was some damage to cortical areas, the areas sustaining unaided breathing – the brainstem – were largely unaffected.

Karen's case highlights the importance of the thalamus for the existence of awareness. The brainstem may play a more important role in the arousal states, but the thalamus is of major importance in establishing awareness of self and the world around us.

Critical thinking activity

Investigating consciousness in animals

Critical thinking focus: critical and creative thinking

Key question: *What methods can we use to investigate whether non-human species have primary consciousness?*

You may want to read this article for more background:

Panksepp, J (2010) Affective consciousness in animals: perspectives on dimensional and primary process emotion approaches. *Proceedings of the Royal Society B: Biological Sciences, 277,* 2905–2907.

Critical thinking review

In short, the non-human animal methods that are used for identifying consciousness are: (a) observational method; (b) experimental method; (c) scanning brain activity/structures. More specifically, some of the following may be used in the investigations.

1. We can try to identify neural structures similar to the human thalamus and cortex.

2. We can try to identify neural activity typical of conscious states in humans.

3. We can try to identify a similar kind of hormonal activity to that produced when humans feel things such as pain.

4. We can try to identify behaviours that suggest that there is a link between how the animal perceives the world, stores the perception in its memory, and acts on it.

Assignments

1. Why did consciousness evolve? Discuss the evolutionary roots of awareness.

2. How does interoceptive awareness link to primary and extended consciousness?

3. What can the study about disorders of awareness tell us about the neural bases for consciousness?

Summary: what you have learned

Now you have finished studying this chapter you should:

– be able to discuss different definitions for consciousness;

– understand how consciousness can be measured scientifically;

– have an understanding of brain activity in different states of consciousness;

– be able to discuss ideas on the evolutionary function of awareness.

Further reading

Panksepp, J (2010) Affective consciousness in animals: perspectives on dimensional and primary process emotion approaches. *Proceedings of the Royal Society B: Biological Sciences*, 277, 2905–2907.

An excellent paper discussing the roots of non-human consciousness.

Edelman, GM (2003) Naturalizing consciousness: a theoretical framework. *Proceedings of the National Academy of Sciences*, 100, 5520–5524.

A good review article about consciousness and the brain.

Craig, AD (2009) How do you feel – now? The anterior insula and human awareness. *Nature reviews. Neuroscience*, 10, 59–70.

An excellent paper talking about the importance of the anterior insula in creating awareness.

www.youtube.com/watch?v=ojpyvpFLN6M

A good video clip on explanations for consciousness.

Chapter 10

Stress and health

Learning outcomes

By the end of this chapter you should:

- *be able to describe how the body responds to stress;*
- *understand the evolutionary importance of stress responses;*
- *be aware of possible pathways that link stress to illness;*
- *be able to identify factors that can mediate the negative effects of stress;*
- *be able to evaluate critically the methodologies used to explore the link between health and stress;*
- *understand the limitations in research that assesses psychosocial interventions that reduce stress and improve well-being;*
- *be aware of future directions of study in this research area, including ways of measuring chronic stress and possible psychosocial interventions to prevent illness;*
- *have developed your critical thinking, organisation and communication skills.*

Introduction

A link between **psychosocial** factors and our health status has long been postulated. As early as AD 200, the physician Galen suggested that women who were more prone to melancholia had a greater tendency to develop 'swellings' of the breasts (indicating breast cancer) than women who were more cheerful. Today biological psychologists have an important role to play in explaining why certain people get ill when exposed to a **pathogen** whereas others remain healthy and why disease outcomes can dramatically differ between people.

Explorations into how exactly psychosocial stressors impact on health were not brought fully into the forefront of psychological research until the 1960s. In 1964, George Solomon published his ground-breaking journal paper entitled 'Emotions, immunity, and disease: a speculative theoretical integration' (Solomon and Moos, 1964) and established the term psychoneuroimmunology. Psychoneuroimmunology is a specific field of research within psychology that aims to uncover the relationship between psychosocial stressors and the immune system (Jemmott, 1985). In the past it was believed that there was a simple link between exposure to stressful environmental factors and health. For example, if a person was exposed to high levels of stressful experiences, such as moving house or the death of a spouse, then they were thought to be at a heightened risk of illness. In this simplistic model, environmental stressors would directly impact on the body's resistance to disease by reducing the number of disease-fighting cells within a person's body. However, we now know that the link between health and stress is not as clear-cut.

In this chapter we will examine the beneficial aspects of the body's response to threat but also consider what happens when responses to stressors become maladaptive. We will also consider factors such as personality type and levels of social support, which have been shown to mediate the effects of stress on health. This chapter will also critically evaluate methodologies used to explore the effect of stress on health and the benefits of psychosocial intervention on disease progression. Finally in this chapter, we will consider the future direction of research, examining how markers of chronic illness might be able to predict illness and psychosocial interventions that might prevent people becoming ill.

Stress

In everyday life we frequently talk about situations that are stressful or factors that cause us stress. However, the term stress is very difficult to define. One reason for this is that what causes people stress is very subjective. For example, some people find speaking in front of an audience very stressful whereas for an actor it is exciting and rewarding. When defining stress, therefore, including the nature of the threat is not important. Stress can be defined as any encounter with a threat that we personally feel unable to deal with. A threat may cause us stress because we may not have the biological ability or the psychological resources to deal with the stressor. However, although a **stressor** can be subjective, some stimuli are known to cause stress in large numbers of people. These include stressors such as job redundancy, natural disasters, marital breakdown, academic examinations, the death of a spouse and moving house.

Although it is not possible to identify threats that will universally induce a stress response, it is possible to refine our definition of stress. First, the term stress can be divided into acute and chronic stress based on the duration of exposure to the stressor.

- *Acute stress* – exposure to a short-term stressor that leads to an immediate physiological response that is present for a short period until the threat has passed.

- *Chronic stress* – exposure to a threat situation where the stressful stimuli are not quickly resolved. The stress response therefore remains elevated for a longer period of time.

The stimuli that induce stress responses in humans can help to refine the definition of stress.

- *Internal stressors* – stress caused by challenges that occur within the body. These could include threats to the body from physical illness or infections, or internal stressors could be the result of psychological pressures such as anxieties about events (such as exam failure) that may or may not occur in the future. Psychological pressures are usually subjective and therefore personal to the person experiencing them.

- *External stressors* – stress that is caused by physical challenges that the body is exposed to. For example, adverse physical stimuli such as extreme cold or high levels of pain can place the human body under stress. External stimuli, such as living in an adverse environment such as a war zone or caring for a terminally ill loved one, can also induce stress.

Exposure to a stressor can induce a number of physiological responses, regardless of whether the stimuli are internally or externally generated. First, we make a personal appraisal of the situation to decide if we are facing a threat. Our decision is based on many factors such as past experiences and our current interpretation of the situation. For example, a low rumbling sound accompanied by the glass beginning to shake in the windows may be interpreted as being caused by a large lorry passing by the building. In this case the stimulus is unlikely to induce a stress response. However, if the same situation occurs in California near the San Andreas fault line, we may interpret the shaking windows and low rumbling sound differently and conclude that we are actually experiencing an earthquake. In this second scenario it is more likely that a stress response would be initiated.

Once a stimulus has been defined as being dangerous the sensory input is passed to the amygdala, which is responsible for the processing of emotional stimuli. If the amygdala confirms that the body is facing a serious threat, then the hypothalamus triggers two main physiological systems that are designed to enhance self-preservation (Selye, 1974). The role of these two systems is to prepare the body to cope with threat (Miller and O'Callaghan, 2002). First is the activation of the sympathomedullary pathway (SAM) that is responsible for the short-term **fight or flight response** (see Figure 10.1).

The actions of the SAM pathway lead to a number of physiological changes that help the body to deal with the threat. As the body needs more oxygen in order to fuel a 'fight or flight' response, the airways in the lungs expand to increase the oxygen intake. The body also needs to release glucose in order to maintain the physical response to the threat. **Adrenaline** triggers the release of glucose from the liver and temporary fat stores within the body. In addition the heart begins to beat faster to allow the blood to be pumped more quickly to the brain and muscles. Increases in glucose and oxygen within the blood lead to enhanced mental processing and alertness.

At the same time as the SAM pathway is activated, the hypothalamus also activates the slower acting **hypothalamic–pituitary–adrenal (HPA) axis**. The HPA axis is designed to maintain a more sustained response to threat (see Figure 10.2).

The response to threat by the SAM pathway is high cost in terms of the energy needed to maintain the response. Therefore the body needs to evaluate whether a sustained response to the perceived

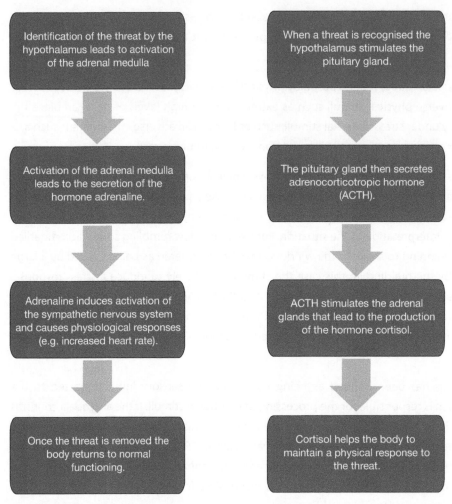

Figure 10.1: *Graphical illustration of the sympathomedullary pathway (SAM)*

Source: Based on Miller and O'Callaghan, 2002.

Figure 10.2: *Graphical illustration of the hypothalamic–pituitary–adrenal (HPA) axis*

Source: Based on Miller and O'Callaghan, 2002.

threat is still required or whether the body can return to normal functioning. The HPA axis helps to maintain a sustained stress response if the brain continues to signal that a threat is present. If the threat is deemed still to be present, the hypothalamus will secrete corticotropin-releasing (CRH). The CRH hormone travels to the pituitary gland and triggers the release of adrenocorticotropic hormone (ACTH). ACTH then causes the adrenal glands to increase the levels of circulating cortisol in the blood. Cortisol helps the body to have the resources needed for a sustained response to threat such as maintaining high levels of blood glucose. If cortisol levels remain high, an appropriate stress response is maintained. If levels of circulating cortisol reduce, the threat is deemed to have been removed and the body returns to normal functioning.

Evolutionary theory – biological importance of stress

There is a tendency to think that stress is unique to the modern world and that it is epidemic in modern society. However, evidence from ancient civilisations suggests that this is not, in fact, the case. Webb and colleagues (2010) took hair samples taken from ten Peruvian mummies and analysed them for levels of the cortisol. The hair samples revealed that the ancient Peruvians appear to have had multiple episodes of stress throughout the final years of their life. These findings suggest that stress was very much a part of ancient Peruvians' daily lives.

The ability to respond to environmental threats is very important. Without the ability to mount a response to a life-threatening situation we would be unable to fight off an attacker or run away from a dangerous situation. An adaptive response to threat results in a boost to physical resources (such as higher levels of circulating blood glucose), which in turn can help us to survive. Other adaptive changes during exposure to threat include up-regulation of the immune system (Segerstrom and Miller, 2004). The likelihood of the body becoming injured and pathogens entering the body is greater when people are in a threat situation. From an evolutionary perspective, therefore, it makes sense for the body to divert resources into preventing infections and accelerating wound healing. However, problems can occur if the body needs to maintain the stress response for a long time in response to a chronic stressor or is unable to return from a heightened response state to normal functioning.

Illness and immunity

It is always puzzling as to why some people get ill when others seem to be immune to a disease or a medical condition. Why do some people develop a cold whereas others who have also been exposed to the same virus do not suffer the annoyance of a week of a running nose and a high temperature? One of the key reasons is that some people appear to have a better functioning immune system than others. But what is the immune system and how does it work?

Immunity is the ability of a person to resist or recover from the effects of a pathogen. Part of the immune system is innate – that is to say, we inherit a certain amount of generic immunity from our parents. The other part of our immune system is developed over time as we learn to identify and destroy pathogens that we come into contact with from different diseases. The adaptability of the immune response means that although we might get very ill the first time we are exposed to a disease, such as chicken pox, the second time we are exposed to the disease our immune response will recognise and know how to destroy the harmful virus.

The immune system is divided into two key components.

- *Natural immunity* is the part of the immune system that is quick acting (minutes to hours) and non-specific, attacking any pathogens that enter the body. It includes cells such as the neutrophil and macrophage that engulf and destroy harmful pathogens. In addition, the natural immune response can release cytokines such as interleukin (IL)-1 that can help the body to recover by inducing a fever or inflammation, or by promoting wound healing. The natural killer cells are another important part of the natural immune system. These cells move in the blood and **lymph**, and seek out and lyse (cause to burst) cancer and virus-infected body cells. Finally, there is the complement system, a group of proteins that bind to **microorganisms** in order to help the body to destroy harmful agents.

- *Specific immunity* is the part of the immune system that takes longer to respond to pathogens and is designed to deal with one specific pathogen. The delay in the specific immune response is why it can take a number of days before we start to get better from diseases such as flu or measles. There are two fundamental adaptive mechanisms within specific immunity – cell-mediated immunity and humoral immunity – and these two immune responses are governed by cells called lymphocytes. There are three types of lymphocytes that mediate specific immunity: T-helper cells, T-cytotoxic cells and B cells.

Pathways from stress to illness

Biological psychologists are now starting to be aware of the harmful effects on health that exposure to long-term stress can have on the human body. However, the precise pathways by which stress can affect health are not fully understood. Over the last 30 years, pathways between exposure to different types of stress and the impact on health have been uncovered. Below a number of these pathways are explored.

Sleep

The pressure on the time we have for sleep has been increasing ever since the invention of the electric light bulb. The modern world means that we do not need to go to bed when it gets dark, so our nightly period of rest can be reduced either by the need to work or from socialising. We are now starting to understand that reductions in the time available for and the quality of sleep can have a major impact on our health. Epidemiologic studies suggest that having less sleep is associated with a greater risk of developing conditions such as diabetes (Ayas et al., 2003).

Research has shown that high levels of psychological stress can impact on both sleep duration and quality. For example, Winwood and Lushington (2006) found that Australian nurses exposed to higher levels of chronic work stress reported poorer sleep quality. Lack of sleep may cause poor health by inducing chronic activation of the HPA axis (Meerlo et al., 2002). Further, reductions in the amount of good-quality sleep we have may impair the release of growth hormone, a hormone that enhances part of immune functioning (Veldhuis and Iranmanesch, 1996). So without good-quality sleep the immune system can become weaker. In turn a weakened immune function can lead to an increased risk of ill health, as our ability to fight off dangerous pathogens is impaired.

Change in lifestyles

Exposure to stressors can impact on health indirectly by causing changes in our lifestyle choices. For example, having a diagnosis of cancer has been shown to lead to a reduction in healthy behaviours such as exercising and eating fruit and vegetables (Mcbride et al., 2000). Further, having to care for a sick parent or having a high-pressure job can put us under time pressures which can reduce behaviours that may have a positive effect on our health. People who are time pressured may not have the ability to exercise or to cook healthy meals. High levels of stress have also been observed to lead to an increased intake of alcohol (Cooper et al., 1992) and an increase in the number of cigarettes that they smoke (Childs and de Wit, 2010).

Allostatic load

Exposure to chronic stressors leads to consistent activation of the HPA axis, which has a high energy cost as the body continually prepares to face the perceived threat. The result of this cumulative strain on the body is known as **allostatic load,** and exposure to a high allostatic load may mean that over time the body becomes unable to respond appropriately to threat. Korte et al. (2005) notes the metaphor suggested by Marius Tausk to illustrate allostatic load. Tausk compared the body's response to chronic stress to a fireman using water to put out a fire. If a fireman uses too much water, then the water can cause more damage than the flames. Further, if too much water is used, the water pressure may be reduced, leading to a lack of water to fight the fire. Just like the fireman using water to put out a fire, the body's stress responses need to be appropriate or problems may occur. If chronic stress leads to the dysregulation of the HPA axis, then this can impact on our ability to mount an adaptive stress response and can lead to a vulnerability to some diseases (Chrousos, 2009).

Impact on immune system

Biological psychologists have been able to see a direct effect of stress exposure on a number of health markers. Acute, short-term stressors appear to lead to an adaptive increase in immune function. For example, laboratory stressors appear to increase cell numbers in some types of lymphocytes (Kiecolt-Glaser and Glaser, 1992). However, when stressors become more chronic they can have a direct influence on the development and progression of diseases (Sklar and Anisman 1981). For example, an Irwin and Livnat (1987) study found that rats exposed to a number of stressors had suppressed T-cell circulation. Changes in immune function have been reported in people exposed to chronic stressors such as **burnout** at work (Lerman et al., 1999) or natural disasters (Solomon et al., 1997). Jennifer Graham and colleagues (2006) suggest that stress has a similar impact on the immune system as aging, with reduced functioning of the innate immunity system (such as natural killer cells production) and lymphocytes (such as white blood cells) being associated with both stress and aging. Chronic stress has also been shown to impact negatively on other measures of the immune system such as the body's ability to mount a response to a vaccination, wound healing and increases in the development of infectious illnesses.

We also know that exposure to chronic stress can impact on mental health, which in turn appears to influence physical health. For example, Irwin et al. (1990) found that depressed patients in hospital had a 50 per cent reduction in natural killer cell activity. Further maladaptive responses to threats such as a natural disaster have been shown to lead to immune dysregulation. For example, hurricane victims who reported higher levels of intrusive thoughts were found to have lower levels of natural killer cell activity (Ironson et al., 1997). Therefore it would appear that stress can impact on the immune system and that changes in mental health as a result of stress exposure may be one way in which this pathway between stress and illness is mediated.

Genetics

Gregor Mendel, a nineteenth-century monk, was the founding father of genetics. He observed that peas retain the traits of their parent and that their characteristics were not influenced by the environment. This observation led to the discovery that biological information can be passed from two parents to their offspring. Genes are arranged like beads on a string called a chromosome. During human reproduction the offspring receives half of their 46 chromosomes from their mother and half from their father. All the genes an individual carries are known as a person's genotype. However, only a portion of our genotype is expressed and this is known as the **phenotype**.

Some diseases can be caused by a flaw in a person's genetic make-up. For example, Huntington's disease is a dominant gene disorder caused by a mutation on chromosome 4, i.e. if you have the gene, you manifest the disorder (Bates, 2005). However, the links between genetics and health are not always as clear-cut. Genes are thought to have moderate influences on disorders such as schizophrenia, mood disorders and anxiety (Plomin and Kosslyn, 2001). Specific gene mutations such as the *BRCA1* and *BRCA2* in breast cancer have now being identified.

In recent years a new field of epigenetics has emerged. Epigenetics is the study of the mechanisms that can switch genes on and off. Research into epigenetics has demonstrated that stressors and/or adverse psychosocial environments can affect gene expression by altering the epigenetic pattern of **DNA methylation** and/or **chromatin structure**. This means that increases in exposure to environmental stressors can cause a change in which genes are expressed, leading to an altered phenotype (Mathews and Janusek, 2011). At this time, however, few studies have been able to establish which components of the immune system can be affected by the epigenetic process.

Prenatal events

One pathway between stress and ill health that has been explored over the past 20 years is the link between the levels of stress that women experience during pregnancy and the health of their infant. Direct links have been established between high levels of stress during pregnancy and an increased likelihood of premature birth (Lobel et al., 2008). Premature births are linked to many negative health outcomes, such as cardiovascular complications and respiratory problems. More recently it has become clear that stress experienced by the mother during pregnancy can have an impact on the unborn children's cognitive and behavioural development. Glover et al. (2010) suggest fetus development can be altered as a result of the stress experienced by the mother, which they term fetal programming. Fetal programming can lead to some changes in the functioning of the child's HPA axis, with high levels of prenatal stress or anxiety being associated with alternated cortisol reactivity in infants' later years. Further, high levels of cortisol experienced prior to birth can lead to learning and attention deficits, anxiety and depressive-like behaviours. For example, King and Laplante (2005) carried out a prospective study on 150 unborn children whose mothers were exposed to a natural disaster – a series of freezing rain storms that affected Southern Quebec in Canada in 1998. The storm caused major devastation, resulting in a high rate of physical injuries, the loss of livelihoods and power shortages. The results of the study suggested that prenatal maternal stress during the storms had a major impact on infant physical functioning as well as having an impact on behavioural and emotional outcomes.

However, the link between maternal stress and infant health is not always easy to ascertain. Weinstock (2008) notes that genetic factors and the postnatal environment can influence the impact of maternal stress on fetal programming. For example, very early life stress can also increase reactivity to stress in later life (Lupien et al., 2009). Children of mothers who are clinically depressed show a risk of heightened activity of the HPA axis (Halligan et al., 2007) as do children who are placed in poor-quality childcare (Vermeer and van IJzendoorn, 2006). Therefore it is very difficult to rule out the postnatal factors and be sure what effect prenatal stress has had on a child. The good news is that the impact of adverse prenatal environments can be reversed in some cases. Gunnar and Quevedo (2007) found that neglected children fostered with a good level of care show normalised glucocorticoid levels after 10 weeks.

Focus on wound healing

Exposure to stress not only leads to a greater likelihood of illness but can also impair recovery for disease and injury. Studies have shown that exposure to acute and to chronic stressors can result in wound healing becoming significantly slower. Studies have found that both the chronic stress of care giving (Kiecolt-Glaser et al., 1995) and the relatively brief stress of academic examinations (Marucha et al., 1998) impede healing.

Critical thinking activity

Evaluating research

Critical thinking focus: analysing and evaluating written text

Key question: *What can Marucha et al.'s (1998) study tell us about wound healing and what are the limitations of the study?*

Read the following paper: Marucha, PT, Kiecolt-Glaser, JK and Favagehi, M (1998) Mucosal wound healing is impaired by examination stress. *Psychosomatic Medicine*, 60 (3), 362–365. A copy of the paper can be found using the following link: http://pni. osumc.edu/KG%20Publications%20%28pdf%29/118.pdf.

What are the benefits of using a small, standardised wound compared to examining healing times in a more naturalistic way such as after an injury or surgery?

Are there any other methodologies that could have been used to find the same results?

At the end of the paper the authors suggest that the study findings have important implications for surgical recovery. What could the implications of the study be on post-surgery care?

Critical thinking review

Philip Marucha and colleagues in their 1998 study show that wound healing takes around 40 per cent longer during times of stress (just before a major exam) compared to a less stressful time, in this case during the summer holidays. The authors highlight changes in the circulating level of an important factor in wound healing (interleukin–1), which was much lower during the exam period. Further, using photographs of the wounds they were able to monitor how quickly the wound healed.

One of the strengths of the experimental design adopted is that all participants in the study were given the same standardised 3.5mm wide by 1.5 mm deep wound, which was inflicted in the same location using the same method. By creating standardised wounds the researchers were able to examine how long a wound takes to heal between the two different time points. Further, the wound was small and healed quickly and so a repeated measures design could be undertaken. It is unlikely that a repeated measures design could be used if more naturalistic wounds were used as people are unlikely to injure themselves in the same manner twice or undergo the same surgery on two different occasions. In addition, comparisons are more difficult to make if the wounds are not standardised.

The effect of stress on disease progression or recovery from illness can be measured in many ways. People can undertake questionnaires to relate their levels of perceived stress and then a number of health outcome measures can be examined. For example, researchers have looked at how self-reported stress levels impact on cancer progression, or recovery from surgery. However, the Marucha et al. (1998) study benefits from having one uniform outcome measure (rate of wound healing) that is clearly defined and can be assessed over a short period of time. When researchers look at outcome measures associated with cancer patients, the outcome measures are much more complex (mortality, frequency of relapse, quality of life), and some of the outcomes need to be monitored for extended periods of time.

The study findings do have some implications for post-surgery recovery. Psychological intervention that can reduce stress might improve recovery rates. If we can reduce the amount of stress experienced by patients immediately after an operation, patients may recover faster, have shorter stays in hospital and have a reduced chance of post-operative complications.

Mediators

Although some pathways between stress and illness have been explored, the impact that environmental stressors have on people has been shown to vary, and research into factors that can mediate the negative effects of stress is important. In the section below the mediating impact of two factors – personality traits and levels of social support – are discussed.

Personality

Trait personality characteristics have been suggested as one possible mediator that can alter the impact of stress on health. In 2001, Deborah Danner and colleagues at the University of Kentucky examined whether having a positive or negative outlook on life can affect your life expectancy. In their study Danner et al. (2001) reviewed short autobiographies written by young nuns before they entered the Sisters of Notre Dame religious congregation in the USA. Danner and her research team reviewed the autobiographies and then divided the nuns into those with a positive outlook (such as Example 1) and those with a more negative emotional outlook (Example 2).

Example 1 (high positive emotion): God started my life off well by bestowing upon me a grace of inestimable value . . . The past year which I have spent as a candidate studying at Notre Dame College has been a very happy one. Now I look forward with eager joy to receiving the Holy Habit of Our Lady and to a life of union with Love Divine.

Example 2 (low positive emotion): I was born on September 26, 1909, the eldest of seven children, five girls and two boys . . . My candidate year was spent in the Motherhouse, teaching Chemistry and Second Year Latin at Notre Dame Institute. With God's grace, I intend to do my best for our Order, for the spread of religion and for my personal sanctification.

The results of Danner et al.'s (2001) study show that positive emotional content in early-life autobiographies was strongly related to age of death. Nuns assessed as having more positive emotional content in their autobiographies were found to have had a longer life. The study therefore highlights that how we approach life can have an impact on our life expectancy. Figure 10.3 illustrates the association between the amount of positive emotion in nuns' autobiographies at age 22 and their longevity.

Another personality characteristic that has been found to impact on health is a person's level of optimism. Optimistic people generally experience daily events in a more positive way and have a

Figure 10.3: *Quartile rankings of the number of positive emotional sentences in autobiographies written by nuns in early life and the probability of survival in late life for 180 participants in Danner et al.'s study (2001)*

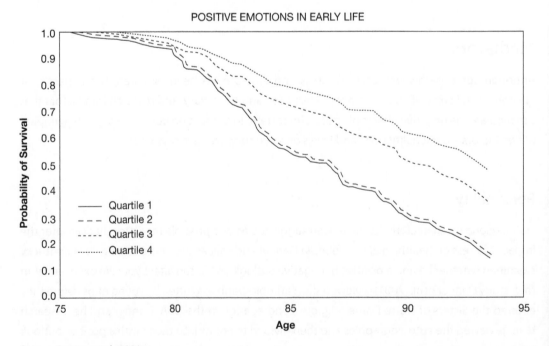

Source: Danner et al., 2001.

global expectation that life will be positive compared to pessimists (Scheier and Carver, 1987). Rasmussen et al. (2009) in a meta-review of 83 studies found that optimism was a significant predictor of positive physical health outcomes. Mika Kivimäki and colleagues (2005) explored the beneficial effects of optimism on the health of 5,007 employees after they had experienced a major life event such as the death or severe illness of a family member. They found those staff members who were more optimistic in their outlook took fewer sick days than their more pessimistic colleagues. One reason why people high in optimism may have better health is that they have better immune functioning. Segerstrom et al. (1998) found that optimists had higher numbers of helper T cells, and more natural killer cell, compared to their more pessimistic colleagues. Segerstrom et al. (1998) suggested that the enhanced immune function found in optimists was due to the more positive way in which they coped with stressors, as they experienced fewer negative moods and undertook more adaptive health behaviours. However, high levels of optimism are not always good for health. If people have unrealistic optimism they may not be interested in reducing behaviours that pose a health risk, such as smoking, as they believe that it is unlikely they will suffer the negative consequences (Weinstein, 1982).

In addition to the more general personality characteristics of emotional outlook and level of optimism, psychologists are also interested in some established personality types. Five main personality types, sometimes known as the 'Big 5' have been identified and are thought to be universally present in both Western and non-Western cultures. These are:

- neuroticism – feelings of anxiety and negative emotions compared to being cool, calm and collected;

- extraversion – being outgoing and being the 'life and soul' of the party compared to being timid and quiet in social settings;

- conscientiousness – being organised and likely to follow rules compared to being impulsive and chaotic;

- agreeableness – being trusting and easygoing compared to being distrustful and independent;

- openness to experience – being open to new ideas and feelings compared to being narrow in your outlook.

In the past, psychologists have tried to link personality types to the likelihood of a person becoming ill. For example, Friedman and Rosenman (1959) defined people who had lower agreeableness and higher neuroticism as having a 'Type A' personality and suggested that those with 'Type A' would be more likely to develop coronary heart disease. Other studies have shown that disease progression can be affected by a person's personality type. For example, Mols et al. (2012) suggested that cancer patients with a Type D personality – defined as the *tendency to experience negative emotions and to inhibit self expression* (Denollet et al., 2006, p970) – may have a poorer quality of life. Their study looked at 3,080 cancer survivors and assessed quality of life and mental health up to ten years post-diagnosis. They found that cancer survivors with a Type D personality are at an increased risk of reporting a poor quality of life and mental health problems.

Personality factors may impact on people's health status by mediating how the person deals with environmental stressors. Some personality traits may lead to a more adaptive response to stress. However, a person's personality type may impact on health in other ways. For example, a patient higher in conscientiousness may have more mental resources to tolerate treatments. Or an extravert may stop taking medication if the medication makes them so drowsy that they cannot take part in social activities. What is clear is that if personality traits can affect illness, onset and progression interventions that take personality characteristics into account will lead to better patient outcomes. For example, people with a more pessimistic outlook on life may need additional support during treatment for a life-threatening illness.

Social support

Social support has been shown to have a powerful influence on mental and physical health. Studies indicate that people with spouses, friends and family members who provide psychological and material resources are in better health than those with fewer positive social relationships. Further, **epidemiological studies** suggest that people with lower levels of social support have higher mortality rates, especially from conditions such as cardiovascular disease (Barth et al., 2010) and cancer (Pinquart and Duberstein, 2010).

Social support can be divided into two main forms.

- *Informal social support*: this type of social support refers to personal networks of family and friends who can help out in practical and emotional ways.

- *Formal social support*: this type of social support refers to the support that can be gained from paid professionals such as social workers or doctors, or from social and community structures such as schools and churches.

Social support can also be divided into:

- perceived support – the perception that support is available if required;

- received support – physical and emotional support that is exchanged within a supportive network of friends and family or from formal social support resources.

One theory suggests that social support has a beneficial effect on health and well-being as it acts as a 'buffer', protecting people from negative events (Cohen and Wills, 1985). Kamarck et al. (1990) found that having a friend present during exposure to a psychological stressor (a simulated job interview) resulted in less cardiovascular reactivity. In another study, participants undertaking a debate on a controversial topic were found to have lower blood pressure if someone was present to give them support during the discussion (Gerin et al., 1992). The importance of social support in helping people to cope with real-world stressors has also been observed in studies looking at **occupational strain**. Regehr (2005) found that informal social support networks were very important in helping paramedics to cope with stressful incidents at work. One paramedic reported: *I have the luxury of having a spouse at home . . . She understands my job well, so if all else was to fail at work, I know I could still go home and I've got a support mechanism there*. Social support has also been found to be important in helping people to deal with acute real-world stressors. Ren and colleagues (1999) found that people with better social support networks before and after exposure to a traumatic event had better health outcomes 12 months later.

Disruption in social support networks has been shown to have a negative impact on health. Lonely students during exams, for example, have been found to have lower NK cell activity compared to their non-lonely peers (Kiecolt-Glaser et al., 1984). Conflict within a close relationship has also been shown to impact negatively on the immune system. For example, wound healing has been found to be impaired in married couples who showed higher levels of conflict (Kiecolt-Glaser et al., 2005). These findings highlight how stressful life events, such as divorce or moving house, can impact on health.

In a stress situation, social support appears to help people appraise the situation as being less threatening, so physiological responses such as increases in blood pressure are not as marked (Sarason et al., 1990). High levels of social support during times of stress also seem to lead to engagement in more positive coping strategies. For example, students with higher levels of social support have been found to be less likely to turn to alcohol to help them cope with exam stress (Steptoe et al., 1996). High levels of social support have also been found to aid recovery from illness and slow down disease progression. People suffering from cardiovascular disease have a lower incidence of depression and better health outcomes if they have good social support networks (Frasure-Smith et al., 2000). Cancer patients also appear to benefit from good social support, with a decreased risk of their cancer reoccurring (Helgeson et al., 1998). Cohen and Janicki-Deverts (2009) suggest that social support has a beneficial effect on health by reducing the stress associated with having a potentially fatal disease.

When assessing the benefits of mediating factors, such as social support, on health, it is important to implement a good experimental design (Cohen and Janicki-Deverts, 2009). It could be argued that lower levels of social support are found in people suffering from serious illness as the illness reduces their ability to maintain their social support networks. This observation highlights the important of **prospective studies**. Studies need to assess people's levels of social support prior to stressor exposure and illness onset. In addition, factors such as age, sex, ethnicity and socio-economic status can impact on both social support levels and health status so they need to be taken into consideration in any studies examining the link between health and stress.

Interventions

Biological psychologists have shown that levels of stress experienced can impact on a person's health. Further, the impact of stress on health can be mediated by factors such as outlook on life or a person's level of social support. Psychologists have therefore argued that interventions that help people to reappraise stressors might also have a positive effect on health outcomes. Psychosocial interventions are normally undertaken after someone has been diagnosed with a serious illness. A diagnosis of cancer, for example, can be a traumatic event that can cause persistent distress (Norton et al., 2005) and can cause the immune system to function less well (Thornton et al., 2007), so interventions that address mood problems, such as anxiety and depression, may not only improve a person's quality of life but also improve their health. For example, Carlson and colleagues (2001) showed that a mindfulness meditation-based stress reduction programme (a mix of meditation, yoga and the body-mind connection training) greatly improved quality of life in seriously ill patients. The participants undertook the training for 1.5 hours each week for seven weeks, plus home study. The results indicated less mood disturbance and fewer symptoms of stress, and these improvements were maintained at the six-month follow-up. Other **psychotherapeutic interventions**, such music therapy, have also been shown to boost levels of salivary immunoglobulin A, a marker of immune function (Burns et al., 2001).

Problems evaluating psychosocial interventions

Assessing the impact of psychosocial interventions on health outcomes is difficult because of the complex methodological issues that need to be considered. In 2006, Nicole Culos-Reed and colleagues completed a pilot study looking at the benefits of yoga for breast cancer survivors. The pilot study indicated that cancer survivors may benefit from undertaking yoga exercises. However, the study does have a number of methodological issues that should be taken into account when considering the findings.

Critical thinking activity

Developing scientific thinking

Critical thinking focus: critical thinking

Key question: *What are the methodological problems associated with evaluating the benefits of psychosocial interventions for health conditions?*

Read the following paper:

Culos-Reed, SN, Carlson, LE, Daroux, LM and Hately-Aldous, S (2006) A pilot study of yoga for breast cancer survivors: physical and psychological benefits.

Psycho-Oncology, 15 (10), 891–897. You can download a copy of the paper from the following URL: https://people.ucalgary.ca/~lcarlso/Yoga%20PON%20Culos-Reed.pdf.

Now try to answer the following questions.

- Do you think that the yoga intervention would work for all cancer sufferers?

- What are the problems associated with comparing the results of this current study with other studies that have assessed the impact of psychosocial interventions?

- How could the researchers improve the design of the study based on your observations of the design of the pilot study?

Critical thinking review

The findings of the study by Nicole Culos-Reed and colleagues is very encouraging as it suggests a simple, low-cost intervention such as yoga classes can have an impact on physical health as well as quality of life and emotional well-being. However, although the results of the study are promising, it has to be remembered that in this pilot study the number of cancer survivors taking part is quite small. Further, the experimental group consisted mainly of female survivors of breast cancer, so the results are difficult to generalise to male cancer survivors and to survivors of other illnesses. In addition, the intervention may be beneficial only to people who enjoy yoga. The benefits of this type of psychosocial intervention may not be evident for people who dislike group exercise classes, for example.

Researchers do face a number of problems when comparing the benefits of different psychosocial interventions. For a start there are many different types of psychosocial interventions, from teaching breathing techniques to support group attendance to walking in the countryside. In addition, even if two studies assess the benefits of the same intervention, the way in which the interventions are administered may differ. For example, in the current study cancer survivors undertook a seven-week practitioner-led yoga course. Other studies that examine the benefits of yoga might give participants a yoga video or a book for unmonitored home study, or participants might have a greater or smaller number of yoga classes. Other problems that make comparisons between interventions difficult are the number of outcome measures that could be used. In the current study the authors have a number of physical outcomes measures as well as some emotional well-being measures. Other researchers might choose to measure the impact of an intervention on a specific part of the immune system or use a longer-term outcome measure, such as cancer reoccurrence rates.

> The authors could improve on this pilot study by using a larger and more diverse population of cancer survivors. For example, the participants in the current pilot study are predominantly females, so a future study could include more male participants to examine if similar beneficial effects of yoga are seen in males. In addition, the intervention was very short (seven weeks), and the effects were only monitored immediately on completion of the intervention. It would be interesting to see the benefits of a longer intervention and how long the benefits continued after the intervention stopped.

Future directions

Over the past 30 years there has been a growing acknowledgement that environmental pressures such as exposure to acute and chronic stressors such as work strain have a major impact on our physical health as well as our mental health. In the future, techniques may be developed that identify people who are under chronic levels of strain and offer them preventative psychosocial intervention that reduces stress and so reduces illness.

Can we use stress markers to see who is going to get ill?

Researchers have the ability to monitor our stress levels in many ways. We can use self-report questionnaires in order to note how many stressors we have been exposed to. Questionnaires that assess the number of daily hassles (such as interpersonal conflicts) or recent major life events (such as moving house or death of a loved one) are frequently used. Other measures might ask us about our general level of perceived stress or how stressful we have found certain stressors or situations. The problem with these subjective measures is that we have no way of knowing if we are at a point where our physiology has started to be compromised by exposure to the stressors. Further measures used to assess stress reactivity, such as measuring circulating cortisol levels in saliva or blood, only give you a measure of how the body is reacting at that moment (Russell et al., 2012).

However, new technologies are currently being developed that allow us to analyse whether the effect of longer-term stress exposure is having an impact on our physiology. One new method that has been developed in the last few years is the ability to measure the levels of cortisol from hair samples. Unlike assessing cortisol in saliva or blood, the cortisol laid down in people's hair gives an objective physiological measure of a person's stress reactivity over the past months (or years if the hair is longer). Hair cortisol has been shown to predict illness. Steudte et al. (2011) found that cortisol in hair was higher in traumatised Ugandan refugees with post-traumatic stress disorder (PTSD) compared to those who did not go on to develop PTSD. More recently, Pereg et al. (2010) found that patients admitted to hospital as a result of a heart attack were more likely to have high hair cortisol levels for the three months prior to the heart attack than patients in hospital for other reasons. This raises the interesting possibility of using hair samples to assess people's stress levels and predicting their likelihood of ill-health.

Preventative psychosocial interventions

Just as today we might have a flu vaccination to stop us catching this year's winter flu, in the future we might be prescribed a psychosocial intervention designed to reduce our stress levels and prevent the onset of illness. It may be that the monitoring of chronic stress markers, such as hair cortisol levels, could identify people who are at high risk of developing impairment in their immune functioning and so risk ill-health. People showing evidence of high chronic stress levels may then be recommended to undertake a psychosocial intervention to reduce stress levels and so prevent illness.

More research is needed into the type of interventions that could reduce stress reactivity and improve health. Some intervention based on current research could be developed. For example, Ward Thompson and colleagues (2012) found that exposure to green spaces correlated with lower levels of self-reported stress and healthy daily cortisol patterns. Other psychosocial interventions that have been shown to reduce stress levels include couples performing head and shoulder massages on each other (Holt-Lunstad et al., 2008) as well as activities such as Tai Chi, brisk walking, meditation and reading (Jin, 1992).

Critical thinking activity

Developing scientific thinking

Critical thinking focus: critical and creative thinking

Key question: *What intervention can reduce stress levels and improve health?*

Although we do not fully understand all the pathways between exposure to stressful events and its impact on health, we do know that people who are exposed to more stressful events have a higher likelihood of becoming ill. Imagine that a local school has noticed that during the exam period a higher number of their students become ill. Using the information in this chapter and other reading you may have completed, identify one psychosocial intervention that you could suggest to the school to reduce the stress levels of students during the exam period. In addition, write a brief summary for the school teachers explaining why you have selected the stress reduction intervention you have chosen and what impact the intervention has been shown to have on health. Remember that you are explaining the information to non-experts so you must keep technical terms to a minimum and explanations simple.

Critical thinking review

This activity helps you assess the suitability of a range of psychosocial interventions to be used with a specific population – in this case, school children. It is important to pick psychosocial interventions that have previously been shown to reduce stress markers that have been linked with physical illness. So you would want to pick an intervention that has been shown in the literature to have an effect not only on emotional well-being but also on markers of physical health, such as the functioning of the immune system.

Some factors that have been shown to impact on how we respond to stress (such as prenatal exposure to stress or personality traits) are not possible to change. Further, you need to select a psychosocial intervention that can be introduced quickly and cheaply, and that is appropriate for school children. For example, enhancing levels of social support for children by introducing lunchtime support groups or running a short course of mindfulness training in the classroom before the exams might be good interventions to select.

This task helps you to develop your written communication skills as you have to put the information into a format that can be understood by non-psychology trained school teachers. The task also involves you applying psychological research to real-world situations.

Skill builder activity

The impact of stress on health and mediating factors

Transferable skill focus: organisational skills and visual communication.

Key question: *How do acute environmental stressors impact on physical health?*

Use the information provided in the chapter to create a **concept map** that shows the impact of acute environmental stressors on one measure of physical health. Also include possible mediators of stress in your visual presentation.

In order to address this task you will need to distinguish between acute and chronic environmental stressors. Then you will need to identify a health marker that is frequently used in the research, such as circulating cortisol levels or natural killer-cell production. Next you will need to identify all the known factors, such as personality, that can modify the impact of the stressor on health.

Skill builder review

This task requires you to extract information from the text and from other reading that you may have done and reorganise it in a visual format. Concept mapping helps you to see logical links between different pieces of research and allows you to develop a clear overview of the research area. You can complete a concept map for chronic stressors or for other health markers if you found this exercise helpful to your learning.

Assignments

1. Discuss the impact of high levels of prenatal stress on infant health.

2. To what extent does the evidence support the suggestion that high levels of environmental stress influence disease progression?

3. Critically discuss the methodological issues that need to be taken into account when assessing the usefulness of psychosocial intervention on health outcomes.

Summary: what you have learned

Now you have finished studying this chapter you should:

- understand how the SAM and HPA systems activate in response to acute stress and how these mechanisms can become dysregulated in the presence of chronic stress;

- understand why stress in important from an evolutionary viewpoint;

- understand the possible pathways that link stress to illness, such as the potential for changes in genetic expression and increases in circulating levels of the stress hormone cortisol;

- understand how the impact of mediators, such as personality traits and social support, can affect how we respond to stressors;

- be able to evaluate critically the methodologies used to explore the link between health and stress;

- understand the limitations in research that assesses psychosocial interventions that reduce stress and improve well-being. These limitations include differences in the participant populations, the types of diseases under investigation, and the length and type of psychosocial intervention used;

– have developed your critical thinking, organisation and communication skills by selecting and writing a summary supporting the use of a psychosocial intervention to help students cope with exam stress. Further, your visual communication and organisation skills will have been developed via the creation of the concept map.

Further reading

Chrousos, GP (2009) Stress and disorders of the stress system. *Nature Reviews. Endocrinology*, 5 (7), 374–381.

This paper gives a detailed review of the cost to the human body of mounting a physiological response to threat.

Cohen, S and Janicki-Deverts, D (2009) Can we improve our physical health by altering our social networks? *Perspectives on Psychological Science*, 4 (4), 375–378.

This paper outlines the key research questions that need to be answered in order to fully explore the link between health and social support.

Danner, DD, Snowdon, DA and Friesen, WV (2001) Positive emotions in early life and longevity: findings from the nun study. *Journal of Personality and Social Psychology*, 80 (5), 804.

Danner and colleagues present an interesting study that explores the link between positive emotion and longevity in a population of North American Catholic nuns.

Lupien, SJ, McEwen, BS, Gunnar, MR and Heim, C (2009) Effects of stress throughout the lifespan on the brain, behaviour and cognition. *Nature Reviews Neuroscience*, 10 (6), 434–445.

This paper examines the impact on the brain of chronic stress experienced during the prenatal period, infancy, childhood, adolescence and adulthood.

Russell, E, Koren, G, Rieder, M and Van Uum, S (2012) Hair cortisol as a biological marker of chronic stress: current status, future directions and unanswered questions. *Psychoneuroendocrinology*, 37 (5), 589–601.

Russell and colleagues discuss the usefulness of hair cortisol in research assessing levels of chronic stress.

Uchino, BN, Bowen, K, Carlisle, M and Birmingham, W (2012) Psychological pathways linking social support to health outcomes: a visit with the 'Ghosts' of research past, present, and future. *Social Science & Medicine*, 74 (7), 949.

This paper reviews studies that have directly tested the psychological mechanisms that might link social support and health.

Glossary

acetylcholine	the first neurotransmitter to have been discovered – it is produced by cholinergic neurons and found in both the central and peripheral nervous systems.
acuity	the precision or sharpness of vision.
adrenal glands	glands found directly above the kidneys in the human body; responsible for the release of certain hormones into the blood supply.
adrenaline	also known as epinephrine – a hormone and a neurotransmitter. Adrenaline is released when people are in stressful situations, and it prepares the body to deal with threats.
afferent	carrying information towards the central nervous system.
agonist	a chemical that triggers responses in a cell by binding to a receptor of the cell.
alexithymia	the inability to consciously experience emotion.
allostatic load	the physiological wear and tear caused by repeated activation of the body's stress responses.
amino acid	an organic compound that is a building block for protein.
amygdala	an almond-shaped area of the brain within the temporal lobe that is believed to govern emotional processing.
anorexia nervosa	an eating disorder most commonly occurring in girls and women, associated with food restriction and a distorted body image.
antagonist	a chemical that blocks a response in the cell caused by an *agonist*.
anterior insular cortex (AI)	part of the cerebral cortex, located deep in the lateral sulcus.
anterograde amnesia	a loss in the ability to encode new memories, most likely to be caused by disease or brain surgery that affects the hippocampus.
anticonvulsant	a drug treatment designed to prevent or treat seizures associated with conditions such as epilepsy.
arcuate fasciculus	bundle of nerve fibres that connects language areas to each other.
attachment	an emotional bond between individuals.

autonomic nervous system (ANS)	involuntary nervous system, controlling visceral functions.
axial section	also called transverse, horizontal, or transaxial plane – divides the brain into superior and inferior parts.
blastocyst	a mass of cells that forms early during development.
bottom-up	a theory that claims that perception relies only on the information contained in the stimulus. This is in contrast to a **top-down** approach to perception.
Broca's area	language area in the frontal lobe of left hemisphere that is active in producing speech.
bulimia nervosa	an eating disorder most commonly occurring in women, associated with binge eating and purging.
burnout	normally related to exhaustion as a result of work pressure, and can lead to problems in both work and home life.
central nervous system (CNS)	the brain and the spinal cord – integrates and coordinates information received from the rest of the body.
cerebral blood flow	the distribution of blood to areas of the brain.
chromatin structure	a combination of DNA and proteins that form the contents of a cell nucleus.
chromosome	a structure made up of DNA and proteins that contain genes and are found in the nucleus of every cell; humans have 46 chromosomes (23 pairs).
cochlear coding	the arrangement of the cochlea whereby low frequency sounds produce maximal stimulation towards the tip of the cochlea, and high frequency sounds produce maximal stimulation towards its base.
concept map	a visual representation of the relationship between two or more key concepts.
contralateral	situated on the opposite side.
convergence	an organisation principle in the retina, where information from more than one receptor cell converges onto one ganglion cell.
convergent evolution	evolutionary processes that independently produce similarities between distant species (e.g. the wings of birds and insects).
coronal section	also known as the frontal plane – divides the brain into ventral and dorsal (or front and back) sections.

cortex	the layered, folded structure of neural tissue, forming the outermost part of the brain – known as the 'thinking' part of the brain.
cortisol	a hormone released by the adrenal glands when the hypothalamic–pituitary–adrenal (HPA) axis is triggered due to exposure to threat.
CT scan	a computerised tomography scan – a series of X-rays showing the structure of parts of the brain or body
dementia	a marked loss of cognitive ability and memory caused by various disorders, such as Alzheimer's disease.
diploid cell	a cell that contains two sets of chromosomes (one from each parent).
DNA	deoxyribonucleic acid – a molecule that contains genetic instructions for proteins needed in the development and growth of an organism.
DNA methylation	within the field of epigenetics this refers to the attachment or substitution of a methyl group to DNA.
dopamine	a neurotransmitter associated with motivation and pleasure.
dopaminergic system	areas that use dopamine as their synaptic transmitter.
duplexity theory of vision	vision is mediated by rod cells at low light levels (e.g. at night), and by cones at higher levels of light (e.g. in the day).
ECG	electrocardiography – the measurement of the electrical activity of the heart, recorded by sensors placed on the skin
EEG	electroencephalography – the recording of brain electrical activity using electrodes placed on the surface of the scalp.
efferent	carrying information away from the central nervous system.
electrophysiology	the study of the electrical activity of the nervous system.
EMG	electromyography – the recording of the electrical activity associated with muscular movements.
emotional stimulus	an object or event that can produce a strong emotional reaction.
endocrine system	cells, tissues and glands that release hormones directly into the bloodstream.
endogenous	substances that are created from within the organism.
enteric nervous system	sub-division of the autonomic nervous system, controlling gastrointestinal processes.

EOG	electrooculography – the recording of the electrical activity associated with eye movements.
epidemiological study	a study that focuses on disease frequencies and potential causes within the human population.
epilepsy	a set of chronic neurologically based medical conditions that cause seizures in the sufferer.
ERP	event-related potential – an analysis technique used with EEG data to measure the timing of brain activity in relation to an external event.
estradiol	the primary form of oestrogen produced by the ovary.
evolutionary fitness	ability to survive and reproduce, passing on genes to the next generation.
exteroceptive	a sensory system that reacts to stimuli from outside the body.
fast adaptors	mechanoreceptors that show adaptation.
fight or flight response	a physiological reaction to danger that prepares the body either to stay and fight or to flee from the threat.
fMRI	functional magnetic resonance imaging – a brain imaging technique used to measure neural activity.
fovea	the area at the centre of the retina that allows for vision of high precision in the centre of the visual field
FOXP2 gene	a gene-encoding protein that is important in speech production.
free-rider	an individual who reaps benefits without paying costs.
function	reason why a trait has evolved; the evolutionary benefits of a trait.
gamete	a sex cell (egg or sperm).
gene	a segment of DNA that is located on a chromosome. Genes act as a set of instructions that allow characteristics to be passed from parents to their offspring.
genetic marker	a sequence of DNA that indicates an increased likelihood of a specific characteristic, trait or event occurring.
genotype	the underlying genetic composition of an individual.
Geschwind's territory	language-related area in the parietal lobule, connecting other brain areas.

glial cell	a cell that maintains the nervous system.
glucocorticoids	a group of corticosteroids (such as cortisol or dexamethasone) produced by the adrenal glands and involved mainly in the metabolism of carbohydrate, protein and fat.
glycogen	a complex carbohydrate used for short-term energy storage.
grey matter	neural tissue found in the brain and spinal cord that contains nerve-cell bodies and nerve fibres. The matter is grey in colour as it does not contain myelin, which gives other areas of neural tissue a white colour.
gyrus	a ridge on the surface of the brain, often surrounded by sulci (see *sulcus*).
haploid cell	a cell that contains one complete set of chromosomes.
hyoid bone	horseshoe-shaped bone in the mid-anterior neck, allowing for speech.
hypothalamic–pituitary–adrenal (HPA) axis	part of the neuroendocrine system that regulates bodily functions such as temperature, immune function and energy use. The HPA axis also plays a major role in helping the body to maintain a response to threat.
hypothalamus	located in the middle of the brain below the thalamus. This cortical area is responsible for the regulation and coordination of many key body functions including the body's response to threat.
inferior parietal lobule	see *Geschwind's territory*.
interoceptive	reacting to stimuli from our internal environments.
interoceptive awareness	awareness of one's bodily states (such as heartbeat, gut sensations).
larynx	the 'voice box', an organ in the neck that is active in breathing and sound production.
lateral sulcus	a fissure that divides frontal and parietal lobes from the temporal lobe.
lip smacking	sound produced by pressing lips together fast, a form of communication used by many primates.
lymph	a clear fluid that contains white blood cells and circulates throughout the lymphatic system. Lymph removes bacteria and some proteins from the tissues and delivers mature lymphocytes into blood system.
macroglia	a constellation of several types of glial cells that maintain the nervous system.

maladaptive behaviour	behaviour that is unhelpful and often counterproductive, whereas adaptive behaviour refers to useful and appropriate behaviour.
mechanoreceptor	a neuron that fires an action potential in response to physical movement.
MEG	magnetoencephalography – recording of the magnetic fields produced by the brain, using sensors placed next to the scalp.
memory consolidation	the process of encoding information from the short-term store into long-term store.
microglia	small glial cells that dispose parts of dead neurons.
microorganism	any organism that is too small to see with the naked eye and so must be viewed under a microscope.
mirror neuron system	neuronal system that 'mirrors' the behaviour of others.
modality	a type of physical energy that can be sensed.
monoamine	a group of neurotransmitters that includes serotonin and dopamine.
MRI	magnetic resonance imaging – a technique to produce detailed pictures of the structure of the brain.
multisensory integration	the study of how signals from the different senses are combined by the brain.
multi-store model of memory	a theoretical model of memory processing suggested by Atkinson and Shiffrin in 1968. It comprises three different memory stores: sensory memory, short-term memory (STM) and long-term memory (LTM).
neurotrophin	protein that regulates the development and maintenance of the nervous system.
nociceptor	somatosensory receptor for pain – free nerve ending that initiates action potentials in the presence of stimuli that cause tissue damage.
non-clinical population	member of the general public who is not suffering from a specific medical condition – whereas a clinical population is a group of people who are suffering from a certain medical condition and are being studied.
obesogenic environment	an environment characterised by widespread availability of inexpensive unhealthy food that contributes to the prevalence of obesity.

occupational strain	a negative physical and/or emotional response to job pressures such as increased workloads or hostile work environments, which can result in physical problems such as hypertension or insomnia.
oxytocin	a neurotransmitter associated with social relationships and bonding.
parasympathetic autonomic nervous system (pANS)	responsible for activities that occur when body is at rest (sexual arousal, tears, digestion, etc).
pathogen	any agent that has the ability to cause disease. The term may relate to viruses, bacteria or fungi.
peripheral nervous system (PNS)	part of the nervous system; consists of nerves from outside of the central nervous system, and connects the central nervous system to other parts of the body.
PET	positron emission tomography. This traces the movement of a radioactive substance in the nervous system, producing detailed pictures about the functional processes in the brain.
phenotype	the expressed, observable physical and behavioural characteristics of an individual, which are part of the underlying genotype.
phonology	branch of linguistics dealing with how sounds are organised in different languages.
phonetics	study of the structural properties of speech sounds.
phylogeny	an evolutionary history of a species.
Prader Willi syndrome	a condition characterised by a constant desire to eat food and motivated by a permanent feeling of hunger.
prospective study	a study that starts at the present time and observes changes within the chosen population over time. Prospective studies within the health psychology field are normally designed to observe who and why healthy people in a population become ill.
proximate explanation	an explanation that looks at HOW something works. In biological psychology, proximate explanations are often dealing with genes, the brain, neurotransmitters and hormones. Proximate explanations are about things that happen in the lifetime of an individual, often within the body of an individual.

psychosocial factors	psychological and social influences that can affect how a person functions.
psychotherapeutic interventions	a set of non-medication-based treatments that use psychological techniques in order to treat mental health disorders.
qualia	the subjective, felt aspects of our mental lives.
receptive field	the region of space in which stimulation will change the firing rate of a neuron.
receptor organ	an organ that contains receptor cells that respond to stimulation (for example, the eyes, the ears).
recursive grammar	the embedding of clauses within sentences.
reticular formation	region of neural networks in the brainstem.
rodent model	research on a rodent, often using invasive techniques that could not be used in humans. The results are used in speculating the causes for human behaviour.
sagittal section	vertical plane that divides the brain into left and right halves.
SCR	skin conductance response – the recording of the electrical activity of the skin, which varies in its moisture level, providing a measure of sympathetic nervous system activity.
semantics	branch of linguistics interested in the meaning of words.
sensory modality	a way of sensing associated with sound, vision, touch, smell or taste.
serotonin	a neurotransmitter with a wide range of functions.
severe language impairment (SLI)	difficulties in understanding, processing and producing language.
sex hormones	a set of hormones such as oestrogen and testosterone that are responsible for the growth or maintenance of the reproductive organs, the development of secondary sex characteristics, and sexual behaviour.
sign language	language that is produced with signs, but still follows a grammatical rule.
single-unit recording	the recording of the electrical activity of a single neuron in the brain, using a microelectrode.
slow adaptors	mechanoreceptors that show no adaptation.

social cognition	processes involved in the encoding, storage and retrieval of social information.
somatic nervous system (SNS)	voluntary nervous system that controls, for example, movements of the body.
spatial resolution	the precision with which a spatial position can measured.
stressor	a stimulus, such as an event or situation, that induces a physiological stress response.
sulcus	a depression, or a furrow, on the surface of the brain.
Sylvian fissure	see *lateral sulcus*.
sympathetic autonomic nervous system (sANS)	prepares the body for 'fight or flight' action.
syntax	the specific structuring of words and sentences.
temporal resolution	the precision with which the time that an event happened can be measured.
testosterone	a sex hormone that exerts both organisational and activational effects.
thalamocortical system	reciprocal connections between thalamus and cortex.
theory of mind	the ability to understand other individuals as intentional creatures.
top-down	an approach to perception that emphasises the importance of contextual factors (expectations, goals, knowledge) in the process of perception, in contrast to a bottom-up approach.
topographic mapping	the ordered projection of cells from the receptor organ to the brain.
transduction	the process of converting a physical stimulus into neural signals.
traumatic memory	emotional memories for life events that have been traumatic, such as car accidents or exposure to natural disasters.
ultimate question	a question that deals with the evolutionary functions of a trait or a behaviour. What reproductive/survival advantages did the trait have for ancestral humans?
vasopressin	a hormone associated with reabsorption of water and blood pressure.

visual agnosia   an impairment in object recognition.

Wernicke's area   language area in the left cerebral cortex that is active in understanding speech.

working memory model   a theoretical model of short-term memory suggested by Baddeley and Hitch (1974).

zygote   two gametes (sperm and egg) joining together to form an initial cell during sexual reproduction.

References

Acevedo, BP, Aron, A, Fisher, HE and Brown, LL (2012) Neural correlates of marital satisfaction and well-being: reward, empathy, and affect. *Clinical Neuropsychiatry*, 9, 20–31.

Adolphs, R (2002a) Neural systems for recognizing emotion. *Current Opinions in Neurobiology*, 12, 169–177.

Adolphs, R (2002b) Recognizing emotion from facial expressions: psychological and neurological mechanisms. *Behavioral and Cognitive Neuroscience Reviews*, 1, 21–61.

Adolphs, R, Tranel, D, Damasio, H and Damasio, A (1994) Impaired recognition of emotion in facial expressions following bilateral damage to the human amygdala. *Nature*, 372, 669–672.

Adolphs, R, Tranel, D, Hamann, S, Young, AW, Calder, AJ, Phelps, EA, Anderson, A, Lee, GP and Damasio, AR (1999) Recognition of facial emotion in nine individuals with bilateral amygdala damage. *Neuropsychologia*, 37, 1111–1117.

Adolphs, R, Tranel, D and Damasio, AR (2003) Dissociable neural systems for recognizing emotions. *Brain and Cognition*, 52, 61–69.

Aiello, AE, Coulborn, RM, Perez, V and Larson, EL (2008) Effect of hand hygiene on infectious disease risk in the community setting: a meta-analysis. *American Journal of Public Health*, 98, 1372–1381.

Alleva, E and Santucci, D (2001) Psychosocial vs 'physical' stress situations in rodents and humans: role of neurotrophins. *Physiology & Behavior*, 73, 313–320.

Al-Shawaf, L and Lewis, DMG (2013) Exposed intestines and contaminated cooks: sex, stress, and satiation predict disgust sensitivity. *Personality and Individual Differences*, 54, 698–702.

Ambadar, Z, Schooler, JW and Cohn, JF (2005) Deciphering the enigmatic face: The importance of facial dynamics in interpreting subtle facial expressions. *Psychological Science*, 16, 403–410.

Anand, BK and Brobeck, JR (1951) Localization of a 'feeding center' in the hypothalamus of the rat. *Proceedings of the Society for Experimental Biology and Medicine*, 77, 323–324.

Archer, J (2004) Sex differences in aggression in real-world settings: a meta-analytic review. *Review of General Psychology*, 8, 291–322.

Archer, J (2006) Testosterone and human aggression: an evaluation of the challenge hypothesis. *Neuroscience and Biobehavioral Reviews*, 30, 319–345.

Armfield, JM (2006) Cognitive vulnerability: a model of the etiology of fear. *Clinical Psychology Review*, 26, 746–768.

Atkinson, RC and Shiffrin, RM (1968) Human memory: a proposed system and its control processes. *The Psychology of Learning and Motivation*, 2, 89–195.

Avena, NM, Rada, P, Moise, N and Hoebel, BG (2006) Sucrose sham feeding on a binge schedule releases accumbens dopamine repeatedly and eliminates the acetylcholine satiety response. *Neuroscience*, 139, 813–820.

Avena, NM, Rada, P and Hoebel, BG (2008) Evidence for sugar addiction: behavioral and neurochemical effects of intermittent, excessive sugar intake. *Neuroscience and Biobehavioral Reviews*, 32, 20–39.

Ayas, NT, White, DP, Al-Delaimy, WK, Manson, JE, Stampfer, MJ, Speizer, FE, Patel, S and Hu, FB (2003) A prospective study of self-reported sleep duration and incident diabetes in women. *Diabetes Care*, 26, 380–384.

Baars, BJ, Banks, WP and Newman, J (eds) (2003a) *Essential sources in the scientific study of consciousness*. Cambridge, MA: MIT Press.

Baars, BJ, Ramsoy, T and Laureys, S (2003b) Brain, conscious experience, and the observing self. *Trends in Neuroscience*, 26, 671–675.

Baddeley, AD and Hitch, G (1974) Working memory. In Bower, GH (ed.) *The psychology of learning and motivation: advances in research and theory* (pp47–89). New York: Academic Press.

Baker, RR and Bellis, MA (1995) *Human sperm competition: copulation, masturbation and infidelity.* London: Chapman & Hall.

Bancroft, J (2002) The medicalization of female sexual dysfunction: the need for caution. *Archives of Sexual Behavior*, 31, 451–455.

Bard, P (1934) On emotional expression after decortication with some remarks on certain theoretical views: Part I. *Psychological Review*, 41, 309–329.

Bartels, A and Zeki, S (2004) The neural correlates of maternal and romantic love. *NeuroImage*, 21, 1155–1166.

Barth, J, Schneider, S and von Känel, R (2010) Lack of social support in the etiology and the prognosis of coronary heart disease: a systematic review and meta-analysis. *Psychosomatic Medicine*, 72, 229–238.

Bartolomei, F, Barbeau, E, Gavaret, M, Guye, M, McGonigal, A, Regis, J and Chauvel, P (2004) Cortical stimulation study of the role of rhinal cortex in déjà vu and reminiscence of memories. *Neurology*, 63 (5), 858–864.

Bartz, J A, Zaki, J, Bolger, N and Oschner, KN (2011) Social effects of oxytocin in humans: context and person matter. *Trends in Cognitive Sciences*, 15, 301–309.

Bates, GP (2005) The molecular genetics of Huntington disease – a history. *Nature Reviews Genetics*, 6, 766–773.

Baxter, MG and Murray, EA (2002) The amygdala and reward. *Nature Review Neuroscience*, 3, 564–573.

Becker, JB (2009) Sexual differentiation of motivation: a novel mechanism? *Hormones and Behavior*, 55, 646–654.

Berger, C, Mehrhoff, FW, Beier, KM and Meinck, HM (2003) Sexual delinquency and Parkinson's disease. *Der Nervenarzt*, 74, 370–375.

Bergh, C, Eklund, T, Soderstcn, P and Nordin, C (1997) Altered dopamine function in pathological gambling. *Psychological Medicine*, 27, 473–475.

Bergman, TJ (2013) Speech-like vocalized lip-smacking in geladas. *Current Biology*, 23, R268–R269.

Bernstein, IL (1999) Taste aversion learning: a contemporary perspective. *Nutrition*, 15, 229–234.

Bernstein, IS, Gordon, TP and Rose, RM (1983) The interaction of hormones, behavior and social context in non-human primates. In Svare, BR (ed.) *Hormones and Aggressive Behavior* (pp 535–561). Plenum: New York.

Berridge, KC (1996) Food reward: brain substrates of wanting and liking. *Neuroscience and Biobehavioural Reviews*, 20, 1–25.

Berridge, KC and Kringelbach, ML (2008) Affective neuroscience of pleasure: reward in humans and animals. *Psychopharmacology*, 199, 457–480.

Berridge, KC and Kringelbach, ML (2013) Neuroscience of affect: brain mechanisms of pleasure and displeasure. *Current Opinion in Neurobiology*, 23, 294–303.

Berridge, KC and Robinson, TE (1998) What is the role of dopamine in reward: hedonic impact, reward learning, or incentive salience? *Brain Research Reviews*, 28, 309–369.

Berwick, RC, Hauser, M and Tattersall, I (2013) Neanderthal language? Just-so stories take center stage. *Frontiers in Psychology*, 4, 671.

Beveridge, TJ, Gill, KE, Hanlon, CA and Porrino, LJ (2008) Parallel studies of cocaine-related neural and cognitive impairment in humans and monkeys. *Philosophical Transactions of the Royal Society of London Series B: Biological Sciences*, 363, 3257–3266.

Bickerton, D (1990) *Language and species*. Chicago, IL: University of Chicago Press.

Blanco, C, Hasin, DS, Petry, N, Stinson, FS and Grant, BF (2006) Sex differences in subclinical and DSM-IV pathological gambling: results from the national epidemiological survey on alcohol and related conditions. *Psychological Medicine*, 36, 943–953.

Boggiano, MM, Chandler, PC, Viana, JB, Oswald, KD, Maldonado, CR and Wauford, PK (2005) Combined dieting and stress evoke exaggerated responses to opioids in binge-eating rats. *Behavioural Neuroscience*, 119, 1207–1214.

Bolhuis, JJ, Okanoya, K and Scharff, C (2010) Twitter evolution: converging mechanisms in birdsong and human speech. *Nature Reviews Neuroscience*, 11, 747–759.

Bonanno, GA, Wortman, CB, Lehman, DR, Tweed, RG, Haring, M, Sonnega, J, Carr, D and Nesse, RM (2002) Resilience to loss and chronic grief: a prospective study from preloss to 18-months postloss. *Journal of Personality and Social Psychology*, 83, 1150–1164.

Bonson, KR, Grant, SJ, Contoreggi, CS, Links, JM, Metcalfe, J, Weyl, HL, Kurian, V, Ernst, M and London, ED (2002) Neural systems and cue-induced cocaine craving. *Neuropsychopharmacology*, 26, 376–386.

Book, AS, Starzyk, KB and Quinsey, VL (2001) The relationship between testosterone and aggression: a meta-analysis. *Aggression and Violent Behavior*, 6, 579–599.

Borg, JS, Lieberman, D and Kiehl, KA (2008) Infection, incest and iniquity: investigating the neural correlates of disgust and morality. *Journal of Cognitive Neuroscience*, 20, 1529–1546.

Bowers, JM, Perez-Pouchoulen, M, Edwards, NS and McCarthy, MM (2013) FOXP2 mediates sex differences in ultrasonic vocalization by rat pups and directs order of maternal retrieval. *The Journal of Neuroscience*, 33, 3276–3283.

Bradley, MM, Codispoti, M, Sabatinelli, D and Lang, PJ (2001) Emotion and motivation II: sex differences in picture processing. *Emotion*, 1, 300–319.

Breiter, HC and Rosen, BR (1999) Functional magnetic resonance imaging of brain reward circuitry in the human. *Annals of New York Academy of Sciences*, 877, 523–547.

Brewer, G and Hendrie, CA (2011) Evidence to suggest that copulatory vocalizations in women are not a reflexive consequence of orgasm. *Archives of Sexual Behavior*, 40, 559–564.

Brody, AL, Olmstead, RE, London, ED, Farahi, J, Meyer, JH, Grossman, P, Lee, GS, Huang, J, Hahn, EL and Mandelkern, MA (2004) Smoking-induced ventral striatum dopamine release. *American Journal of Psychiatry*, 16, 1211–1218.

Bruce, V and Young, A (1986) Understanding face recognition. *British Journal of Psychology*, 77, 305–327.

Bruck, JN (2013) Decades-long social memory in bottlenose dolphins. *Proceedings of the Royal Society B: Biological Sciences*, 280, 1768.

Bruer, JT (1998) Brain and child development: time for some critical thinking. *Public Health Reports*, 113, 388–397.

Brunner, R, Schaefer, D, Hess, K, Parzer, P, Resch, F and Schwab, S (2006) Effect of high-dose cortisol on memory functions. *Annals of the New York Academy of Sciences*, 1071 (1), 434–437.

Burek, MJ and Oppenheim, RW (1996) Programmed cell death in the developing nervous system. *Brain Pathology*, 6 (4), 427–446.

Burns, SJ, Harbuz, MS, Hucklebridge, F and Bunt, L (2001) A pilot study into the therapeutic effects of music therapy at a cancer help center. *Alternative Therapies in Health and Medicine*, 7, 48.

Buss, C, Wolf, OT, Witt, J and Hellhammer, DH (2004) Autobiographic memory impairment following acute cortisol administration. *Psychoneuroendocrinology*, 29 (8), 1093–1096.

Buss, DM (1988a) From vigilance to violence: tactics of mate retention in American undergraduates. *Ethology and Sociobiology*, 9, 291–317.

Buss, DM (1988b) Love acts: the evolutionary biology of love. In Sternberg, R and Barnes, M (eds) *The psychology of love* (pp100–118). New Haven, CT: Yale University Press.

Buss, DM (2000) *The dangerous passion: why jealousy is as necessary as love or sex*. London: Bloomsbury.

Buss, DM, Larsen, RJ, Westen, D and Semmelroth, J (1992) Sex differences in jealousy: evolution, physiology and psychology. *Psychological Science*, 3, 251–255.

Buss, DM, Shackelford, T K, Kirkpatrick, L A, Chloe, J, Hasegawa, T and Bennett, K (1999) Jealousy and beliefs about infidelity: tests of competing hypotheses in the United States, Korea, and Japan. *Personal Relationships*, 6, 125–150.

Buzsaki, G (2006) *Rhythms of the Brain*. Oxford: Oxford University Press.

Cabanac, M, Cabanac, AJ and Parent, A (2009) The emergence of consciousness in phylogeny. *Behavioural Brain Research*, 198, 267–272.

Cacioppo, JT, Berntson, GG, Larsen, JT, Poehlmann, KM and Ito, TA (2000) The psychophysiology of emotion. *Handbook of Emotions*, 2, 173–191.

Cahill, L and McGaugh, JL (1998) Mechanisms of emotional arousal and lasting declarative memory. *Trends in Neurosciences*, 21 (7), 294–299.

Calder, AJ, Young, AW, Rowland, D, Perrett, DI, Hodges, JR and Etcoff, NL (1996) Facial emotion recognition after bilateral amygdala damage: differentially severe impairment of fear. *Cognitive Neuropsychology*, 13, 699–745.

Canli, T, Zhao, Z, Brewer, J, Gabrieli, JD and Cahill, L (2000) Event-related activation in the human amygdala associates with later memory for individual emotional experience. *Journal of Neuroscience*, 20 (19), RC99–1.

Canli, T, Desmond, JE, Zhao, Z and Gabrieli, JD (2002) Sex differences in the neural basis of emotional memories. *Proceedings of the National Academy of Sciences of the United States of America*, 99, 10789–10794.

Cannas, A, Solla, P, Floris, G, Tacconi, P, Loi, D, Marcia, E and Marrosu, MG (2006) Hypersexual behaviour, frotteurism, and delusional jealousy in a young Parkinsonian patient during dopaminergic therapy with pergolide: a rare case of iatrogenic paraphilia. *Progress in Neuropharmacology & Biological Psychiatry*, 30, 1539–1541.

Cannon, WB (1915) *Bodily changes in pain, hunger, fear and rage*. New York: D Appleton & Co.

Cannon, WB (1927) The James-Lange theory of emotions: a critical examination and an alternative theory. *The American Journal of Psychology*, 39, 106–124.

Cannon, WB and Washburn, AL (1912) An explanation of hunger. *American Journal of Physiology – Legacy Content*, 29, 441–451.

Carlson, LE, Ursuliak, Z, Goodey, E, Angen, M and Speca, M (2001) The effects of mood and symptoms of stress in cancer outpatients: 6-month follow-up. *Supportive Care in Cancer*, 9, 112–123.

Carter, CS (1992) Oxytocin and sexual behaviour. *Neuroscience and Biobehavioural Reviews*, 16, 131–144.

Case, TI, Repacholi, BM and Stevenson, RJ (2006) My baby doesn't smell as bad as yours: the plasticity of disgust. *Evolution and Human Behavior*, 27, 357–365.

Caspi, A and Moffitt, T E (2006) Gene–environment interactions in psychiatry: joining forces with neuroscience. *Nature Reviews Neuroscience*, 7, 583–590.

Castellanos, EH, Charboneau, E, Dietrich, MS, Park, S, Bradley, BP, Mogg, K and Cowan, RL (2009) Obese adults have visual attention bias for food cue images: evidence for altered reward system function. *International Journal of Obesity*, 33, 1063–1073.

Catani, M and Jones, DK (2005) Perisylvian language networks of the human brain. *Annals of neurology*, 57, 8–16.

Chalmers, DJ (1995) Facing up to the problem of consciousness. *Journal of Consciousness Studies*, 2, 200–219.

Chen, Q, Heston, JB, Burkett, ZD and White, SA (2013) Expression analysis of the speech-related genes FOXP1 and FOXP2 and their relation to singing behavior in two songbird species. *The Journal of Experimental Biology*, 216, 3682–3692.

Cherrier, MM, Matsumoto, AM, Amory, JK, Asthana, S, Bremner, W, Peskind, ER, Raskind, MA and Craft, S (2005) Testosterone improves spatial memory in men with Alzheimer disease and mild cognitive impairment. *Neurology*, 64 (12), 2063–2068.

Childs, E and de Wit, H (2010) Effects of acute psychosocial stress on cigarette craving and smoking. *Nicotine & Tobacco Research*, 12, 449–453.

Chivers, ML, Rieger, G, Latty, E and Bailey, JM (2004) A sex difference in the specificity of sexual arousal. *Psychological Science*, 15, 736–744.

Choplin, JM and Motyka Joss, L (2012) Simultaneous and sequential comparisons of food quantity and consumption. *Eating Behaviors*, 13, 310–316.

Christiansen, MH and Kirby, S (2003) Language evolution: consensus and controversies. *Trends in Cognitive Sciences*, 7, 300–307.

Chrousos, GP (2009) Stress and disorders of the stress system. *Nature Reviews. Endocrinology*, 5, 374–381.

Clark, A. (2013). Whatever next? Predictive brains, situated agents, and the future of cognitive science. *Behavioural and Brain Sciences*, 36, 181–204.

Cobb, J (1979) Morbid jealousy. *British Journal of Hospital Medicine*, 21, 511–518.

Cobey, KD, Pollet, TV, Roberts, CS and Buunk, AP (2011) Hormonal birth control use and relationship jealousy: evidence for estrogen dosage effects. *Personality and Individual Differences*, 50, 315–317.

Cobey, KD, Buunk, AP, Roberts, SC, Klipping, C, Appels, N, Zimmerman, Y, Coelingh Bennink, HJT and Pollet, TV (2012) Reported jealousy differs as a function of menstrual cycle stage and contraceptive pill use: a within-subjects investigation. *Evolution and Human Behavior*, 33, 395–401.

Cobos, P, Sanchez, M, Garcia, C, Nieves Vera, M and Vila, J (2002) Revisiting the James versus Cannon debate on emotion: startle and autonomic modulation in patients with spinal cord injuries. *Biological Psychology*, 61, 251–269.

Cohen, E and Haun, D (2013) The development of tag-based cooperation via a socially acquired trait. *Evolution and Human Behavior*, 34, 230–235.

Cohen, S and Janicki-Deverts, D (2009) Can we improve our physical health by altering our social networks? *Perspectives on Psychological Science*, 4, 375–378.

Cohen, S and Wills, TA (1985) Stress, social support, and the buffering hypothesis. *Psychological Bulletin*, 98, 310.

Cohen-Bendahan, CC, van de Beek, C and Berenbaum, SA (2005) Prenatal sex hormone effects on child and adult sex-typed behavior: methods and findings. *Neuroscience Biobehavioural Review*, 29, 353–384.

Collignon, O, Girard, S, Gosselin, F, Roy, S, Saint-Amour, D, Lassonde, M and Lepore, F (2008) Audio-visual integration of emotion expression. *Brain Research*, 1242, 126–135.

Comer, SD, Collins, ED, MacArthur, RB and Fischman, MW (1999) Comparison of intravenous and intranasal heroin self-administration by morphine-maintained humans. *Psychopharmacology*, 143, 327–338.

Cooper, J, Gordon, IJ and Pike, AW (2000) Strategies for the avoidance of faeces by grazing sheep. *Applied Animal Behaviour Science*, 69, 15–33.

Cooper, ML, Russell, M, Skinner, JB, Frone, MR and Mudar, P (1992) Stress and alcohol use: moderating effects of gender, coping, and alcohol expectancies. *Journal of Abnormal Psychology*, 101, 139.

Corballis, M (2007) The uniqueness of human recursive thinking: the ability to think about thinking may be the critical attribute that distinguishes us from all other species. *American Scientist*, 95, 240–248.

Corballis, MC (2010) Mirror neurons and the evolution of language. *Brain and Language*, 112, 25–35.

Corbetta, M (1998) Frontoparietal cortical networks for directing attention and the eye to visual locations: identical, independent, or overlapping neural systems? *Proceedings of the National Academy of Sciences*, 95, 831–838.

Corkin, S (1984) Lasting consequences of bilateral medial temporal lobectomy: clinical course and experimental findings in HM. *Seminars in Neurology*, 4 (2), 249–259.

Cosmides, L and Tooby, J (2000) Evolutionary psychology and the emotions. In Lewis, M and Haviland-Jones, JM (eds) *Handbook of Emotions* (pp 91–115). New York: Guilford Press.

Cottrell, CA and Neuberg, SL (2005). Different emotional reactions to different groups: a sociofunctional threat-based approach to 'prejudice'. *Journal of Personality and Social Psychology*, 88, 770–789.

Cowen, P (2011) Has psychopharmacology got a future? *The British Journal of Psychiatry*, 198, 333–335.

Craig, AD (2002) How do you feel? Interoception: the sense of the physiological condition of the body. *Nature Reviews Neuroscience*, 3, 655–666.

Craig, AD (2009) How do you feel – now? The anterior insula and human awareness. *Nature reviews. Neuroscience*, 10, 59–70.

Crawford, LL and Domjan, M (1993) Sexual approach conditioning: omission contingency tests. *Animal Learning & Behavior*, 21, 42–50.

Crick, F and Koch, C (2003) A framework for consciousness. *Nature Neuroscience*, 6, 119–126.

Critchley, HD, Wiens, S, Rotshtein, P, Öhman, A and Dolan, RJ (2004) Neural systems supporting interoceptive awareness. *Nature Neuroscience*, 7, 189–195.

Cromwell, HC and Schultz, W (2003) Effects of expectations for different reward magnitudes on neuronal activity in primate striatum. *Journal of Neurophysiology*, 89, 2823–2838.

Cross, CP and Campbell, A (2011) Women's aggression. *Aggression and Violent Behavior*, 16, 390–398.

Culos-Reed, SN, Carlson, LE, Daroux, LM and Hately-Aldous, S (2006) A pilot study of yoga for breast cancer survivors: physical and psychological benefits. *Psycho-Oncology*, 15, 891–897.

Curtis, V, Aunger, R and Rabie, T (2004) Evidence that disgust evolved to protect from risk of disease. *Proceedings of the Royal Society Biological Sciences of London, Series B: Biological Sciences*, 271, S131-S133.

Dallman, MF, Pecoraro, NC and la Fleur, SE (2005) Chronic stress and comfort foods. Self-medication and abdominal obesity. *Brain, Behavior and Immunity*, 19, 275–280.

Daly, M and Wilson, M (1988) *Homicide*. Hawthorne, NY: Aldine de Gruyter.

Daly, M and Wilson, M (1994) Evolutionary psychology of male violence. In Archer, J (ed.) *Male violence* (pp253–288). London: Routledge.

Damasio, AR (1998) Investigating the biology of consciousness. *Philosophical Transactions of the Royal Society of London. Series B: Biological Sciences*, 353, 1879–1882.

Damasio, AR, Grabowski, TJ, Bechara, A, Damasio, H, Ponto, LL, Parvizi, J and Hichwa, RD (2000) Subcortical and cortical brain activity during the feeling of self-generated emotions. *Nature Neuroscience*, 3, 1049–1056.

Danner, DD, Snowdon, DA and Friesen, WV (2001) Positive emotions in early life and longevity: findings from the nun study. *Journal of Personality and Social Psychology*, 80, 804.

Darwin, C (1872) *The expression of the emotions in man and animals*. London: John Murray.

Davidson, RJ, Kabat-Zinn, J, Schumacher, J, Rosenkranz, M, Muller, D, Santorelli, SF et al. (2003) Alterations in brain and immune function produced by mindfulness meditation. *Psychosomatic Medicine*, 65, 564–570.

Davies, M and Whalen, PJ (2001) The amygdala: vigilance and emotion. *Molecular Psychiatry*, 6, 13–34.

Debiec, J (2005) Peptides of love and fear: vasopressin and oxytocin modulate the integration of information in the amygdala. *Bioessays*, 27, 869–873.

Debiec, J (2007) From affiliative behaviors to romantic feelings: a role of nanopeptides. *FEBS Letters*, 581, 2580–2586.

de Boer, A, van Buel, EM and Ter Horst, GJ (2012) Love is more than just a kiss: a neurobiological perspective on love and affection. *Neuroscience*, 201, 114–124.

de Boer, SF, van der Vegt, BJ and Koolhaas, JM (2003) Individual variation in aggression of feral rodent strains: a standard for the genetics of aggression and violence? *Behavior Genetics*, 33, 485–501.

DeBruine, LM, Jones, BC and Perrett, DI (2005) Women's attractiveness judgments of self-resembling faces change across the menstrual cycle. *Hormones and Behavior*, 47, 379–383.

Dediu, D and Levinson, SC (2013) On the antiquity of language: the reinterpretation of Neandertal linguistic capacities and its consequences, *Frontiers in Psychology*, 4, 397.

de Jong, PJ and Merckelbach, H (1998) Blood-injection-injury phobia and fear of spiders: domain specific individual differences in disgust sensitivity. *Personality and Individual Differences*, 24, 153–158.

Del Giudice, M and Belsky, J (2011) Parent–child relationships. In Salmon, C and Shackelford, TK (eds) *The Oxford handbook of evolutionary family psychology* (pp65–82). Oxford: Oxford University Press.

Dennett, DC (1988) Quining qualia. In Marcel, AJ and Bisiach, E (eds) *Consciousness in contemporary science* (pp42–77). Oxford: Clarendon Press.

Denollet, J, Pedersen, SS, Vrints, CJ and Conraads, VM (2006) Usefulness of type D personality in predicting five-year cardiac events above and beyond concurrent symptoms of stress in patients with coronary heart disease. *The American Journal of Cardiology*, 97, 970–973.

Deriziotis, P and Fisher, SE (2013) Neurogenomics of speech and language disorders: the road ahead. *Genome Biology*, 14, 1–12.

Deschner, T, Heistermann, M, Hodges, K and Boesch, C (2004) Female sexual swelling size, timing of ovulation, and male behavior in wild West African chimpanzees. *Hormones and Behavior*, 46, 204–215.

D'Esposito, M, Detre, JA, Alsop, DC, Shin, RK, Atlas, S and Grossman, M (1995) The neural basis of the central executive system of working memory. *Nature*, 378 (6554), 279–281.

Dewart, T, Frank, B and Schmeidler, J (2006) The impact of 9/11 on patients in New York City's substance abuse treatment programs. *American Journal of Drug and Alcohol Abuse*, 32, 665–672.

Diamond, ME, Petersen, RS and Harris, JA (1999) Learning through maps: functional significance of topographic organization in primary sensory cortex. *Journal of Neurobiology*, 41 (1), 64–68.

Dimitropoulos, A and Schultz, RT (2008) Food-related neural circuitry in Prader-Willi syndrome: response to high versus low calorie foods. *Journal of Autism and Developmental Disorders*, 38, 1642–1653.

Dobzhansky, T (1973) Nothing in biology makes sense except in the light of evolution. *American Biology Teacher*, 35, 125–129.

Doherty, RW, Hatfield, E, Thompson, K and Choo, P (1994) Cultural and ethnic influences on love and attachment. *Personal Relationships*, 1, 391–398.

Dolan, RJ, Morris, JS and de Gelder, B (2001) Crossmodal binding of fear in voice and face. *Proceedings of the National Academy of Sciences of the United States of America*, 98, 10006–10010.

Domjan, M, Blesbois, E and Williams, J (1998) The adaptive significance of sexual conditioning: Pavlovian control of sperm release. *Psychological Science*, 9, 411–415.

Dreifuss, JJ, Dubois-Dauphin, M, Widmer, H and Raggenbass, M (1992) Electrophysiology of oxytocin actions on central neurons. *Annals of the New York Academy of Science*, 652, 46–57.

Driver, J and Noesselt, T (2008) Multisensory interplay reveals crossmodal influences on 'sensory-specific' brain regions, neural responses, and judgments. *Neuron*, 10, 11–23.

Dubois J and VanRullen, R (2012) Visual trails: do the doors of perception open periodically? *PLOS Biology*, 9, e1001056.

Dunbar, R (1998) *Grooming, gossip, and the evolution of language*. Cambridge, MA: Harvard University Press.

Easton, JA, Schipper, LD and Shackelford, TK (2007) Morbid jealousy from an evolutionary psychological perspective. *Evolution and Human Behavior*, 28, 399–402.

Edelman, GM (1987) *Neural Darwinism: the theory of neuronal group selection*. New York: Basic Books.

Edelman, GM (2003) Naturalizing consciousness: a theoretical framework. *PNAS*, 100, 5520–5524.

Edwards, S and Self, DW (2006) Monogamy: dopamine ties the knot. *Nature Neuroscience*, 9, 7–8.

Eibl-Eibesfeldt, I (1970) *Ethology: the biology of behaviour*. New York: Holt, Rinehart, & Winston.

Ekman, P (1973) Cross-culture studies of facial expression. In Ekman, P (ed.) *Darwin and facial expression: a century of research in review* (pp162–222). New York: Academic Press.

Ekman, P (1992) An argument for basic emotions. *Cognition & Emotion*, 6, 169–200.

Ekman, P and Friesen, WV (1975) *Unmasking the face: a guide to recognizing emotions from facial clues*. Englewood Cliffs, NJ: Prentice-Hall.

Ekman, P, Levenson, RW and Friesen, WV (1983) Autonomic nervous system activity distinguishes among emotions. *Science*, 221, 1208–1210.

Else-Quest, NM, Hyde, JS, Goldsmith, HH and van Hulle, CA (2006) Gender differences in temperament: a meta-analysis. *Psychological Bulletin*, 132, 33–72.

Emanuele, E, Politi, P, Bianchi, M, Minoretti, P, Bertona, M and Geroldi, D (2006) Raised plasma nerve growth factor levels associated with early-stage romantic love. *Psychoneuroendocrinology*, 31, 288–294.

Engelmann, M, Landgraf, R and Wotjak, CT (2004) The hypothalamic-neurohypophysial system regulates the hypothalamic-pituitary-adrenal axis under stress: an old concept revisited. *Frontiers in Neuroendocrinology* 25, 132–149.

Ephraim, PL, Wegener, ST, MacKenzie, EJ, Dillingham, TR and Pezzin, LA (2005) Phantom pain, residual limb pain and back pain in amputees: results of a national survey. *Archives of Physical Medicine and Rehabilitation*, 86, 1910–1919.

Ertman, N, Andreano, JM and Cahill, L (2011) Progesterone at encoding predicts subsequent emotional memory. *Learning & Memory*, 18 (12), 759–763.

Esch, T and Stefano, GB (2005) Love promotes health. *Neuroendocrinology Letters*, 26, 264–267.

Everitt, B, Belin, D, Economidou, D, Pelloux, Y, Dalley, J and Robbins, T (2008) Neural mechanisms underlying the vulnerability to develop compulsive drug-seeking habits and addiction. *Philosophical Transactions of the Royal Society B: Biological Sciences*, 363, 3125–3135.

Fabes, RA, Eisenberg, N, Jones, S, Smith, M, Guthrie, I, Poulin, R, Shepard, S and Friedman, J (1999) Regulation, emotionality, and preschoolers' socially competent peer interactions. *Child Development*, 70, 432–442.

Fairburn, CG, Shafran, R and Cooper, Z (1999) A cognitive behavioural theory of anorexia nervosa. *Behaviour Research and Therapy*, 37, 1–13.

Fedio, P and Van Buren, JM (1974) Memory deficits during electrical stimulation of the speech cortex in conscious man. *Brain & Language*, 1 (1), 29–42.

Fehér, O, Wang, H, Saar, S, Mitra, PP and Tchernichovski, O (2009) De novo establishment of wild-type song culture in the zebra finch. *Nature*, 459, 564–568.

Feinberg, DR, Jones, BC, Law-Smith, MJ, Moore, FR, DeBruine, LM, Cornwell, RE, Hillier, SG and Perrett, DI (2006) Menstrual cycle, trait estrogen level, and masculinity preferences in the human voice. *Hormones and Behavior*, 49, 215–222.

Ferguson, CJ (2008) An evolutionary approach to understanding violent antisocial behavior: diagnostic implications for duel-process etiology. *Journal of Forensic Psychology Practice*, 8, 321–343.

Fessler, DMT (2002) Reproductive immunosuppression and meat eating. *Rivista di Biologia (Biology Forum)*, 94, 407–430.

Fessler, DMT and Navarrete, CD (2003) Domain-specific variation in disgust sensitivity across the menstrual cycle. *Evolution and Human Behavior*, 24, 406–417.

Fessler, DMT, Eng, SJ and Navarrete, CD (2005) Elevated disgust sensitivity in the first trimester of pregnancy: evidence supporting the compensatory prophylaxis hypothesis. *Evolution and Human Behavior*, 26, 344–351.

Field, TM and Walden, TA (1982) Production and discrimination of facial expressions by preschool children. *Child Development*, 1299–1311.

Field, TM, Woodson, R, Greenberg, R and Cohen, D (1982) Discrimination and imitation of facial expression by neonates. *Science*, 218, 179–181.

Finn, AS, Sheridan, MA, Kam, CLH, Hinshaw, S and D'Esposito, M (2010) Longitudinal evidence for functional specialization of the neural circuit supporting working memory in the human brain. *The Journal of Neuroscience*, 30 (33), 11062–11067.

Fisher, H (2004) *Why we love: the nature and chemistry of romantic love.* New York: Holt.

Fisher, SE and Marcus, GF (2006) The eloquent ape: genes, brains and the evolution of language. *Nature Reviews Genetics*, 7, 9–20.

Fitch, W, Huber, L and Bugnyar, T (2010) Social cognition and the evolution of language: constructing cognitive phylogenies. *Neuron*, 65, 795–814.

Flaxman, SM and Sherman, PW (2000) Morning sickness: a mechanism for protecting mother and embryo. *Quarterly Review of Biology*, 75, 113–148.

Flegal, KM and Troiano, RP (2000) Changes in the distribution of body mass index of adults and children in the US population. *International Journal of Obesity*, 24, 807–818.

Fleischman, DS and Fessler, DMT (2011) Progesterone's effects on the psychology of disease avoidance: support for the compensatory behavioural prophylaxis hypothesis. *Hormones and Behaviour*, 59, 271–275.

Foster, DL and Nagatini, S (1999) Physiological perspectives on leptin as a regulator of reproduction: role in timing puberty. *Biology of Reproduction*, 60, 205–215.

Fox, E, Derakshan, N and Shoker, L (2008) Trait anxiety modulates the electrophysiological indices of rapid orienting towards angry faces. *NeuroReport*, 19, 259–263.

Fox, MW (1970) A comparative study of the development of facial expressions in canids; wolf, coyote and foxes. *Behaviour*, 36, 49–73.

Franken, IH and Muris, P (2005) Individual differences in reward sensitivity are related to food craving and relative body weight in healthy women. *Appetite*, 45, 198–201.

Frasure-Smith, N, Lespérance, F, Gravel, G, Masson, A, Juneau, M, Talajic, M and Bourassa, MG (2000) Social support, depression, and mortality during the first year after myocardial infarction. *Circulation*, 101, 1919–1924.

Friedman, M and Rosenman, R H (1959) Association of specific overt behavior pattern with blood and cardiovascular findings blood cholesterol level, blood clotting time, incidence of arcus senilis, and clinical coronary artery disease. *Journal of the American Medical Association*, 169, 1286–1296.

Frijda, NH (1986) *The emotions.* Cambridge: Cambridge University Press.

Frith, U and Frith, C (2010) The social brain: allowing humans to boldly go where no other species has been. *Philosophical Transactions of the Royal Society B: Biological Sciences*, 365, 165–176.

Gabrieli, JD (1998) Cognitive neuroscience of human memory. *Annual Review of Psychology*, 49 (1), 87–115.

Gagnon, KT, Geuss, MN and Stefanucci, JK (2013) Fear influences perceived reaching to targets in audition, but not vision. *Evolution and Human Behavior*, 34, 49–54.

Galef, BG and White, DJ (2000) Evidence of social effects on mate choice in vertebrates. *Behavioural Processes*, 51, 167–175.

Gangestad, SW, Thornhill, R and Garver, CE (2002) Changes in women's sexual interests and their partner's mate-retention tactics across the menstrual cycle: evidence for shifting conflicts of interest. *Proceedings of the Royal Society of London Series B: Biological Sciences*, 269, 975–982.

Gauthier, I, Skudlarski, P, Gore, JC and Anderson, AW (2000) Expertise for cars and birds recruits brain areas involved in face recognition. *Nature Neuroscience*, 3, 191–197.

Gearhardt, AN, Treat, TA, Hollingworth, A and Corbin, WR (2012) The relationship between eating-related individual differences and visual attention to foods high in added fat and sugar. *Eating Behaviors*, 13, 371–374.

Geary, DC, DeSoto, CM, Hoard, MK, Skaggs Sheldon, M and Lynne Cooper, M (2001) Estrogens and relationship jealousy. *Human Nature*, 12, 299–320.

Georgiadis, JR and Kringelbach, ML (2012) The human sexual response cycle: brain imaging evidence linking sex to other pleasures. *Progress in Neurobiology*, 98, 49–81.

Georgiadis, JR, Kortekaas, R, Kuipers, R, Nieuwenburg, A, Pruim, J, Reinders, AATS and Holstege, G (2006) Regional blood flow changes associated with clitorally induced orgasm in healthy women. The *European Journal of Neuroscience*, 24, 3305–3316.

Georgiadis, JR, Farrell, MJ, Boessen, R, Denton, DA, Gavrilescu, M, Kortekaas, R, Renken, RJ, Hoogduin, JM and Egan, G (2010) Dynamic subcortical blood flow during male sexual activity with ecological validity: a perfusion fMRI study. *NeuroImage*, 50, 208–216.

Gerin, W, Pieper, C, Levy, R and Pickering, TG (1992). Social support in social interaction: a moderator of cardiovascular reactivity. *Psychosomatic Medicine*, 54, 324–336.

Ghazanfar, AA and Schroeder, CE (2006) Is neocortex essentially multisensory? *Trends in Cognitive Sciences*, 10, 278–285.

Giammanco, M, Tabacchi, G, Giammanco, S, Di Majo, D and La Guardia, M (2005) Testosterone and aggressiveness. *Medical Science Monitor: International Medical Journal of Experimental and Clinical Research*, 11, RA136-RA145.

Gibson, JJ (1966) *The senses considered as perceptual systems*. Boston, MA: Houghton Mifflin.

Gizewski, ER, Krause, E, Karama, S, Baars, A, Senf, W and Forsting, M (2006) There are differences in cerebral activation between females in distinct menstrual phases during viewing of erotic stimuli: a fMRI study. *Experimental Brain Research*, 174, 101–108.

Glover, V, O'Connor, TG and O'Donnell, K (2010) Prenatal stress and the programming of the HPA axis. *Neuroscience & Biobehavioral Reviews*, 35 (1), 17–22.

Goddard, MR, Godfray, HC and Burt, A (2005) Sex increases the efficacy of natural selection in experimental yeast populations. *Nature*, 434, 636–640.

Golden, NH and Carlson, JL (2008) The pathophysiology of amenorrhea in the adolescent. *Annals of the New York Academy of Sciences*, 1135, 163–178.

Goldman-Rakic, PS and Leung, H-C (2002) Functional architecture of the dorsolateral prefrontal cortex in monkeys and humans. In Stuss, DT and Knight, RT (eds) *Principles of frontal lobe function* (pp85–95). Oxford: Oxford University Press.

Goodman, A (2008) Neurobiology of addiction: an integrative review. *Biochemical Pharmacology*, 75, 266–322.

Gordon-Weeks, PR (2000) *Neuronal growth cones*. Cambridge: Cambridge University Press.

Gossop, M, Griffiths, P, Powis, B, and Strang, J (1992) Severity of dependence and route of administration of heroin, cocaine and amphetamines. *British Journal of Addiction*, 87, 1527–1536.

Gottschalk, M and Ellis, L (2009) Evolutionary and genetic explanations of violent crime. In Ferguson, C (ed.) *Violent crime: clinical and social implications*. Thousand Oaks, CA: Sage.

Gould, SJ (1997) The exaptive excellence of spandrels as a term and prototype. *Proceedings of the National Academy of Sciences*, 94, 10750–10755.

Graham, JE, Christian, LM and Glaser, J K (2006) Stress, age, and immune function: toward a lifespan approach. *Journal of Behavioral Medicine*, 29, 389–400.

Grammer, K, Jutte, A and Fischmann, B (1997) Der Kampf der geschlechter und der Krieg der signale. In Karnitscheider, B (ed.) *Liebe, Lust und Leidenschaft: Sexualitat im Spiegal der Wissenschaft* (pp9–35). Stuttgart: Hirzel.

Grant, JA, Courtemanche, J, Duerden, EG, Duncan, GH and Rainville, P (2010) Cortical thickness and pain sensitivity in zen meditators. *Emotion*, 10, 43–53.

Greely, H, Sahakian, B, Harris, J, Kessler, RC, Gazzaniga, M, Campbell, P and Farah, MJ (2008) Towards responsible use of cognitive-enhancing drugs by the healthy. *Nature*, 456 (7223), 702–705.

Greeno, GG and Wing, RR (1994) Stress-induced eating. *Psychological Bulletin*, 115, 444–464.

Gregory, R (1974) *Concepts and mechanisms of perception*. London: Duckworth.

Groesz, LM, McCoy, S, Carl, J, Saslow, L, Stewart, J, Adler, N, Laraia, B and Epel, E (2012) What is eating you? Stress and the drive to eat. *Appetite*, 58, 717–721.

Guerrieri, R, Nederkoorn, C and Jansen, A (2008) The interaction between impulsivity and a varied food environment: its influence on food intake and overweight. *International Journal of Obesity*, 32, 708–714.

Guerrieri, R, Stanczyk, N, Nederkoorn, C and Jansen, A (2012) Reward-sensitive women overeat in a varied food environment, but only when hungry. *Eating Behaviors*, 13, 317–320.

Gunnar, M and Quevedo, K (2007) The neurobiology of stress and development. *Annual Review Psychology*, 58, 145–173.

Guo, G, Roettger, ME and Shih, JC (2007) Contributions of the DAT1 and DRD2 genes to serious and violence delinquency among adolescents and young adults. *Human Genetics*, 121, 125–136.

Gutierrez, R and Giner-Sorolla, R (2007) Anger, disgust, and presumption of harm as reactions to taboo-breaking behaviors, *Emotion*, 7, 853–868.

Gutman, Y (2007) Mediational effects of alexithymia on the relationship between personality pathology and couple functioning. *Dissertation Abstracts International: Section B: The Sciences and Engineering*, 68, 8397.

Guttman, H and Laporte, L (2002) Alexithymia, empathy, and psychological symptoms in a family context. *Comprehensive Psychiatry*, 43, 448–455.

Guyer, AE, Monk, CS, McClure-Tone, EB, Nelson, EE, Roberson-Nay, R, Adler, AD, Fromm, SJ, Pine, DS, and Ernst, M (2008) A developmental examination of amygdala response to facial expressions. *Journal of Cognitive Neuroscience*, 20, 1565–1582.

Habel, U, Windischberger, C, Derntl, B, Robinson, S, Kryspin-Exner, I, Gur, RC and Moser, E (2007) Amygdala activation and facial expressions: explicit emotion discrimination versus implicit emotion processing. *Neuropsychologia*, 45, 2369–2377.

Halligan, SL, Herbert, J, Goodyer, I and Murray, L (2007) Disturbances in morning cortisol secretion in association with maternal postnatal depression predict subsequent depressive symptomatology in adolescents. *Biological Psychiatry*, 62, 40–46.

Hampson, E and Morley, EE (2013) Estradiol concentrations and working memory performance in women of reproductive age. *Psychoneuroendocrinology*, 38 (12), 2897–2904.

Hamshere, M L, Holmans, P A, McCarthy, G M, Jones, L A, Murphy, K C, Sanders, R D et al. (2011) Phenotype evaluation and genomewide linkage study of clinical variables in schizophrenia. *American Journal of Medical Genetics Part B: Neuropsychiatric Genetics*, 156, 929–940.

Harding, CF (1983) Hormonal influences on avian aggressive behavior. In Svare, B (ed.) *Hormones and aggressive behavior* (pp435–467). New York: Plenum.

Hare, B, and Tomasello, M (2005) Human-like social skills in dogs? *Trends in Cognitive Sciences*, 9, 439–444.

Harlow, SD (2000) Menstruation and menstrual disorders: the epidemiology of menstruation and menstrual dysfunction. In Goldman, M and Hatch, M (eds) *Women and Health* (pp99–113). San Diego, CA: Academic Press.

Harris, CR (2002) Sexual and romantic jealousy in heterosexual and homosexual adults. *Psychological Science*, 13, 7–12.

Harrison, NR, Wuerger, SM and Meyer, GF (2010). Reaction time facilitation for horizontally moving auditory-visual stimuli. *Journal of Vision*, 10, 1–21.

Hatfield, E and Rapson, RL (1996) *Love and sex: cross-cultural perspectives*. Needham Heights, MA: Allyn & Bacon.

Hatfield, E and Rapson, RL (2002) Passionate love and sexual desire: cultural and historical perspectives. In Vangelisti, AL and Reis, HT (eds) *Stability and change in relationships: advances in personal relationships* (pp306–324). New York: Cambridge University Press.

Hauk, O, Johnsrude, I and Pulvermuller, F (2004) Somatotopic representation of action words in human motor and premotor cortex. *Neuron*, 41, 301–307.

Hauser, MD and Fitch, WT (2003) What are the uniquely human components of the language faculty? *Studies in the Evolution of Language*, 3, 158–181.

Hauser, MD, Chomsky, N and Fitch, WT (2002) The faculty of language: what is it, who has it, and how did it evolve? *Science*, 298, 1569–1579.

Havlicek, J, Roberts, SC and Flegr, J (2005) Women's preference for dominant male odour: effects of menstrual cycle and relationship status. *Biology Letters*, 1, 256–259.

Haxby, JV, Hoffman, EA and Gobbini, MI (2000) The distributed human neural system for face perception. *Trends in Cognitive Science*, 4, 223–233.

Hayes, CJ, Stevenson, RJ and Coltheart, M (2007) Disgust and Huntington's disease. *Neuropsychologia*, 45, 1135–1151.

Hayes, KJ and Hayes, C (1952) Imitation in a home-raised chimpanzee. *Journal of Comparative and Physiological Psychology*, 45, 450–459.

Healey, KM, Pinkham, AE, Richard, JA and Kohler, CG (2010) Do we recognize facial expressions of emotions from persons with schizophrenia? *Schizophrenia Research*, 122, 144–150.

Heidbreder, CA, Gardner, EL, Zheng-Xiong, X, Thanos, PK, Mugnaini, M, Hagan, JJ and Ashby, CR (2005) The role of central dopamine D_3 receptors in drug addiction: a review of pharmacological evidence. *Brain Research Reviews*, 49, 77–105.

Helgeson, VS, Cohen, S and Fritz, HL (1998) Social ties and cancer. *Psycho-oncology*, 99–109.

Hess, RA, Bunick, D, Lee, KH, Bahr, J, Taylor, JA, Korach, KS and Lubahn, DB (1997) A role for oestrogens in the male reproductive system. *Nature*, 390, 509–512.

Hetherington, AW and Ranson, SW (1940) Hypothalamic lesions and adiposity in the rat. *Anatomical Record*, 78, 149–172.

Hill, A, and Ward, S (1988) Origin of the Hominidae: the record of African large hominoid evolution between 14 My and 4 My. *American Journal of Physical Anthropology*, 31, 49–83.

Hill, JO and Peters, JC (1998) Environmental contributions to the obesity epidemic. *Science*, 280, 1371–1374.

Hockett, CF and Altmann, S (1968) A note on design features. In Sebeok, TA (ed.), *Animal communication; techniques of study and results of research* (pp61–72). Bloomington, IN: Indiana University Press.

Hoffman, HA (2010) Early developmental patterning sets the stage for brain evolution. *PNAS*, 107 (22), 9919–9920.

Hohmann, GW (1966) Some effects of spinal cord lesions on experienced emotional feelings. *Psychophysiology*, 3, 143–156.

Hollis, KL, Pharr, VL, Dumas, MJ, Britton, GB and Field, J (1997) Classical conditioning provides paternity advantage for territorial male blue gouramis (Trichogaster trichopterus). *Journal of Comparative Psychology*, 111, 219–225.

Holman, SD and Goy, RW (1995) Experiential and hormonal correlates of care-giving in rhesus macaques. In Pryce, CR, Martin, RD and Skuse, D (eds) *Motherhood in human and nonhuman primate: biosocial determinants* (pp87–93). Basel: Karger.

Holt-Lunstad, J, Birmingham, WA and Light, KC (2008) Influence of a 'warm touch' support enhancement intervention among married couples on ambulatory blood pressure, oxytocin, alpha amylase, and cortisol. *Psychosomatic Medicine*, 70, 976–985.

Hu, R, Eskandar, E and Williams, Z (2009) Role of deep brain stimulation in modulating memory formation and recall. *Neurosurgical Focus*, 27(1), E3.

Huang, CL, Hsiao, S, Hwu, HG and Howng, SL (2012) The Chinese Facial Emotion Recognition Database (DFERD): a computer-generated 3-D paradigm to measure the recognition of facial emotional expressions at different intensities. *Psychiatry Research*, 200, 928–932.

Hubel, DH and Wiesel, TN (1962) Receptive fields, binocular interaction and functional architecture in the cat's visual cortex. *Journal of Physiology*, 160, 106–154.

Humphreys, TP, Wood, LM and Parker, JDA (2009) Alexithymia and satisfaction in intimate relationships. *Personality and Individual Differences*, 46, 43–47.

Hyman, SE and Malenka, RC (2001) Addiction and the brain: the neurobiology of compulsion and its persistence. *National Review of Neuroscience*, 2, 695–703.

Hyman, SE, Malenka, RC and Nestler, EJ (2006) Neural mechanisms of addiction: the role of reward-related learning and memory. *Annual Review of Neuroscience*, 29, 565–598.

IJzerman, H and Semin, GR (2009) The thermometer of social relations mapping social proximity on temperature. *Psychological Science*, 20, 1214–1220.

Ingelfinger, FJ (1944) The late effects of total and subtotal gastrectomy. *New England Journal of Medicine*, 231, 321–327.

Insel, TR and Hulihan, TJ (1995) A gender-specific mechanism for pair bonding: oxytocin and partner preference formation in monogamous voles. *Behavioral Neuroscience*, 109, 782–789.

Ironson, G, Wynings, C, Schneiderman, N, Baum, A, Rodriguez, M, Greenwood, D and Fletcher, MA (1997) Post-traumatic stress symptoms, intrusive thoughts, loss, and immune function after Hurricane Andrew. *Psychosomatic Medicine*, 59, 128–141.

Irwin, J, and Livnat, S (1987) Behavioral influences on the immune system: stress and conditioning. *Progress in Neuro-Psychopharmacology and Biological Psychiatry*, 11, 137–143.

Irwin, M, Patterson, T, Smith, TL, Caldwell, C, Brown, SA, Gillin, JC, and Grant, I (1990) Reduction of immune function in life stress and depression. *Biological Psychiatry*, 27, 22–30.

Iverson, JM and Goldin-Meadow, S (2005) Gesture paves the way for language development. *Psychological Science*, 16, 367–371.

James, W (1884) What is an emotion? *Mind*, 9, 188–205.

James, W (1890) *The Principles of Psychology*, 2. New York: Henry Holt.

Janik, VM (2013) Cognitive skills in bottlenose dolphin communication. *Trends in cognitive sciences*, 17, 157–159.

Jansen, A, Theunissen, N, Slechten, K, Nederkoorn, C, Boon, B, Mulkens, S, and Roefs, A (2003) Overweight children overeat after exposure to food cues. *Eating Behaviors*, 4, 197–209.

Jemmott, JB (1985) Psychoneuroimmunology: the new frontier. *American Behavioral Scientist*, 28, 497–509.

Jin, P (1992) Efficacy of Tai Chi, brisk walking, meditation, and reading in reducing mental and emotional stress. *Journal of Psychosomatic Research*, 36, 361–370.

Kabat-Zinn, J (1996) *Full catastrophe living: how to cope with stress, pain and illness using mindfulness meditation*. London, Piatkus.

Kamarck, TW, Manuck, SB, and Jennings, JR (1990) Social support reduces cardiovascular reactivity to psychological challenge: a laboratory model. *Psychosomatic Medicine*, 52, 42–58.

Kamitani, Y and Tong, F (2005) Decoding the visual and subjective contents of the human brain. *Nature Neuroscience*, 8, 679–685.

Kanovsky, P, Bares, M, Pohanka, M, and Rektor, I (2002) Penile erections and hypersexuality induced by pergolide treatment in advanced, fluctuating Parkinson's disease. *Journal of Neurology*, 249, 112–114.

Kanwisher, N and Yovel, G (2006) The fusiform face area: a cortical region specialized for the perception of faces. *Philosophical Transactions of the Royal Society of London B*, 361, 2109–2128.

Kanwisher, N, McDermott, J and Chun, MM (1997) The fusiform face area: a module in human extrastriate cortex specialized for face perception. *Journal of Neuroscience,* 17, 4302–4311.

Kauer, JA, and Malenka, RC (2007) Synaptic plasticity and addiction. *National Review of Neuroscience*, 8, 844–858.

Kaye, WH, Fudge, JL and Paulus, M (2009) New insights into symptoms and neurocircuit function of anorexia nervosa. *Nature Reviews Neuroscience*, 10, 573–584.

Kelly, SD, Özyürek, A and Maris, E (2010) Two sides of the same coin speech and gesture mutually interact to enhance comprehension. *Psychological Science*, 21, 260–267.

Keri, S and Kiss, I (2011) Oxytocin response in a trust game and habituation of arousal. *Physiology & Behavior*, 102, 221–224.

Kiecolt-Glaser, JK and Glaser, R (1992) Psychoneuroimmunology: can psychological interventions modulate immunity? *Journal of Consulting and Clinical Psychology*, 60 (4), 569.

Kiecolt-Glaser, JK, Garner, W, Speicher, C, Penn, GM, Holliday, J and Glaser, R (1984) Psychosocial modifiers of immunocompetence in medical students. *Psychosomatic Medicine*, 46 (1), 7–14.

Kiecolt-Glaser, JK, Marucha, PT, Mercado, AM, Malarkey, WB and Glaser, R (1995) Slowing of wound healing by psychological stress. *The Lancet*, 346, 1194–1196.

Kiecolt-Glaser, JK, Loving, TJ, Stowell, JR, Malarkey, WB, Lemeshow, S, Dickinson, SL and Glaser, R (2005) Hostile marital interactions, proinflammatory cytokine production, and wound healing. *Archives of General Psychiatry*, 62 (12), 1377.

Kilts, CD, Egan, G, Gideon, DA, Ely, TD and Hoffman, JM (2003) Dissociable neural pathways are involved in the recognition of emotion in static and dynamic facial expressions. *Neuroimage*, 18, 156–168.

King, S and Laplante, DP (2005) The effects of prenatal maternal stress on children's cognitive development: Project Ice Storm. *Stress: The International Journal on the Biology of Stress*, 8, 35–45.

King, SL and Janik, VM (2013) Bottlenose dolphins can use learned vocal labels to address each other. *Proceedings of the National Academy of Sciences*, 110, 13216–13221.

Kirschbaum, C, Wolf, OT, May, M, Wippich, W and Hellhammer, DH (1996) Stress-and treatment-induced elevations of cortisol levels associated with impaired declarative memory in healthy adults. *Life sciences*, 58 (17), 1475–1483.

Kivimäki, M, Vahtera, J, Elovainio, M, Helenius, H, Singh-Manoux, A and Pentti, J (2005) Optimism and pessimism as predictors of change in health after death or onset of severe illness in family. *Health Psychology*, 24, 413.

Knecht, S, Flöel, A, Dräger, B, Breitenstein, C, Sommer, J, Henningsen, H, Ringelstein, B and Pascual-Leone, A (2002) Degree of language lateralization determines susceptibility to unilateral brain lesions. *Nature Neuroscience*, 5, 695–699.

Knutson, B, Fong, GW, Bennett, SM, Adams, CM and Hommer, S (2003) A region of media prefrontal cortex tracks monetarily rewarding outcomes: characterization with rapid event related fMRI. *NeuroImage*, 18, 263–272.

Ko, C-H, Liu, G-C, Hsiao, S, Yen, J-Y, Yang, M-J, Lin, W-C, Yen, C-F and Chen S-S (2009) Brain activities associated with gaming urge of online gaming addiction. *Journal of Psychiatric Research*, 43, 739–747.

Kohler, CG, Turner, TT, Gur, RE and Gur, RC (2004) Recognition of facial emotions in neuropsychiatric disorders. *CNS Spectrums*, 9, 267–274.

Kokkonen, P, Karvonen, JT, Veijola, J, Laksy, K, Jokelainen, J, Jarvelin, M and Joukamass, M (2001) Prevalence and sociodemographic correlates of alexithymia in a population sample of young adults. *Comprehensive Psychiatry*, 42, 471–476.

Komisaruk, BR, Whipple, B, Crawford, A, Liu, WC, Kalnin, A and Mosier, K (2004) Brain activation during vaginocervical self-stimulation and orgasm in women with complete spinal cord injury: fMRI evidence of mediation by the vagus nerves. *Brain Research*, 1024, 77–88.

Konow, A and Pribram, KH (1970) Error recognition and utilisation produced by injury to the frontal cortex in man. *Neuropsychologia*, 8, 489–491.

Koob, GF (2004) Allostatic view of motivation: Implications for psychopathology. *Nebraska Symposium of Motivation*, 50, 1–18.

Koob, GF (2009) Brain stress systems in the amygdala and addiction. *Brain Research*, 1293, 61–75.

Koob, GF and LeMoal, M (1997) Drug abuse: hedonic homeostatic dysregulation. *Science*, 278, 52–58.

Korte, SM, Koolhaas, JM, Wingfield, JC and McEwen, BS (2005) The Darwinian concept of stress: benefits of allostasis and costs of allostatic load and the trade-offs in health and disease. *Neuroscience & Biobehavioral Reviews*, 29, 3–38.

Kosslyn, SM, Digirolamo, GJ, Thompson, WL and Alpert, NM (1998) Mental rotation of objects versus hands: neural mechanisms revealed by positron emission tomography. *Psychophysiology*, 35, 151–161.

Kosten, TR, Scanley, BE, Tucker, KA, Oliveto, A, Prince, C, Sinha, R, Potenza, MN, Skudlarski, P and Wexler, BE (2006) Cue-induced brain activity changes and relapse in cocaine dependent patients. *Neuropsychopharmacology*, 31, 644–650.

Koukounas, E, and McCabe, MP (2001) Sexual and emotional variables influencing sexual response to erotica: a psychophysiological investigation. *Archives of Sexual Behavior*, 30, 393–408.

Kozel, FA, Johnson, KA, Laken, SJ, Grenesko, EL, Smith, JA, Walker, J and George, MS (2009) Can simultaneously acquired electrodermal activity improve accuracy of fMRI detection of deception? *Social Neuroscience*, 4(6), Dec, 510–517.

Kranz, GS, Kasper, S and Lanzenberger, R (2010) Reward and the serotonergic system. *Neuroscience*, 166, 1023–1035.

Kuhle, BX, Smedley, KD and Schmitt, DP (2009) Sex differences in the motivation and mitigation of jealousy-induced interrogations. *Personality and Individual Differences*, 46, 499–502.

Kuhlmann, S, Piel, M and Wolf, OT (2005) Impaired memory retrieval after psychosocial stress in healthy young men. *The Journal of Neuroscience*, 25 (11), 2977–2982.

Kurtz, AB and Johnson, PT (1999) Case 7: hydranencephaly. *Radiology*, 210, 419–422.

Kuruppuarachchi, KALA and Seneviratne, AN (2011) Organic causation of morbid jealousy. *Asian Journal of Psychiatry*, 4, 258–260.

Lacroix, R, Eason, E and Melzack, R (2000) Nausea and vomiting during pregnancy: a prospective study of its frequency, intensity and patterns of change. *American Journal of Obstetrics and Gynecology*, 182, 931–937.

Lamm, C and Singer, T (2010) The role of anterior insular cortex in social emotions. *Brain Structure and Function*, 214, 579–591.

Landis, D and O'Shea, WA (2000) Cross-cultural aspects of passionate love: an individual differences analysis. *Journal of Cross-Cultural Psychology*, 31, 752–777.

Lane, RD, Sechrest, L, Reidel, R, Weldon, V, Kaszniak, A and Schwartz, GE (1996) Impaired verbal and nonverbal emotion recognition in alexithymia. *Psychosomatic Medicine*, 58, 203–210.

Lange, CG (1885/1912) The mechanisms of the emotions. In Rand, B (ed.) *The classical psychologists* (pp672–684). Boston, MA: Houghton Mifflin.

Langford, DJ, Bailey, AL, Chanda, ML, Clarke, SE, Drummond, TE, Echols, S, Glick, S, Ingrao, J, Klassen-Ross, T, Lacriox-Fralish, ML, Matsumiya, L, Sorge, RE, Sotocinal, SG, Tabeka, JM, Wong, D, van den Maagdenberg, AM, Ferrari, MD, Craig, KD and Mogil, JS (2010) Coding of facial expressions of pain in the laboratory mouse. *Nature Methods*, 7, 447–449.

Larsen, JK, Brand, N, Bermond, B and Hijman, R (2003) Cognitive and emotional characteristics of alexithymia: a review of neurobiological studies. *Journal of Psychosomatic Research*, 54, 533–541.

Laufs, H, Lengler, U, Hamandi, K, Kleinschmidt, A and Krakow, K (2006) Linking generalized spike-and-wave discharges and resting state brain activity by using EEG/fMRI in a patient with absence seizures. *Epilepsia*, 47, 444–448.

Lazar, SW, Kerr, CE, Wasserman, RH, Gray, JR, Greve, DN, Treadway, MT et al. (2005) Meditation experience is associated with increased cortical thickness. *Neuroreport*, 16, 1893.

Leckman, JF and Mayes, LC (1999) Preoccupations and behaviors associated with romantic and parental love: perspectives on the origin of obsessive-compulsive disorder. *Child and Adolescent Psychiatry Clinics of North America*, 8, 635–665.

Lenroot, RK and Giedd, JN (2010) Sex differences in the adolescent brain. *Brain and Cognition*, 72, 46–55.

Levi-Montalcini, R (1982) Developmental neurobiology and the natural history of nerve growth facor. *Annual Review of Neuroscience*, 5, 341–362.

Levine, R, Sato, S, Hashimoto, T and Verma, J (1995) Love and marriage in eleven cultures. *Journal of Cross-Cultural Psychology*, 26, 554–571.

Lerman, Y, Melamed, S, Shragin, Y, Kushnir, T, Rotgoltz, Y, Shirom, A and Aronson, M (1999) Association between burnout at work and leukocyte adhesiveness/aggregation. *Psychosomatic Medicine*, 61, 828–833.

Lim, MM and Young, LJ (2006) Neuropeptidergic regulation of affiliative behavior and social bonding in animals. *Hormones and Behavior*, 50, 506–517.

Lipkind, D, Marcus, GF, Bemis, DK, Sasahara, K, Jacoby, N, Takahasi, M et al. (2013) Stepwise acquisition of vocal combinatorial capacity in songbirds and human infants. *Nature*, 498, 104–108.

Little, AC, Jones, BC and Burris, RP (2007) Preferences for masculinity in male bodies change across the menstrual cycle. *Hormones and Behavior*, 51, 633–639.

Lloyd, EA (2005) *The case of the female orgasm: bias in the science of evolution*. Cambridge, MA: Harvard University Press.

Lobel, M, Cannella, DL, Graham, JE, DeVincent, C, Schneider, J and Meyer, BA (2008) Pregnancy-specific stress, prenatal health behaviors, and birth outcomes. *Health Psychology*, 27, 604.

Lupien, SJ, McEwen, BS, Gunnar, MR and Heim, C (2009) Effects of stress throughout the lifespan on the brain, behaviour and cognition. *Nature Reviews Neuroscience*, 10 (6), 434–445.

Luria, AR, Pribram, KH and Homskaya, ED (1964) An experimental analysis of the behavioural disturbance produced by a left frontal arachnoidal endothelioma (meningioma). *Neurophysiologia*, 2, 257–280.

Lyn, H and Savage-Rumbaugh, S (2012) The use of emotion symbols in language-using apes. In Watanabe, S and Kuczaj, S (eds) *Emotions of animals and humans* (pp113–127). Tokyo: Springer.

Lyons, M, Healy, N and Bruno, D (2013) It takes one to know one: Relationship between lie detection and psychopathy. *Personality and Individual Differences*, 55, 676–679.

Macht, M (2008) How emotions affect eating: a five-way model. *Appetite*, 50, 1–11.

MacLean, EL and Hare, B (2012) Bonobos and chimpanzees infer the target of another's attention. *Animal Behaviour*, 83, 345–353.

Macmillan, M (2008) Phineas Gage: unravelling the myth. *The Psychologist*, 21 (9), 828–831.

MacNeilage, PF (1998) The frame/content theory of evolution of speech production. *Behavioral and Brain Sciences*, 21, 499–511.

Maguire, EA, Frackowiack, RS and Frith, CD (1997) Recalling routes around London: activation of the right hippocampus in taxi drivers. *The Journal of Neuroscience*, 17(18), 7103–7110.

Maguire, EA, Woollett, K and Spiers, HJ (2006) London taxi drivers and bus drivers: a structural MRI and neuropsychological analysis. *Hippocampus*, 16 (12), 1091–1101.

Mah, K and Binik, YM (2005) Are orgasms in the mind or the body? Psychosocial versus physiological correlates of orgasmic pleasure and satisfaction. *Journal of Sex and Marital Therapy*, 31, 187–200.

Majerus, S, Gill-Thwaites, H, Andrews, K and Laureys, S (2005) Behavioral evaluation of consciousness in severe brain damage. *Progress in Brain Research*, 150, 397–413.

Mak, YE, Simmons, KB, Gitelman, DR and Small, DM (2005) Taste and olfactory intensity perception changes following left insular stroke. *Behavioral Neuroscience*, 119, 1693–1700.

Mallinckrodt, B and Wei, M (2005) Attachment, social competencies, social support, and psychological distress. *Journal of Counseling Psychology*, 52, 358–367.

Manning, JT, Scutt, D, Whitehouse, GH, Leinster, SJ and Walton, JM (1996). Asymmetry and the menstrual cycle in women. *Ethology and Sociobiology*, 17, 129–143.

Manuck, SB, Kaplan, JR and Lotrich, FE (2006) Brain serotonin and aggressive disposition in humans and nonhuman primates. In Nelson, RJ (ed.) *Biology of aggression* (pp65–113). New York: Oxford University Press.

Marazziti, D, Akiskal, HS, Rossi, A and Cassano, GB (1999) Alteration of the platelet serotonin transporter in romantic love. *Psychological Medicine*, 29, 741–745.

Marcus, GF and Fisher, SE (2003) FOXP2 in focus: what can genes tell us about speech and language? *Trends in Cognitive Sciences*, 7, 257–262.

Marcus, MD and Kalarchian, MA (2003) Binge eating in children and adolescents. *International Journal of Eating Disorders*, 34, S47-S57.

Marks, IM (1987) *Fears, phobias and rituals*. New York: Oxford University Press.

Martin, RD (2007) The evolution of human reproduction: a primatological perspective. *American Journal of Physical Anthropology*, 134, 59–84.

Marucha, PT, Kiecolt-Glaser, JK and Favagehi, M (1998) Mucosal wound healing is impaired by examination stress. *Psychosomatic Medicine*, 60, 362–365.

Mathews, HL and Janusek, LW (2011) Epigenetics and psychoneuroimmunology: mechanisms and models. *Brain, Behavior, and Immunity*, 25, 25–39.

Maynard Smith, J and Szathmary, E (1997) *The major transitions in evolution*. Oxford: Oxford University Press.

Mazur, A and Booth, A (1998) Testosterone and dominance in men. *Behavioral and Brain Sciences*, 21, 353–397.

Mcbride, CM, Clipp, E, Peterson, BL, Lipkus, IM and Demark_Wahnefried, W (2000) Psychological impact of diagnosis and risk reduction among cancer survivors. *Psycho-Oncology*, 9, 418–427.

McCall, GS and Shields, N (2008) Examining the evidence from small-scale societies and early prehistory and implications for modern theories of aggression and violence. *Aggression and Violent Behavior*, 13, 1–9.

McClure, SM, Berns, GS, and Montague, PR (2003a) Temporal prediction errors in a passive learning task activate human striatum. *Neuron*, 38, 339–346.

McClure, SM, Daw, ND and Montague, PR (2003b) A computational substrate for incentive salience. *Trends in Neuroscience*, 25, 423–428.

McDonald, PW and Prkachin, KM (1990) The expression and perception of facial emotion in alexithymia: a pilot study. *Psychosomatic Medicine*, 52, 199–210.

McFie, J and Zangwill, OL (1960) Visual-constructive disabilities associated with lesions of the left cerebral hemisphere. *Brain: A Journal of Neurology*, 83, 243–260.

Meerlo, P, Koehl, M, Van der Borght, K and Turek, F W (2002) Sleep restriction alters the hypothalamic_pituitary_adrenal response to stress. *Journal of Neuroendocrinology*, 14, 397–402.

Melzack, R (1993) Pain: past, present and future. *Canadian Journal of Experimental Psychology*, 47, 615–629.

Melzack, R (2011) The story of pain. *The Psychologist*, 24, 470–471.

Menzies, RG and Clarke, JC (1995) The etiology of phobias: a nonassociative account. *Clinical Psychology Review*, 15, 23–48.

Mercer, KD, Selby, M and McClung, J (2005) The effects of psychopathy, violence and drug use on neuropsychological functioning. *American Journal of Forensic Psychology*, 23, 65–86.

Merker, B (2007) Consciousness without a cerebral cortex: a challenge for neuroscience and medicine. *Behavioral and Brain Sciences*, 30, 63–81.

Meule, A and Kubler, A (2012) Food cravings in food addiction: the distinct role of positive reinforcement. *Eating Behaviors*, 13, 252–255.

Meule, A, Westenhofer, J and Kubler, A (2011) Food cravings mediate the relationship between rigid, but not flexible control of eating behavior and dieting success. *Appetite*, 57, 582–584.

Meule, A, Lutz, A, Vogele, C and Kubler, A (2012) Food cravings discriminate differentially between successful and unsuccessful dieters and non-dieters; validation of the Food Cravings Questionnaire in German. *Appetite*, 58, 88–97.

Meyer, G, Harrison, N and Wuerger, S (2013) The time course of auditory–visual processing of speech and body actions: Evidence for the simultaneous activation of an extended neural network for semantic processing. *Neuropsychologia*, 51, 1716–1725.

Miczek, KA and Fish, WW (2006) Monoamines, GABA, glutamate and aggression. In Nelson, RJ (ed.) *Biology of aggression* (pp114–149). New York: Oxford University Press.

Mihm, M, Gangooly, S and Muttukrishna, S (2011) The normal menstrual cycle in women. *Animal Reproductive Science*, 124, 229–236.

Miklósi, A, Topál, J and Csányi, V (2004) Comparative social cognition: what can dogs teach us? *Animal Behaviour*, 67, 995–1004

Mikulincer, M and Goodman, GS (eds) (2006) *Dynamics of romantic love: attachment, caregiving and sex*. New York: Guildford Press.

Miller, DB and O'Callaghan, JP (2002) Neuroendocrine aspects of the response to stress. *Metabolism*, 51, 5–10.

Milligan, D, Drife, JO and Short, RV (1975) Changes in breast volume during normal menstrual cycle and after oral contraceptives. *British Medical Journal*, 4, 494–496.

Milner, AD and Goodale, MA (1995) *The visual brain in action*. Oxford: Oxford Press.

Milner, B, Corkin, S and Teuber, HL (1968) Further analysis of the hippocampal amnesic syndrome: 14-year follow-up study of HM. *Neuropsychologia*, 6 (3), 215–234.

Mineka, S and Ohman, A (2002) Phobias and preparedness: the selective, automatic and encapsulated nature of fear. *Biological Psychiatry*, 52, 927–937.

Mineka, S, Davidson, M, Cook, M and Keir, R (1984) Observational conditioning of snake fear in rhesus monkeys. *Journal of Abnormal Psychology*, 93, 355–372.

Mizuno, K, Tanaka, M, Ishii, A, Tanabe, HC, Onoe, H, Sadato, N and Watanabe, Y (2008) The neural basis of academic achievement motivation. *NeuroImage*, 42, 369–378.

Mols, F, Thong, MS, de Poll-Franse, LVV, Roukema, JA and Denollet, J (2012) Type D (distressed) personality is associated with poor quality of life and mental health among 3080 cancer survivors. *Journal of Affective Disorders*, 136, 26–34.

Moncrieff, J and Cohen, D (2009) How do psychiatric drugs work? *BMJ: British Medical Journal*, 338.

Mong, JA and Pfaff, DW (2003) Hormonal and genetic influences underlying arousal as it drives sex and aggression in animal and human brains. *Neurobiology of Aging*, 24, S83-S88.

Montebarocci, O, Codispoti, M, Baldaro, B and Rossi, N (2004) Adult attachment style and alexithymia. *Personality and Individual Differences*, 36, 499–507.

Monteleone, GT, Phan, KL, Nusbaum, HC, Fitzgerald, D, Irick, JS, Fienberg, SE and Cacioppo, JT (2009) Detection of deception using fMRI: better than chance, but well below perfection. *Social Neuroscience*, 4 (6), Dec, 528–538.

Moore, TM, Scarpa, A and Raine, A (2002) A meta-analysis of serotonin metabolite 5-HIAA and antisocial behavior. *Aggressive Behavior*, 28, 299–316.

Morin, A (2007) Consciousness is more than wakefulness. *Behavioral and Brain Sciences*, 30, 99.

Morley, KI and Hall, WD (2003) Is there a genetic susceptibility to engage in criminal acts? *Trends and Issues in Crime and Justice*, 263.

Morris, JS, Ohman, A and Dolan, RJ (1999) A subcortical pathway to the right amygdala mediating 'unseen' fear. *Proceedings of the National Academy of Sciences of the United States of America*, 96, 1680–1685.

Moser, E, Derntl, B, Robinson, S, Fink, B, Gur, RC and Grammer, K (2007) Amygdala activation at 3T in response to human and avatar facial expressions of emotions. *Journal of Neuroscience methods*, 161, 126–133.

Mottaghy, FM, Krause, BJ, Kemna, LJ, Töpper, R, Tellmann, L, Beu, M, Pascual-Leone, A and Müller-Gärtner, HW (2000) Modulation of the neuronal circuitry subserving working memory in healthy human subjects by repetitive transcranial magnetic stimulation. *Neuroscience Letters,* 280 (3), 167–170.

Mullen, PE and Maack, LH (1985) Jealousy, pathological jealousy, and aggression. In Farrington, DP and Gunn, J (eds) *Aggression and dangerousness* (pp103–126). New York: John Wiley.

Muschamp, JW, Dominguez, JM, Sato, SM, Shen, RY and Hull, EM (2007) A role for hypocretin (orexin) in male sexual behaviour. *The Journal of Neuroscience,* 27, 2837–2845.

Nairne, JS and Pandeirada, JN (2008) Adaptive memory: remembering with a Stone Age brain. *Current Directions in Psychological Science,* 17 (4), 239–243.

Nairne, JS, Thompson, SR and Pandeirada, JN (2007) Adaptive memory: survival processing enhances retention. *Journal of Experimental Psychology: Learning, Memory, and Cognition,* 33 (2), 263.

Nakamura, K, Matsumoto, M and Hikosaka, O (2008) Reward-dependent modulation of neuronal activity in the primate dorsal raphe nucleus. *The Journal of Neuroscience,* 28, 5331–5343.

Nederkoorn, C, Smulders, FT and Jansen, A (2000) Cephalic phase responses, craving and food intake in normal subjects. *Appetite,* 35, 45–55.

Nederkoorn, C, Braet, C, van Eijs, Y, Tanghe, A and Jansen, A (2006) Why obese children cannot resist food: the role of impulsivity. *Eating Behaviors,* 7, 315–322.

Need, AC, Attix, DK, McEvoy, JM, Cirulli, ET, Linney, KN, Wagoner, AP and Goldstein, DB (2008) Failure to replicate effect of Kibra on human memory in two large cohorts of European origin. *American Journal of Medical Genetics Part B: Neuropsychiatric Genetics,* 147 (5), 667–668.

Newbury, DF, Fisher, SE and Monaco, AP (2010) Recent advances in the genetics of language impairment. *Genome Medicine,* 2, 6.

Newman, E, O'Connor, DB and Conner, M (2007) Daily hassles and eating behaviour: the role of cortisol reactivity status. *Psychoneuroendocrinology,* 32, 125–132.

Ngun, TC, Ghahramani, N, Sanchez, FJ, Blocklandt, S and Vilain, E (2011) The genetics of sex differences in brain and behavior. *Frontiers in Neuroendocrinology,* 32, 227–246.

Nichols, DE (2004) Hallucinogens. *Pharmacology & Therapeutics,* 101, 131–181.

Nijs, IMT, Franken, IHA and Muris, P (2010) Food-related Stroop interference in obese and normal weight individuals: behavioral and electrophysiological indices. *Eating Behaviors,* 11, 258–265.

Noriuchi, M, Kikuchi, Y and Senoo, A (2008) The functional neuroanatomy of maternal love: mother's response to infant's attachment behaviors. *Biological Psychiatry,* 63, 415–423.

Norton, TR, Manne, SL, Rubin, S, Hernandez, E, Carlson, J, Bergman, C and Rosenblum, N (2005) Ovarian cancer patients' psychological distress: the role of physical impairment, perceived unsupportive family and friend behaviors, perceived control, and self-esteem. *Health Psychology,* 24, 143.

Oaten, M, Stevenson, RJ and Case TI (2009) Disgust as a disease avoidance mechanism: a review and model. *Psychological Bulletin,* 135, 303–321.

Oatley, K and Johnson-Laird, PN (1987) Towards a cognitive theory of emotions. *Cognition and Emotion,* 1, 29–50.

O'Brien, CP (2008) Evidence-based treatments of addiction. *Philosophical Transactions of the Royal Society B: Biological Sciences,* 363, 3277–3286.

O'Connor, MF, Wellisch, DK, Stanton, AL, Eisenberger, NI, Irwin, MR and Lieberman, MD (2008) Craving love? Enduring grief activates brain's reward center. *Neuroimage,* 42, 969–972.

Ogura, K, Shinohara, M, Ohno, K and Mori, E (2008) Frontal behavioral syndromes in Prader-Willi syndrome. *Brain Development,* 30, 469–476.

Ogura, K, Fujii, T, Abe, N, Hosokai, Y, Shinohara, M, Fukuda, H and Mori, E (2013) Regional cerebral blood flow and abnormal eating behavior in Prader-Willi syndrome. *Brain and Development*, 35, 427–434.

Ohman, A and Minkea, S (2001) Fears, phobias, and preparedness: toward an evolved module of fear and fear learning. *Psychological Review*, 108, 483–522.

Olatunji, BO, Haidt, J, McKay, D and David, B (2008) Core, animal-reminder, and contamination disgust: three kinds of disgust with distinct personality, behavioral, physiological and clinical correlates. *Journal of Research in Personality*, 42, 1243–1259.

Olazabal, DE and Young, LJ (2006) Species and individual differences in juvenile female alloparental care are associated with oxytocin receptor density in the striatum and the lateral septum. *Hormones and Behavior*, 49, 681–687.

Olds, J and Milner, P (1954) Positive reinforcement produced by electrical stimulation of septal area and other areas of the brain. *Journal of Comparative and Physiological Psychology*, 47, 419–427.

Ouimette, P, Coolhart, D, Funderburk, JS, Wade, M and Brown, PJ (2007) Precipitants of first substance use in recently abstinent substance use disorder patients with PTSD. *Addictive Behaviour*, 32, 1719–1727.

Pacheco-Lopez, G and Bermudez-Rattoni, F (2011) Brain-immune interactions and the neural basis of disease-avoidant ingestive behaviour. *Philosophical Transactions of the Royal Society B: Biological Sciences*, 366, 3389–3406.

Packard, MG and Knowlton, BJ (2002) Learning and memory functions of the basal ganglia. *Annual Review of Neuroscience*, 25 (1), 563–593.

Paland, S and Lynch, M (2006) Transitions to asexuality result in excess amino acid substitutions. *Science*, 311, 990–992.

Panksepp, J (1998) *Affective neuroscience: the foundations of human and animal emotions*. New York: Oxford University Press.

Panksepp, J (2005) Affective consciousness: core emotional feelings in animals and humans. *Consciousness and Cognition*, 14, 30–80.

Panksepp, J and Biven, L (2012) *The archaeology of mind: neuroevolutionary origins of human emotions*. New York: WW Norton & Co

Panlilio, LV, Goldberg, SR, Gilman, JP, Jufer, R, Cone, EJ and Schindler, CW (1998) Effects of delivery rate and non-contingent infusion of cocaine on cocaine self-administration in rhesus monkeys. *Psychopharmacology*, 137, 253–258.

Papassotiropoulos, A, Stephan, D, Huentelman, M, Hoerndli, F, Craig, D, Pearson, J, Huynh, K, Brunner, F, Corneveaux, J, Osborne, D, Wollmer, M, Aerni, A, Coluccia, D, Hanggi, J, Mondadori, C, Buchmann, A, Reiman, E, Caselli, R, Henke, K and de Quervain, D (2006) Common Kibra alleles are associated with human memory performance. *Science*, 314 (5798), 475–478.

Parker, JD, Keefer, KV, Taylor, GJ and Bagby, RM (2008) Latent structure of the alexithymia construct: a taxometric investigation. *Psychological Assessment*, 20, 385–396.

Parker, PD, Prkachin, KM and Prkachin, GC (2005) Processing of facial expressions of negative emotion in alexithymia: the influence of temporal constraint. *Journal of Personality*, 73, 1087–1107.

Parvizi, J and Damasio, A (2001) Consciousness and the brainstem. *Cognition*, 79, 135–160.

Pawlowski, B, and Jasienska, G (2005) Women's preferences for sexual dimorphism in height depend on menstrual cycle phase and expected duration of relationship. *Biological Psychology*, 70, 38–43.

Pazol, K (2003) Mating among the Kakamega Forest blue monkeys (Cercopithecus mitis): does female sexual behavior function to manipulate paternity assessment? *Behaviour*, 140, 473–499.

Pedersen, CA (1997) Oxytocin control of maternal behavior regulation by sex steroids and offspring stimuli. *Annals of the New York Academy of Sciences*, 807, 126–145.

Pedersen, CA (2004) Biological aspects of social bonding and the roots of human violence. *Annals of the New York Academy of Sciences*, 1036, 106–127.

Pelchat, ML, Johnson, A, Chan, R, Valdez, J and Ragland, JD (2004) Images of desire: food-craving activation during fMRI. *Neurolmage*, 23, 1486–1493.

Penfield, W (1968) Engrams in the human brain: mechanisms of memory. *Proceedings of the Royal Society of Medicine*, 61 (8), 831.

Penfield, W and Boldrey, E (1937) Somatic motor and sensory representation in the cerebral cortex of man as studied by electrical stimulation. *Brain*, 60, 389–443.

Pepperberg, IM (2012) Abstract concepts: data from a grey parrot. *Behavioural processes*, 93, 82–90.

Pereg, D, Gow, R, Mosseri, M, Lishner, M, Rieder, M, Van Uum, S, and Koren, G (2011) Hair cortisol and the risk for acute myocardial infarction in adult men. *Stress*, 14, 73–81.

Peters, S, Derryberry, EP and Nowicki, S (2012) Songbirds learn songs least degraded by environmental transmission. *Biology Letters*, 8, 736–739.

Pfaff, DW, Martin, EM and Faber, D (2012) Origins of arousal: roles for medullary reticular neurons. *Trends in Neurosciences*, 35, 468–476.

Phillips, ML, Young, AW, Senior, C, Brammer, M, Andrew, C, Calder, AJ, Bullmore, ET, Perrett, DI, Rowland, D, Williams, SC, Gray, JA and David, AS (1997) A specific neural substrate for perceiving facial expressions of disgust. *Nature*, 389, 495–498.

Piasecki, TM (2006) Relapse to smoking. *Clinical Psychology Review*, 26, 196–215.

Pietrzak, RH, Laird, JD, Stevens, DA and Thompson, NS (2002) Sex differences in human jealousy: a coordinated study of forced-choice, continuous rating-scale, and physiological responses on the same subjects. *Evolution and Human Behavior*, 23, 83–94.

Pilley, JW and Reid, AK (2011) Border collie comprehends object names as verbal referents. *Behavioural Processes*, 86, 184–195.

Pinker, S (1994) *The language instinct*. London: Allen Lane.

Pinker, S (2010) The cognitive niche: coevolution of intelligence, sociality, and language. *Proceedings of the National Academy of Sciences*, 107, 8993–8999.

Pinquart, M and Duberstein, PR (2010) Associations of social networks with cancer mortality: a meta-analysis. *Critical Reviews in Oncology/Hematology*, 75 (2), 122–137.

Pipitone, RN, and Gallup, GG Jr (2008) Women's voice attractiveness varies across the menstrual cycle. *Evolution and Human Behavior*, 29, 268–274.

Platek, SM and Shackelford, TK (2006) *Female infidelity and paternal uncertainty: evolutionary Perspectives on male anti-cuckoldry tactics*. Cambridge: Cambridge University Press.

Plomin, R and Kosslyn, SM (2001) Genes, brain and cognition. *Nature Neuroscience*, 4, 1153–1154.

Pollick, AS and de Waal, FB (2007) Ape gestures and language evolution. *Proceedings of the National Academy of Sciences*, 104, 8184–8189.

Pringle, A, Cooper, MJ, Browning, M and Harmer, CJ (2012) Effects of low dose tryptophan depletion on emotional processing in dieters. *Eating Behaviors*, 13, 154–157.

Prkachin, GC, Casey, C and Prkachin, KM (2009) Alexithymia and perception of facial expressions of emotion. *Personality and Individual Differences*, 46, 412–417.

Rainville, P, Bechara, A, Naqvi, N and Damasio, AR (2006) Basic emotions are associated with distinct patterns of cardiorespiratory activity. *International Journal of Psychophysiology*, 61, 5–18.

Rakic, P (2003) Development and evolutionary adaptations of cortical radial glia. *Cerebral Cortex*, 13, 541–549.

Rasmussen, HN, Scheier, MF and Greenhouse, JB (2009) Optimism and physical health: a meta-analytic review. *Annals of Behavioral Medicine*, 37, 239–256.

Rees, G (2007) Neural correlates of the contents of visual awareness in humans. *Philosophical Transactions of the Royal Society B: Biological Sciences*, 362, 877–886.

Regehr, C (2005) Bringing the trauma home: spouses of paramedics. *Journal of Loss and Trauma*, 10, 97–114.

Rempel, JK and Baumgartner, B (2003) The relationship between attitudes towards menstruation and sexual attitudes, desires and behavior in women. *Archives of Sexual Behavior*, 32, 155–163.

Ren, XS, Skinner, K, Lee, A and Kazis, L (1999) Social support, social selection and self-assessed health status: results from the veterans health study in the United States. *Social Science & Medicine*, 48, 1721–1734.

Ritter, RS and Preston, JL (2011) Cross gods and icky atheism: disgust responses to rejected religious beliefs. *Journal of Experimental Social Psychology*, 47, 1225–1230.

Robinson, S J, Sünram-Lea, S I, Leach, J and Owen-Lynch, P J (2008) The effects of exposure to an acute naturalistic stressor on working memory, state anxiety and salivary cortisol concentrations. *Stress: The International Journal on the Biology of Stress*, 11, 115–124.

Roder, S, Brewer, G and Fink, B (2009) Menstrual cycle shifts in women's self-perception and motivation: a daily report method. *Personality and Individual Differences*, 47, 616–619.

Rohlfs, P and Ramirez, JM (2006) Aggression and brain asymmetries: a theoretical review. *Aggression and Violent Behavior*, 11, 283–297.

Rohner, RP and Britner, PA (2002) Worldwide mental health correlates of parental acceptance-rejection: review of cross-cultural and intracultural evidence. *Cross-Cultural Research*, 36, 16–47.

Rolls, ET (1994) Neural processing related to feeding in primates. In Legg, C and Booth, D (eds) *Appetite: Neural and Behavioral Basis* (pp11–53). Oxford: Oxford University Press.

Rolls, ET (2000) The orbitofrontal cortex and reward. *Cerebral Cortex*, 10, 284–294.

Rosenbaum, TY (2007) Pelvic floor involvement in male and female sexual dysfunction and the role of pelvic floor rehabilitation in treatment: a literature review. *The Journal of Sexual Medicine*, 4, 4–13.

Rozin, P, Haidt, J and McCauley, CR (2000) Disgust. In Lewis, M and Haviland, J (eds) *Handbook of emotions* (pp637–653). New York: Guilford Press.

Russell, E, Koren, G, Rieder, M and Van Uum, S (2012) Hair cortisol as a biological marker of chronic stress: current status, future directions and unanswered questions. *Psychoneuroendocrinology*, 37, 589–601.

Rutherford, HJV, Mayes, LC and Potenza, MN (2010) Neurobiology of adolescent substance abuse: implications for prevention and treatment. *Child & Adolescent Psychiatric Clinics of North America*, 19, 479–492.

Sacks, O (1985) *The man who mistook his wife for a hat*. London: Picador.

Sagarin, BJ, Martin, AL, Coutinho, SA, Edlund, JE, Patel, L, Skowronski, JJ and Zengel, B (2012) Sex differences in jealousy: a meta-analytic examination. *Evolution and Human Behavior*, 33, 595–614.

Said, CP, Haxby, JV and Todorov, A (2011) Brain systems for assessing the affective value of faces. *Philosophical Transactions of the Royal Society B: Biological Sciences*, 366, 1660–1670.

Sarason, IG, Sarason, BR and Pierce, GR (1990) Social support: the search for theory. *Journal of Social and Clinical Psychology*, 9, 133–147.

Sato, W, Kubota, Y, Okada, T, Murai, T, Yoshikawa, S and Sengoku, A (2002) Seeing happy emotion in fearful and angry faces: qualitative analysis of facial expression recognition in a bilateral amygdala-damaged patient. *Cortex*, 38, 727–742.

Scarr, S and Salapatek, P (1970) Patterns of fear development during infancy. *Merril-Palmer Quarterly*, 16, 53–90.

Schaller, M, Miller, GE, Gervais, WM, Yager, S and Chen, E (2010) Mere visual perception of other people's disease symptoms facilitates a more aggressive immune response. *Psychological Science*, 21, 649–652.

Scharlemann, JP, Eckel, CC, Kacelnik, A and Wilson, RK (2001) The value of a smile: game theory with a human face. *Journal of Economic Psychology*, 22, 617–640.

Scheier, ME and Carver, CS (1987) Dispositional optimism and physical well_being: the influence of generalized outcome expectancies on health. *Journal of Personality*, 55, 169–210.

Schenk, T and McIntosh, RD (2010) Do we have independent visual streams for perception and action? *Cognitive Neuroscience*, 1, 52–62.

Schiff, ND (2008) Central thalamic contributions to arousal regulation and neurological disorders of consciousness. *Annals of the New York Academy of Sciences*, 1129, 105–118.

Schiff, ND and Plum, F (2000) The role of arousal and 'gating' systems in the neurology of impaired consciousness. *Journal of Clinical Neurophysiology*, 17, 438–452.

Schmitt, DP, Alcalay, L, Allik, J, Angleiter, A, Ault, L, Austers, I et al. (2004) Patterns and universals of mate poaching across 53 nations: the effects of sex, culture, and personality on romantically attracting another person's partner. *Journal of Personality and Social Psychology*, 86, 560–584.

Schutzwohl, A (2006) Sex differences in jealousy: information search and cognitive preoccupation. *Personality and Individual Difference*, 40, 285–292.

Schwarz, S and Hassebrauck, M (2008) Self-perceived and observed variations in women's attractiveness throughout the menstrual cycle: a diary study. *Evolution and Human Behavior*, 29, 282–288.

Scoville, WB and Milner, B (1957) Loss of recent memory after bilateral hippocampal lesions. *Journal of Neurology, Neurosurgery, and Psychiatry*, 20 (1), 11.

Sear, R and Mace, R (2008) Who keeps children alive? A review of the effects of kin on child survival. *Evolution and Human Behavior*, 29, 1–18.

Segerstrom, SC and Miller, GE (2004) Psychological stress and the human immune system: a meta-analytic study of 30 years of inquiry. *Psychological Bulletin*, 130, 601.

Segerstrom, SC, Taylor, SE, Kemeny, ME and Fahey, JL (1998) Optimism is associated with mood, coping, and immune change in response to stress. *Journal of Personality and Social Psychology*, 74, 1646.

Seligman, ME (1970) On the generality of the laws of learning. *Psychological Review*, 77, 406–418.

Seligman, MEP (1971) Phobias and preparedness. *Behavior Therapy*, 2, 307–320.

Selye, H (1974) *Stress without distress*. New York: Lippincott.

Senior, C, Lau, A and Butler, MJR (2007) The effects of the menstrual cycle on social decision making. *International Journal of Psychophysiology*, 63, 186–191.

Seth, AK and Baars, BJ (2005) Neural Darwinism and consciousness. *Consciousness and Cognition*, 14, 140–168.

Shackelford, TK, Buss, DM and Bennett, K (2002) Forgiveness or breakup: sex differences in responses to a partner's infidelity. *Cognition and Emotion*, 16, 299–307.

Shams. L, Kamitani, Y and Shimojo, S (2000) Illusions: What you see is what you hear. *Nature*, 408, 788.

Shankle, WR, Landing, BH, Rafii, MS, Schiano, A, Chen, JM and Hara, J (1998) Evidence for a post-natal doubling of neuron number in the developing human cerebral cortex between 15 months and 6 years. *Journal of Theoretical Biology*, 191, 115–140.

Shapira, NA, Lessig, MC, He, AG, James, GA, Driscoll, DJ and Liu, Y (2005) Satiety dysfunction in Prader-Willi syndrome demonstrated by fMRI. *Journal of Neurology, Neurosurgery and Psychiatry*, 76, 260–262.

Sherwin, BB, Gelfand, MM and Brender, W (1985) Androgen enhances sexual motivation in females: a prospective, crossover study of sex steroid administration in surgical menopause. *Psychosomatic Medicine*, 47, 339–351.

Siddique, T and Deng, HX (1996) Genetics of amyotrophic lateral sclerosis. *Human Molecular Genetics*, 5, 1465–1470.

Siegal, EH and Stefanucci, JK (2011) A little bit louder now: negative affect increases perceived loudness. *Emotion*, 11, 1006.

Sifneos, PE (1973) The prevalence of 'alexithymic' characteristics in psychosomatic patients. *Psychotherapy and Psychosomatics*, 22, 255–262.

Singer, W (2001) Consciousness and the binding problem. *Annals of the New York Academy of Sciences*, 929, 123–146.

Sklar, LS and Anisman, H (1981) Stress and cancer. *Psychological. Bulletin*, 89, 369.

Small, CM, Manatunga, AK and Marcus, M (2007) Validity of self-reported menstrual cycle length. *Annals of Epidemiology*, 17, 163–170.

Small, DM, Zatorre, RJ, Dagher, A, Evans, AC and Jones-Gotman, M (2001) Changes in brain activity related to eating chocolate: from pleasure to aversion. *Brain*, 124, 1720–1733.

Small, MF (1996) 'Revealed' ovulation in humans? *Journal of Human Evolution*, 30, 483–488.

Smeets, E, Roefs, A and Jansen, A (2009) Experimentally induced chocolate craving leads to an attentional bias in increased distraction but not in speeded detection. *Appetite*, 53, 370–375.

Smith, P (2007) Why has aggression been thought of as maladaptive? In Hawley, P, Little, T and Rodkin, P (eds) *Aggression and adaptation: the bright side to bad behavior* (pp65–83). Mahwah NJ: Lawrence Erlbaum.

Smolka, MN, Buhler, M, Klein, S, Zimmerman, U, Mann, K, Heinz, A and Braus, DF (2006) Severity of nicotine dependence modulates cue-induced brain activity in regions involved in motor preparation and imagery. *Psychopharmacology*, 184, 577–588.

Solms, M and Panksepp, J (2012) The 'Id' knows more than the 'Ego' admits: neuropsychoanalytic and primal consciousness perspectives on the interface between affective and cognitive neuroscience. *Brain Sciences*, 2, 147–175.

Solomon, GF and Moos, RH (1964) Emotions, immunity, and disease: a speculative theoretical integration. *Archives of General Psychiatry*, 11, 657.

Solomon, GF, Segerstrom, SC, Grohr, P, Kemeny, M and Fahey, J (1997) Shaking up immunity: psychological and immunologic changes after a natural disaster. *Psychosomatic Medicine*, 59, 114–127.

Spiteri, E, Konopka, G, Coppola, G, Bomar, J, Oldham, M, Ou, J et al. (2007) Identification of the transcriptional targets of FOXP2, a gene linked to speech and language, in developing human brain. *The American Journal of Human Genetics*, 81, 1144–1157.

Steele, J, Ferrari, PF and Fogassi, L (2012) From action to language: comparative perspectives on primate tool use, gesture and the evolution of human language. *Philosophical Transactions of the Royal Society B: Biological Sciences*, 367, 4–9.

Stefanucci, JK and Proffitt, DR (2009) The roles of altitude and fear in the perception of height. *Journal of Experimental Psychology. Human Perception and Performance*, 35, 424–438.

Stein, BE and Arigbede, MO (1972) Unimodal and multimodal response properties of neurons in the cat's superior colliculus. *Experimental Neurology*, 36, 179–196.

Steiner, JE, Glaser, D, Hawilo, ME and Berridge, KC (2001) Comparative expression of hedonic impact: affective reactions to taste by human infants and other primates. *Neuroscience & Biobehavioral Reviews*, 25, 53–74.

Stellar, E (1954) The physiology of motivation. *Psychological Review*, 61, 5.

Stemmler, G (2004) Physiological processes during emotion. In Philippot, P and Feldman, RS (eds) *The regulation of emotion* (pp33–70). Mahwah, NJ: Erlbaum.

Steptoe, A, Wardle, J, Pollard, TM, Canaan, L and Davies, GJ (1996) Stress, social support and health-related behavior: a study of smoking, alcohol consumption and physical exercise. *Journal of Psychosomatic Research*, 41, 171–180.

Sterelny, K (2012) Language, gesture, skill: the co-evolutionary foundations of language. *Philosophical Transactions of the Royal Society B: Biological Sciences*, 367, 2141–2151.

Steudte, S, Kolassa, IT, Stalder, T, Pfeiffer, A, Kirschbaum, C and Elbert, T (2011) Increased cortisol concentrations in hair of severely traumatized Ugandan individuals with PTSD. *Psychoneuroendocrinology*, 36, 1193–1200.

Stevenson, RJ, Case, TI and Oaten, MJ (2009) Frequency and recency of infection and their relationship with disgust and contamination sensitivity. *Evolution and Human Behavior*, 30, 363–368.

Stevenson, RJ, Hodgson, D, Oaten, MJ, Barouei, J and Case, TI (2011) The effect of disgust on oral immune function. *Psychophysiology*, 48, 900–907.

Stevenson, RJ, Hodgson, D, Oaten, MJ, Moussavi, M, Langberg, R, Case, TI and Barouei, J (2012) Disgust elevates core body temperature and up-regulates certain oral immune markers. *Brain, Behaviour, and Immunity*, 26, 1160–1168.

Stoessel, C, Stiller, J, Bleich, S, Boensch, D, Doerfler, A, Garcia, M, Richter-Schmidinger, T, Kornhuber, J and Forster, C (2011) Differences and similarities on neuronal activities of people being happily and unhappily in love: a functional magnetic resonance imaging study. *Neuropsychobiology*, 64, 52–60.

Stoleru, S, Redoute, J, Costes, N, Lavenne, F, Bars, DL, Dechaud, H, Forest, MG, Pugeat, M, Cinotti, L and Pujol, JF (2003) Brain processing of visual sexual stimuli in men with hypoactive sexual desire disorder. *Psychiatry Research: Neuroimaging*, 124, 67–86.

Summers, CH and Winberg, S (2006) Interactions between the neural regulation of stress and aggression. *The Journal of Experimental Biology*, 209, 4581–4589.

Swinderen, BV (2005) The remote roots of consciousness in fruit-fly selective attention? *Bioessays*, 27, 321–330.

Taglialatela, JP, Russell, JL, Schaeffer, JA and Hopkins, WD (2011) Chimpanzee vocal signaling points to a multimodal origin of human language. *PloS one*, 6, e18852.

Takahashi, H, Matsuura, M, Yahata, N, Koeda, M, Suhara, T and Okubo, Y (2006) Men and women show distinct brain activations during imagery of sexual and emotional infidelity. *Neuroimage*, 32, 1299–1307.

Taneka, SC, Doya, K, Okada, G, Ueda, K, Okamoto, Y and Yamawaki, S (2004) Prediction of immediate and future rewards differentially recruits cortico-basal ganglia loops. *Nature Neuroscience*, 7, 887–893.

Teramitsu, I and White, SA (2006) FOXP2 regulation during undirected singing in adult songbirds. *The Journal of Neuroscience*, 26, 7390–7394.

Tetley, A, Brunstrom, J and Griffiths, P (2009) Individual differences in food-cue reactivity: the role of BMI and everyday portion-size selections. *Appetite*, 52, 614–620.

Thornhill, R, Gangestad, SW, Miller, R, Scheyd, G, McCollough, JK, and Franklin, M (2003) Major histocompatibility complex genes, symmetry, and body scent attractiveness in men and women. *Behavioral Ecology*, 14, 668–678.

Thornton, LM, Andersen, BL, Crespin, TR and Carson, WE (2007) Individual trajectories in stress covary with immunity during recovery from cancer diagnosis and treatments. *Brain, Behavior, and Immunity*, 21, 185–194.

Toates, F (2006) *Biological psychology*, 2nd edn. Barcelona: Prentice Hall.

Tops, M, Van Der Pompe, G, Wijers, AA, Den Boer, JA, Meijman, TF and Korf, J (2004) Free recall of pleasant words from recency positions is especially sensitive to acute administration of cortisol. *Psychoneuroendocrinology*, 29(3), 327–338.

Trautmann, SA, Fehr, T and Herrmann, M (2009) Emotions in motion: dynamic compared to static facial expressions of disgust and happiness reveal more widespread emotion-specific activations. *Brain Research*, 1284, 100–115.

Trivers, RL (1972) Parental investment and sexual selection. In Campbell, B (ed.) *Sexual selection and the descent of man* (pp139–179). Chicago, IL: Aldine.

Tsuang, MT, Lyons, MJ, Meyer, JM, Doyle, T, Eisen, SA, Goldberg, J, True, W, Lin, N, Roomey, R and Eaves, L (1998) Co-occurrence of abuse of different drugs in men: the role of drug-specific and shared vulnerabilities. *Archives of General Psychiatry*, 55, 967–972.

Tylka, TL and Subich, LM (2002) Exploring young women's perceptions of the effectiveness and safety of maladaptive weight control techniques. *Journal of Counseling and Development*, 80, 101–110.

Tylka, TL, Eneli, IU, Kroon van Diest, AM and Lumeng, JC (2013) Which adaptive maternal eating behaviors predict child feeding practices? An examination with mothers of 2- to 5- year old children. *Eating Behaviors*, 14, 57–63.

Uchino, BN, Bowen, K, Carlisle, M and Birmingham, W (2012) Psychological pathways linking social support to health outcomes: a visit with the 'Ghosts' of research past, present, and future. *Social Science & Medicine* 74, 949.

Ungerleider, LG and Mishkin, M (1982) Two cortical visual systems. In Ingle, DJ, Goodale, MA and Mansfield, RJW (eds) *Analysis of visual behavior* (pp549–586). Cambridge, MA: MIT Press.

Uomini, NT and Meyer, GF (2013) Shared brain lateralization patterns in language and Acheulean stone tool production: a functional transcranial Doppler ultrasound study. *PloS one*, 8, e72693.

van Lankveld, JJ and Smulders, FT (2008) The effect of visual sexual content on the event-related potential. *Biological Psychology*, 79, 200–208.

Van Zoeren, JG and Stricker, EM (1977) Effects of preoptic, lateral hypothalamic, or dopamine-depleting lesions on behavioural thermoregulation in rats exposed to the cold. *Journal of Comparative and Physiological Psychology*, 91 (5), 989–999.

Vanderschuren, LJ and Everitt, BJ (2005) Behavioral and neural mechanisms of compulsive drug seeking. *European Journal of Pharmacology*, 526, 77–88.

Veldhuis, JD and Iranmanesh, A (1996) Physiological regulation of the human growth hormone (GH)-insulin-like growth factor type I (IGF-I) axis: predominant impact of age, obesity, gonadal function, and sleep. *Sleep*, 19, S221-S224.

Vermeer, HJ and van IJzendoorn, MH (2006) Children's elevated cortisol levels at daycare: a review and meta-analysis. *Early Childhood Research Quarterly*, 21, 390–401.

Vestergaard-Poulsen, P, Van Beek, M, Skewes, J, Bjarkam, CR, Stubberup, M, Bertelsen, J et al. (2009) Long-term meditation is associated with increased gray matter density in the brain stem. *Neuroreport*, 20, 170–174.

Vidaltamavo, R, Bargas, J, Covarrubias, L, Hernandez, A, Galarraga, E, Guitierrez-Ospina, G and Drucker-Colin, R (2010) Stem cell therapy for Parkinson's disease: a road map for a successful future. *Stem Cells Dev*, 19 (3), 311–320.

Volavka, J, Bilder, R and Nolan, K (2004). Catecholamines and aggression: the role of COMT and MAO polymorphisms. *Annals of the New York Academy of Sciences*, 1036, 393–398.

Vuilleumier, P (2002) Facial expression and selective attention. *Current Opinion in Psychiatry*, 15, 291–300.

Wager, TD, Luan Phan, K, Liberzon, I and Taylor, SF (2003) Valence, gender, and lateralization of functional brain anatomy in emotion: a meta-analysis of findings from neuroimaging. *NeuroImage*, 19, 513–531.

Wagner, H and Lee, V (1999) Facial behavior alone and in the presence of others. In Philippot, P, Feldman, RS and Coats, EJ (eds) *The social context of nonverbal behavior* (pp 262–286). New York: Cambridge University Press.

Wallen, K (2001) Sex and context: hormones and primate sexual motivation. *Hormones and Behavior*, 40, 339–357.

Wallis, JD (2007) Orbitofrontal cortex and its contribution to decision making. *Annual Review of Neuroscience*, 30, 31–56.

Wang, GJ, Tomasi, D, Backus, W, Wang, R, Telang, F, Geliebter, A, Korner, J, Bauman, A, Fowler, JS, Thanos, PK, and Volkow, ND (2008) Gastric distension activates satiety circuitry in the human brain. *Neuroimage*, 39, 1824–1831.

Wang, XT (2002) Risk as reproductive variance. *European and Human Behavior*, 23, 35–57.

Wansink, B, Cheyney, MM and Chan, N (2003) Exploring comfort food preferences across age and gender. *Physiology & Behavior*, 79, 739–747.

Ward Thompson, C, Roe, J, Aspinall, P, Mitchell, R, Clow, A and Miller, D (2012) More green space is linked to less stress in deprived communities: evidence from salivary cortisol patterns. *Landscape and Urban Planning*, 105, 221–229.

Warne, JP (2009) Shaping the stress response: interplay of palatable food choices, glucocorticoids, insulin, and abdominal obesity. *Molecular and Cellular Endocrinology*, 300, 137–146.

Warner, LH (1927) A study of sex behavior in the white rat by means of the obstruction method. *Comparative Psychology Monographs*, 4, 1–67.

Webb, E, Thomson, S, Nelson, A, White, C, Koren, G, Rieder, M and Van Uum, S (2010) Assessing individual systemic stress through cortisol analysis of archaeological hair. *Journal of Archaeological Science*, 37, 807–812.

Weddell, RA, Miller, JD and Trevarthen, C (1990) Voluntary emotional facial expressions in patients with focal cerebral lesions. *Neuropsychologia*, 28, 49–60.

Weinstein, ND (1982) Unrealistic optimism about susceptibility to health problems. *Journal of Behavioral Medicine*, 5, 441–460.

Weinstock, M (2008) The long-term behavioural consequences of prenatal stress. *Neuroscience & Biobehavioral Reviews*, 32 (6), 1073–1086.

Welling, LLM, Puts, DA, Roberts, SC, Little, AC and Burriss, RP (2012) Hormonal contraceptive use and mate retention behavior in women and their male partners. *Hormones and Behavior*, 61, 114–120.

Whalen, PJ, Shin, LM, McInerney, SC, Fischer, H, Wright, CI and Rauch, SL (2001) A functional MRI study of human amygdala responses to facial expressions of fear versus anger. *Emotion*, 1, 70–83.

Whatson, T and Sterling, V (1998) *Development and flexibility*. Berlin: Springer.

Wicker, B, Keysers, C, Plailly, J, Royet, JP, Gallese, V and Rizzolatti, G (2003) Both of us disgusted in my insula: the common neural basis of seeing and feeling disgust. *Neuron*, 40, 655–664.

Wilcox, AJ, Weinberg, CR and Baird, DD (1995) Timing of sexual intercourse in relation to ovulation: effects on the probability of conception, survival of the pregnancy, and sex of the baby. *New England Journal of Medicine*, 333, 1517–1521.

Willems, RM and Hagoort, P (2007) Neural evidence for the interplay between language, gesture, and action: a review. *Brain and Language*, 101, 278–289.

Williams, LE and Bargh, JA (2008) Experiencing physical warmth promotes interpersonal warmth. *Science*, 322, 606–607.

Williams, LM, Phillips, ML, Brammer, MJ, Skerrett, D, Lagopoulos, J, Rennie, C, Bahramali, H, Olivieri, G, David, AS, Peduto, A and Gordon, E (2001) Arousal dissociates amygdala and hippocampal fear responses: evidence from simultaneous fMRI and kin conductance recording. *NeuroImage*, 14, 1070–1079.

Williams, LM, Barton, MJ, Kemp, AH, Liddell, BJ, Peduto, A, Gordon, E and Bryant, RA (2005) Distinct amygdala-autonomic arousal profiles in response to fear signals in healthy males and females. *NeuroImage*, 28, 618–626.

Williams, LM, Kemp, AH, Felmingham, K, Liddell, BJ, Palmer, DM and Bryant, RA (2007) Neural biases to covert and overt signals of fear: dissociation by trait anxiety and depression. *Journal of Cognitive Neuroscience*, 19, 1595–1608.

Wilson, ME, Fisher, J, Fischer, A, Lee, V, Harris, RB and Bartness, TJ (2008) Quantifying food intake in socially housed monkeys: social status effects on caloric consumption. *Physiology & Behavior*, 94, 586–594.

Wilson, SJ, Sayette, MA and Fiez, JA (2004) Prefrontal responses to drug cues: a neurocognitive analysis. *Natural Neuroscience*, 7, 211–214.

Wilson, SM, Saygin, AP, Sereno, MI and Iacoboni, M (2004) Listening to speech activates motor areas involved in speech production. *Nature Neuroscience*, 7, 701–702.

Winslow, JT, Hastings, N, Carter, CS, Harbaugh, CR and Insel, TR (1993) A role for central vasopressin in pair bonding in monogamous prairie voles. *Nature*, 365, 545–548.

Winwood, PC and Lushington, K (2006) Disentangling the effects of psychological and physical work demands on sleep, recovery and maladaptive chronic stress outcomes within a large sample of Australian nurses. *Journal of Advanced Nursing*, 56, 679–689.

Witelson, SF, Beresh, H and Kigar, DL (2006) Intelligence and brain size in 100 postmortem brains: sex lateralization and age factors. *Brain*, 129, 386–398.

Woodson, JC (2002) Including 'learned sexuality' in the organization of sexual behavior. *Neuroscience and Biobehavioral Reviews*, 26, 69–80.

Wrangham, RW, Wilson, ML and Muller, MN (2006) Comparative rates of violence in chimpanzees and humans. *Primates*, 47, 14–26.

Wubben, MJJ, de Cremer, D and van Dijk, E (2009) How emotion communication guides reciprocity: establishing cooperation through disappointment and anger. *Journal of Experimental Social Psychology*, 45, 987–990.

Xu, X, Aron, A, Brown, L, Cao, G, Feng, T and Weng, X (2011) Reward and motivation systems: a brain mapping study of early-stage intense romantic love in Chinese participants. *Human Brain Mapping*, 32, 249–257.

Xu, X, Brown, L, Aron, A, Cao, G, Feng, T, Acevedo, B and Weng, X (2012) Regional brain activity during early-stage intense romantic love predicted relationship outcomes after 40 months: an fMRI assessment. *Neuroscience Letters*, 526, 33–38.

Yalachkov, Y, Kaiser, J and Naumer, MJ (2012) Functional neuroimaging studies in addiction: multisensory drug stimuli and neural cue reactivity. *Neuroscience and Biobehavioral Reviews*, 36, 825–835.

Yesavage, JA, Mumenthaler, MS, Taylor, JL, Friedman, L, O'Hara, R, Sheikh, J, Tinklenberg, J and Whitehouse, PJ (2002) Donepezil and flight simulator performance: effects on retention of complex skills. *Neurology*, 59 (1), 123–125.

Yoshimoto, K, McBride, W J, Lumeng, L and Li, T-K (1991) Alcohol stimulates the release of dopamine and serotonin in the nucleus accumbens. *Alcohol*, 9, 17–22.

Young, LJ and Wang, Z (2004) The neurobiology of pair bonding. *Nature Neuroscience*, 7, 1048–1054.

Zald, DH (2003) The human amygdala and the emotional evaluation of sensory stimuli. *Brain Research Review*, 41, 88–123.

Zaretskaya, N, Thielscher, A, Logothetis, NK and Bartels, A (2010) Disrupting parietal function prolongs dominance durations in binocular rivalry. *Current Biology*, 20, 2106–2111.

Zeki, S (2007) The neurobiology of love. *FEBS Letters*, 581, 2575–2579.

Zhou, W and Chen, D (2008) Encoding human sexual chemosensory cues in the orbitofrontal and fusiform cortices. *The Journal of Neuroscience*, 28, 14416–14421.

Index

Pages containing relevant figures and tables are given in italic.